Lecture Notes in Computer Science   10600

Commenced Publication in 1973
Founding and Former Series Editors:
Gerhard Goos, Juris Hartmanis, and Jan van Leeuwen

More information about this series at http://www.springer.com/series/8677

James Noble · Ralph Johnson
Uwe Zdun · Eugene Wallingford (Eds.)

Transactions on Pattern Languages of Programming IV

 Springer

Editors-in-Chief
James Noble
Victoria University of Wellington
Wellington, New Zealand

Ralph Johnson
Siebel Center for Computer Science
Urbana, IL, USA

Editors
Uwe Zdun
University of Vienna
Vienna, Austria

Eugene Wallingford
University of Northern Iowa
Cedar Falls, IA, USA

ISSN 0302-9743   ISSN 1611-3349 (electronic)
Lecture Notes in Computer Science
ISSN 1869-6015   ISSN 2511-6444 (electronic)
Transactions on Pattern Languages of Programming
ISBN 978-3-030-14290-2   ISBN 978-3-030-14291-9 (eBook)
https://doi.org/10.1007/978-3-030-14291-9

Library of Congress Control Number: 2019932783

This Springer imprint is published by the registered company Springer Nature Switzerland AG
The registered company address is: Gewerbestrasse 11, 6330 Cham, Switzerland

Preface

Welcome to the fourth issue of *LNCS Transactions on Pattern Languages of Programming*. Software patterns are an effective means for improving the quality of software design and engineering and communication among the people building them. Patterns capture the best practices of software design, making them available to all software engineers.

LNCS Transactions on Pattern Languages of Programming publishes papers on patterns and pattern languages as applied to software design, development, and use, throughout all phases of the software life cycle, from requirements and design to implementation, maintenance and evolution. The primary focus of the *LNCS Transactions on Pattern Languages of Programming* is on patterns, pattern collections, and pattern languages themselves. The journal also includes reviews, survey articles, criticisms of patterns and pattern languages, as well as other research on patterns and pattern languages.

This issue includes six articles that went through two phases of review and improvement. First, the articles were workshopped at one of the PLoP conferences where (after an initial peer review) they received suggestions for improvement in a shepherding process and in a writer's workshop. Then the articles were substantially extended by the authors, and these extended versions were peer-reviewed again by at least three reviewers per article.

This edition of *LNCS Transactions on Pattern Languages of Programming* marks a transition in editorship: The founding editors-in-chief, James Noble and Ralph Johnson, will retire after this issue and the current editors, Eugene Wallingford and Uwe Zdun, will become the new editors-in-chief. We thank James and Ralph for their efforts during the founding period of *LNCS Transactions on Pattern Languages of Programming*.

We thank the anonymous reviewers who helped in the peer-review process of this issue.

January 2019

James Noble
Eugene Wallingford
Uwe Zdun

Contents

Contents

Patterns for Light-Weight Fault Tolerance and Decoupled Design in Distributed Control Systems

Pekka Alho[1(✉)] and Jari Rauhamäki[2]

[1] Department of Intelligent Hydraulics and Automation,
Tampere University of Technology, Tampere, Finland
pekka.alho@iki.fi
[2] Department of Automation Science and Engineering,
Tampere University of Technology, Tampere, Finland
jari.rauhamaki@gmail.com

Abstract. Distributed control systems comprise networked computing units that monitor and control physical processes in feedback loops. Reliability of these systems is affected by dynamic and complex computing environments where connections and system configurations may change rapidly. Diverse redundancy can be effective in improving system dependability, but it is susceptible to common mode failures and development costs for design diversity are often seen as prohibitive. In this paper we present three patterns that can be used to provide light-weight form of fault tolerance to improve system dependability and resilience by providing ability to cope with unexpected events and faults. These patterns are presented together with a pattern language that shows how they relate to other fault tolerance patterns.

Keywords: Dependability · Distributed systems · Fault tolerance ·
Real-time systems · Reliability

1 Introduction

Distributed control systems are continuously gaining importance, as more and more devices and machines are equipped with embedded systems that control their operation. Computers in these control systems are increasingly more powerful and networked, providing intelligence and interoperability. Examples of such systems range from large mobile machines to groups of robots and intelligent sensor networks. These cyber-physical systems (CPSs) interact with environment and physical processes, influencing many parts of our lives either directly or indirectly. Therefore they need to be *dependable,* which can be measured with the attributes of availability, reliability, safety, integrity and maintainability [1]. However, with the increased functionality and intelligence, the complexity of these systems is also increased, meaning that the development process becomes more demanding and dependability becomes more costly to achieve and verify. Another significant feature of CPSs is that they often have strict timing constraints, which may put limitations on the architecture.

© Springer Nature Switzerland AG 2019
J. Noble et al. (Eds.): TPLOP IV, LNCS 10600, pp. 1–21, 2019.
https://doi.org/10.1007/978-3-030-14291-9_1

Many critical systems that have failed catastrophically are well-known – examples such as Therac-25 radiation therapy machine and the explosion of Ariane 5 rocket are infamous, whereas highly reliable systems receive little recognition, even though their study might give valuable ideas for the design and architecture of new software. One example of such systems can be found in telephony applications, namely Ericsson AXD301 Asynchronous Transfer Mode (ATM) switches that achieved nine nines (99.9999999%) service availability, running software written in Erlang [2]. Erlang's highly decoupled actor model and fault handling based on supervisors have inspired especially. Let it crash and Service manager patterns found in this paper.

This paper presents three software patterns that can be used to improve control system dependability – the third pattern is called DATA-CENTRIC ARCHITECTURE – and shows how they fit in the existing literature by addressing the specific needs of CPSs. The approach promoted by these three patterns is based on implementing a decoupled architectural design with supporting fault mitigation and handling. The decoupled architecture can also be used to gradually introduce additional fault tolerance solutions such as checkpointing and rejuvenation to the system, until a sufficient level of reliability has been achieved [3]. Our patterns were originally encountered in the research of remote handling control systems for robotic manipulators, but all patterns have examples of other known uses as well. These examples are presented in the corresponding sections of the patterns.

One reason why development of CPSs is difficult is because the systems typically consist of dynamic service chains that operate on wide range of platforms, which complicates management of end-to-end deadlines. Moreover, modern middleware provide capabilities to flexibly change service deployment on these subsystems, but some configurations may be inefficient or even unusable if communication links become overloaded. While adaptability has benefits, these uncertainties nevertheless complicate assurance of reliability and predictability of the system. Therefore, CPSs benefit from a design that makes the overall system more robust, whereas more traditional fault tolerance solutions, such as hardware redundancy, are arguably better suited for static safety-critical subsystems.

Data-centric approach is one way to increase decoupling between communicating units. However, data-centric design as a central communication paradigm, as well as the concept of CPS, is still fairly novel in the domain of distributed control systems. Although control systems are by nature data-centric (read sensor data and desired output, send actuator command, etc.), this has usually been from point A to point B. The patterns in this paper capture some of the ways that reliability-related challenges faced in developing more intelligent and adaptable distributed control systems have been solved. Next chapter shows how our patterns fit the gaps in the existing pattern literature, by addressing needs specific to CPSs.

2 Context of the Patterns

Fault tolerance cannot be implemented without redundancy of some kind. To have fault tolerance for e.g. computer failures, we would need at least two computers – if one fails the other one can detect the error and try to correct it. Software faults on the other hand are typically development faults, which are harder to detect and correct than hardware faults. To have good coverage for software faults, diverse redundancy (e.g. N-version programming) is needed, but it has been criticized of being susceptible to common mode failures [4]. Moreover, development costs for design diversity are often seen as prohibitive.

Patterns in this paper present an alternative approach to fault tolerance, based on dividing the system into highly decoupled modules and implementing lightweight form of fault tolerance. We present an architectural pattern called DATA-CENTRIC ARCHITECTURE as one way to achieve a high level of decoupling. One of the key points of decoupling is that it should by itself improve reliability by limiting fault propagation and improving modularity and understandability of the system. In a way, modular approach can be seen similar to compartmentalization of ships – without compartments, every leak can sink the ship. An example of a software system that uses modularity to successfully implement fault isolation and resilience is the MINIX 3 operating system released in 2005 [5]. Driver management of MINIX 3 is presented as one of the known uses of SERVICE MANAGER.

Modular and decoupled architecture can also be used to implement other reliability-improving patterns like SERVICE MANAGER and LET IT CRASH documented in this paper or other well-known patterns like LEAKY BUCKET COUNTER [6], WATCHDOG [6, 7], etc. The short descriptions of the patterns presented in this paper are listed in the Table 1. List of all referenced patterns with descriptions can be found in an appendix.

Table 1. Pattern descriptions

Pattern	Description
DATA-CENTRIC ARCHITECTURE	How to implement reliable and scalable distributed control system? Build the system from autonomous modules that communicate by sharing data that is based on a well-designed and consistent data model
SERVICE MANAGER	How to detect faults and restart modules or processes after a failure? Implement a service manager that can monitor, start and stop modules
LET IT CRASH	How to react to failures without crashing the whole system? Flush the corrupted state by "crashing" the process instead of writing extensive error handling code. Let some other process like service manager do the error recovery e.g. by restarting the crashed process

DATA-CENTRIC ARCHITECTURE provides the decoupled architectural model needed to use LET IT CRASH for fault handling. The SERVICE MANAGER pattern provides a way for trying recovery after failures, in addition to providing error detection and monitoring. The idea of crashing a process suggested by LET IT CRASH may sound like a risky action to take. However, the idea is to offer recovery from transient physical and interaction faults (sometimes called Heisenbugs), ability to keep the system as a whole functioning, even if some internal process would crash, and possibility to hot-swap code and bug-fixes. The downside of this approach is of course that it is not suited for fail-operate systems such as flight controllers that must be operational all the time – this type of systems would be the right domain to apply design diversity.

In order to show how these patterns fit the existing literature, we have built a pattern language for fault tolerance in CPSs that references related patterns and pattern languages, shown in Fig. 1. Entry point to the language is the need for introducing fault tolerance to the system in order to improve its dependability. The three main starting points are MINIMIZE HUMAN INTERVENTION [6], REDUNDANCY [6] and UNITS OF MITIGATION [6], but the REDUNDANCY branch has been not been explored in-depth since it presents somewhat different approach from the three patterns found in this paper. Recovery types have also been condensed to a single concept. Some of the connections presented in the original sources have been reorganized in order to better fit in this context, and the figure shows only one of the possible combinations of the patterns. Connections to other patterns and pattern languages can be checked from the references in Table 2 found in the appendix.

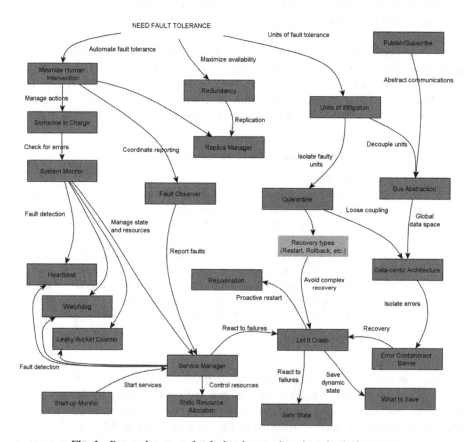

Fig. 1. Pattern language for fault tolerance in cyber-physical systems

The pattern language shows how the patterns presented in this paper build on top of existing patterns and support implementing fault recovery and SAFE STATE [7] in CPSs. Gaps identified in the pattern language are related to CPSs being networked systems with real-time requirements and safety concerns. Fault handling needs extra attention since control system cannot try complex fault recovery routines that could have unforeseen consequences. Instead, a better approach is to QUARANTINE [6] the faults locally and stop their propagation, even if that would mean losing some functionality either temporarily or permanently.

There are several existing patterns that have similar purposes as SERVICE MANAGER, such as FAULT OBSERVER [6], REPLICA MANAGER [15], SERVICE CONFIGURATOR [16] and SYSTEM MONITOR [6]. However, CPSs benefit from more active management component that can try to react to the failures within system specifications – because they typically have timing-critical control loops and state machines – to mitigate faults and stop their propagation in the system.

Finally, to implement the fault handling, units need a loosely coupled architecture that is robust to failures and supports fault detection. The patterns in the pattern language work together by building on the top of features provided by other patterns as shown in Fig. 1 but all of the patterns can also be used in other contexts besides distributed control systems. Other well-known fault tolerance patterns also work well in combination with the presented patterns. Besides the patterns presented here, other typical examples related to reliability of CPSs include implementation for fault detection, fault reporting, sending and acknowledgement of commands, etc. but have been left out of this paper.

3   Patterns

3.1   Data-Centric Architecture

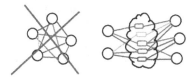

Intent. Implement an architecture based on autonomous modules (e.g. services, processes or applications) that communicate by sharing properly modeled data.

Context. You are developing a distributed control system that consists of several subsystems and needs to interact with other heterogeneous systems such as mobile machines or plant systems. The system has CPU and memory resources available to run an operating system – rather than being based on a basic time-triggered scheduler used in resource-constrained embedded systems. Failures in control functions (e.g. boom or manipulator control) may cause damage to the environment and equipment, meaning that some subsystems may be categorized as safety or mission-critical.

Problem. How to implement a reliable and scalable distributed control system?

Forces

- *Throughput*: Some time-critical data such as sensor measurements may be updated with short period, producing large amounts of communication.
- *Scalability*: New nodes and subsystems can join the system any time; assumptions about interfaces between modules should be minimized.
- *Changeability*: System configuration and functionality might change. Changing interfaces in a tightly coupled system requires code changes at both ends (and at all clients), so assumptions about expected behavior should be minimized. Point-to-point protocol based client-server architectures (e.g. sockets or remote method invocation) are not ideal because of complexity and coupling introduced.
- *Maintainability and long expected life-cycle*: The control system has long expected lifetime and needs to be maintainable and extensible in the future – if subsystems are added or substituted, changes to existing modules need to be minimized. System should be easy to understand and modify without breaking it.
- *Maintainability*: Implementing custom communication channels and protocols should be avoided.
- *Reusability*: Same modules could be used in other control system implementations.
- *Interoperability*: Distributed control systems consist of and/or need to communicate with heterogeneous platforms.
- *Testability*: Tightly coupled modules are difficult to test because they are more dependent on other modules.
- *Availability*: The system as a whole should remain available, even if some subsystems or processes experience failures.
- *Reliability*: A single fault in the control system software should not endanger functionality of the whole system (i.e. no single point of failures).
- *Reliability*: Faults should be detected and their propagation prevented.
- *Real-time performance*: Control system interacts with the real world and needs to react in a deterministic manner.
- *Safety*: Need to detect if a module has crashed or is down (not releasing new information) so that the system can enter SAFE STATE in a controlled fashion. Safety-critical and non-safety-critical subsystems cannot be tightly coupled, since errors may propagate.
- *Quality of service*: Different subsystems may have different requirements for quality of service[1] (QoS) policies. There is an impedance mismatch between e.g. real-time control systems that operate on a timescale of milliseconds and enterprise/high level systems that are several orders of magnitude slower.

---

[1] QoS policies provide the ability to specify various parameters such as rate of publication, rate of subscription, reliability, data lifespan, transport priority, etc. to control end-to-end connection properties. Policies can be matched on a request vs. offered basis.

Solution. Build the system from autonomous modules that communicate by sharing data that is based on a well-designed and consistent data model.
Implement communication between modules as sharing of data, instead of sending point-to-point messages or request-reply service calls. Data-centric approach is based on minimizing dependencies between modules by removing direct inter-module references and hiding module-specific behavior. This can be achieved by delegating data-handling to a middleware solution that supports publishing of data to topics in a distributed data space and making applications tolerate unavailability of dependencies. Asynchronous messaging is a well-known way to reduce coupling of systems, but data-centric approach increases this further by removing the concept of recipient from the publisher.

Modules should be built to be autonomous and not expect that other services are always started in a specific order and available. Service/module composition may change during runtime; there are patterns for managing the configurations (e.g. SERVICE CONFIGURATOR). Developer should avoid assumption about state of the dependencies, i.e. other services. Dependencies may not always be available and this must be taken into account in the application code so that the service will react accordingly if its dependency is down because it is in the process of starting, failed, manually shut down, etc.

Management of the global data space is externalized to the middleware that implements a topic-based PUBLISH/SUBSCRIBE model. Middleware disseminates data to all participating nodes, acting as a single source of up-to-date system-wide state information. It acts as a single source of up-to-date state information in the system, instead of applications managing state separately.

Modules do not need to know recipients of the data when publishing it, which reduces coupling. Instead of sending data directly to a recipient, it is published to a topic. Data can be e.g. sensor measurements, events or commands, but it must follow a shared information model which is represented as topics in the actual system implementation. Publishers register as data writers to a topic and interested subscribers can join the topic as data readers. Single topic can have multiple instances, which are identified by a key value, and can have multiple readers and writers, as shown in Fig. 2.

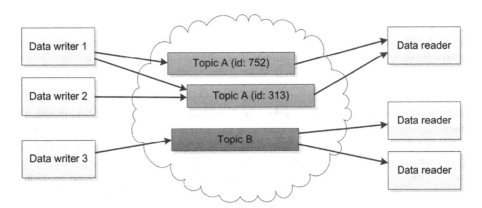

Fig. 2. Data is published to topics that can have multiple data writers and readers. Topic A has two instances, identified by the id number key value.

Since the middleware decouples the modules, publisher might assume that a subscriber is listening when it is not. If a publisher needs to know that data has been received, it should monitor status of the subscriber (published to another topic). This might be true, for example, with commands sequences where commands must be completed before sending the next one.

Instead of designing callable methods for components, you must design how to represent the state of the system and the external or internal events that can affect it. This is captured in a common data model, which contains the essential elements of the physical system and application logic. Conceptually the data model is similar to class diagram in object-oriented programming since it consists of identifying entity types, which have data attributes assigned to them, and associations. The difference is that the data model focuses on data instead of behavior. Data model ensures that communication between modules is unambiguous and interoperable. Appropriate QoS attributes can also be attached to the data model.

Communication and application logic are separated since network communications are delegated to a "data bus" formed by the publish/subscribe middleware (Fig. 3), so that the application logic can focus on the core functionality. Middleware takes care of maintaining the data up-to-date, automatically updating new nodes that join. If the middleware uses a central server as a message BROKER [8], it becomes a single-point-of-failure and possibly a bottleneck. Therefore, choose a decentralized middleware solution, if possible, to avoid this problem.

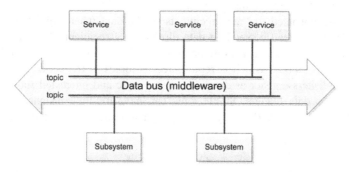

Fig. 3. Middleware implementation as a virtual data bus that has no central components or brokers. Services and subsystems can join topics as publishers and/or subscribers.

Granularity of modules and interactions are important design decisions that affect failure consequences, performance and reusability of modules. Fine-grained autonomous modules (large number of smaller modules) are easier to reuse and make it easier to isolate faults, but limiting the number of modules and interactions helps to avoid potential performance issues. Modules communicating only locally can be more fine-grained than ones communicating remotely, although the data model should not include location dependencies. Fine-grained interactions give more flexibility, as it will be possible to treat data items separately. Coarse-grained interactions are usually preferred between remote modules in order to avoid overhead, but data that is updated rapidly should be separated from data with slow update rates in order to avoid unnecessary use of bandwidth. Further control over system granularity can be achieved by dividing it to domains.

Compared to message-centric publish/subscribe, one of the differences in data-centric model is that data samples published to topics are transparent to the middleware. In message-centric model, middleware does not know or care about message contents and communication is point-to-point by nature which introduces coupling between modules, although some message-centric middleware also support publishing of messages to topics. Data-centric communication is based on a data model that expresses the state of the system. Since data is interpreted through the model, it is platform-independent and middleware can prioritize, filter and manage the data based on its contents and QoS policies, replacing part of the application logic. Although developing a data model adds to upfront planning efforts, systems with long-term lifecycles benefit in terms of maintainability and evolvability.

Consequences

+ Publishers do not need to know about subscribers.
+ Interoperability between heterogeneous platforms since data is interpreted through the data model.
+ Decoupled design provides error confinement and other benefits such as improved maintainability.
+ Modules can be changed dynamically because late joiners receive new data automatically; ability to hot-swap code can be easily implemented.
+ An application or subsystem can be shut down without impacting the overall operation of the system.
+ Network transport layer is abstracted as communications are externalized to middleware, which reduces communication related code and simplifies implementation.
+ Gives developers control of data delivery with QoS management; QoS can be used e.g. to guarantee reliable delivery (eventually) or that available data is kept up-to-date with best effort. Former would be useful for sending status changes or commands, whereas latter could be used for sensor measurement for which guaranteeing delivery of outdated samples makes no sense.
+ Reusability is improved since modules are using shared memory and have their own namespaces, etc.
+ Publish/subscribe based middleware scales effectively since recipients for data are not explicitly defined.
+ Performance gains can be achieved on multi-core machines since modules can be easily parallelized and they communicate asynchronously.
± Needs good and consistent data models that must be managed and maintained, but a well-thought-out data model improves maintainability and makes reuse of the code easier.
− A publisher might assume that a subscriber is listening when it is not.

- Sending of commands is not as straightforward as in client-server architectures since commands need to be parsed from the data. However, interactions can be modeled as operation codes sent between two modules.
- Parsing of data complicates debugging because it adds another potential source for faults. If data is parsed incorrectly, origin of fault may not be self-evident.
- Extra code needed when compared to more monolithic applications since modules cannot presume that all dependencies are started in specific order and available all the time.
- Serialization and deserialization of the data structures for transmission may add overhead.
- Faults in the middleware itself complicate testing and are hard to detect.
- Middleware solutions add some overhead to message size and use system resources.
- Possible vendor lock-in to the middleware provider

Known uses. Data Distribution Service for Real-Time Systems (DDS) is decentralized and data-centric middleware based on the publish/subscribe model. DDS is aimed at mission-critical and embedded systems that have strict performance and reliability requirements. Therefore, its implementations have typically been optimized and tested to suit the needs of these systems. DDS is used as the information backbone in the Thales TACTICOS naval combat management system that integrates various subsystems such as weapons, sensors, counter measures, communication, navigation, etc. to a "system of systems". Applications are distributed dynamically over a pool of computers in order to provide combat survivability and avoid single-point-of-failures. System configuration can be adapted for use in various mission configurations, onboard & simulator training, and different ship types.

Related Patterns. BUS ABSTRACTION [7], and PUBLISHER-SUBSCRIBER.

MEDIATOR [9] increases decoupling in a similar fashion, but is designed to decrease connections between objects locally.

Decoupled modules in DATA-CENTRIC ARCHITECTURE act as UNITS OF MITIGATION, parts that contain errors and error recovery.

3.2   Service Manager

Also Known as. SUPERVISOR.

Intent. Service manager starts, stops, and monitors processes locally and takes care of resource allocation for systems that need high availability and real-time performance.

Context. You are developing a system with highly decoupled architecture (e.g. using DATA-CENTRIC ARCHITECTURE) that consists of large number of processes or tasks (services). These processes have dependencies and therefore need to be started in specific order. Process composition may change dynamically during runtime because your system will have intelligent functionality, it needs to adapt to new situations, or different functionalities need to be tested without stopping/restarting the whole system.

You know rough upper-limit estimates for how much system resources such as memory and CPU time the processes will use.

The system has long expected life-cycle. It is likely to be deployed on a remote location, for example a forest or a control cubicle, making direct physical interaction with the system a bothersome task.

If you have a real-time operating system and a task gets stuck in a while loop or some other control structure, it freezes the whole system as other lower priority processes (including input devices and network connections) cannot get CPU time. In this case, the only option is usually to restart the whole computer manually.

Problem. How to ensure that all dynamic modules in your control system are running correctly and you have enough system resources to achieve deterministic real-time performance?

Forces

- *Availability*: The system as a whole should remain available, even if some subsystems or processes experience failures, in order to able to use other parts of the system that are not connected to the failed subsystem. The system must detect faults and try to mitigate them automatically. If a failure needs immediate reaction from a human operator, the system will not scale cost-efficiently and reliably.
- *Data logging/testability*: If a process fails, the failure should be detected and logged.
- *Real-time performance*: The control system needs to respond in a deterministic and predicable manner. Predictability includes system behavior when a fault is triggered.
- *System resources*: Control systems are typically deployed on embedded devices that have limited memory and CPU resources available. They may need to be monitored in order to guarantee the real-time performance of the system.

Solution. Implement a service manager that can monitor, start and stop local modules.
Create a local parent process (the service manager) that is responsible for starting, stopping and monitoring its child processes. The basic idea of the service manager is to keep its child processes alive by restarting them when necessary. Location of the service manager is on the same computer as the child processes in order to keep implementation simple. Therefore, all computers in the system need their own,

independently functioning, service managers. The service manager is given the highest process priority in the system or put in the kernel so that a faulty real-time process cannot prevent it from functioning by consuming all available CPU time.

Start the child processes based on a fixed order or a dependency table read from a configuration file, similar to START-UP MONITOR [7], and/or implement a user interface that can be used to start and stop processes.

Use the service manager to allocate resources like CPU time and memory for the child processes and monitor their use. Expected maximum resource consumption can be specified in the same configuration file that is used for starting services. New processes are not started if there are not enough resources available. If a process consumes more resources than expected, it can be restarted, triggering error handling according to the LET IT CRASH pattern. Resource use can be followed e.g. with proc filesystem or *getrusage* call in Unix-like systems.

Since one of the key functionalities of service manager is to monitor processes for failures, error detection can be based on additional or alternative techniques besides resource monitoring. This can be done with e.g. operating system features, HEARTBEAT [6, 7] or WATCHDOG.

If fault recovery fails, service manager should mitigate the fault by QUARANTINING the faulty module. If the fault is persistent, LEAKY BUCKET COUNTER can be used to limit the number of restarts.

If the service manager is deployed on a system that uses DATA-CENTRIC ARCHITECTURE, service startup interfaces can be implemented through the middleware. Since the middleware abstracts the location of the data, it can be used to remotely start dependencies. For example, service manager SM_A must start a service called S1. However, it has a dependency called S2 which cannot be found locally, so the service manager publishes a start request for S2. A second service manager SM_B on another computer notices the request, starts S2 and publishes information about the successful startup. SM_A receives information that S2 is available and starts S1.

The implementation for service manager needs to be kept fairly simple, since it acts as a single point of failure locally. This conflicts with the need to use of configuration files, making resource checks, and providing user interface, so they should be based on external components or libraries that have been proven in use.

Consequences

+ Detects and initializes recovery from transient faults that cause a process to consume too much system resources or become unresponsive.
+ Ensures other processes stay alive and have sufficient resources.
+ Simplifies starting procedure of complex system that consists of large number of processes, making possible to start and stop a large number of processes automatically and in a specific order.
+ Cost-efficiency: the same service manager implementation can be reused on several systems.
+ Supports logging and reporting of errors so that they do not go undetected.
− Cannot detect faults that cause erroneous output for monitored components.
− Cannot recover persistent faults such as development and physical faults, e.g. computer failures.

- Potential single point of failure that may stop the entire system from working if services are incorrectly terminated.
- Restarting a service may cause the system to behave in non-deterministic way and miss deadlines, which is a failure for a hard real-time system. However, it should be noted that the failure would have likely caused the system to miss the deadlines or exhibit some other unwanted behavior even without service restart.
- Resource utilization needs to be estimated for the processes in order to set limits.
- Service manager uses system resources and may reduce performance

Known uses. Node State Manager (NSM) for in-vehicle infotainment systems: GENIVI Alliance (http://genivi.org/) is a non-profit consortium promoting open-source platform for the automotive in-vehicle infotainment industry. Reference implementation of the platform includes NSM that is responsible for information regarding the current running state of the embedded system. NSM component collates information from multiple sources and uses this to determine the current state of the node. It is the highest level of escalation on the node and will therefore command the reset and supply control logic. It is notified of errors and other status signals from components that are responsible for monitoring system health in different ways. NSM also provides shutdown management by signaling applications to shut down.

MINIX 3.0 driver manager: MINIX is a POSIX conformant operating system, based on a microkernel that has minimal amount of software executing in the kernel mode. Most of the operating system runs in user mode as independent processes, including processes for the file system, process manager, and device drivers. The system uses a special component known as the driver manager to monitor and control all services and drivers in the system [5]. Driver manager is the parent process for all components, so it can detect their crashes (based on POSIX signals). Additionally the driver manager can check the status of selected drivers periodically using HEARTBEAT messages. When a failure is detected, the driver manager automatically replaces the malfunctioning component with a fresh copy without needing to reboot the computer. The driver manager can also be explicitly instructed to replace a malfunctioning component with a new one.

Monit (http://mmonit.com/monit/) is an open source tool that can function as a service manager in non-real time systems. Following code listing shows an example configuration for Spamassassin daemon that restarts the daemon if its memory or CPU usage exceeds 50% for 5 monitoring cycles:

```
check process spamd with pidfile /var/run/spamd.pid
    start program = "/etc/init.d/spamd start"
    stop  program = "/etc/init.d/spamd stop"
    if 5 restarts within 5 cycles then timeout
    if cpu usage > 50% for 5 cycles then restart
    if mem usage > 50% for 5 cycles then restart
    depends on spamd_bin
    depends on spamd_rc
```

Related Patterns. FAULT OBSERVER [6], HEARTBEAT, SAFE STATE, SOMEONE IN CHARGE [6], START-UP MONITOR, STATIC RESOURCE ALLOCATION [7], and WATCHDOG.

To see how to design an application in a way that it can be easily restarted at any time, see LET IT CRASH.

MANAGER design pattern [10] can be used to manage multiple objects of same type – the idea is similar to SERVICE MANAGER (keep track of entities and provide unified interface for them) but the MANAGER focuses on different scope, i.e. managing entities (objects) of the same type and does not include resource monitoring or fault detection.

SERVICE CONFIGURATOR is very similar to SERVICE MANAGER in many regards. However, the main use cases for SERVICE CONFIGURATOR are, as the name implies, related to reconfiguration of the system, whereas SERVICE MANAGER aims to improve fault tolerance of the system by managing (monitoring & restarting) services. In CPSs, dynamic reconfiguration of the system can often be undesirable due to possible safety implications. An example of SERVICE CONFIGURATOR is the device driver system in modern OSs. A comparable implementation of the to SERVICE MANAGER is the driver manager in MINIX, which adds the management (fault detection & restart) aspect to device drivers.

SERVICE MANAGER can QUARANTINE a module by stopping it if a fault is detected. and recovery does not work.

SYSTEM MONITOR [6] can be used to study behavior of system or specific tasks and make sure they operate correctly, e.g. by using HEARTBEAT or WATCHDOG. If a monitored task stops, SYSTEM MONITOR reports the error. Compared to it, SERVICE MANAGER has a more active role in managing the tasks.

REPLICA MANAGER [15] provides the necessary mechanisms for the replica management in systems that use active node replication, i.e. REDUNDANCY, whereas SERVICE MANAGER does not make presumptions about the use of redundancy.

3.3 Let It Crash

   𝔍𝔲𝔰𝔱 𝔞 𝔣𝔩𝔢𝔰𝔥 𝔴𝔬𝔲𝔫𝔡.

Also Known as. CRASH-ONLY [11], FAIL-FAST, LET IT FAIL or OFFENSIVE PROGRAMMING.

Intent. Avoid complex error handling for unspecified errors. Instead, crash the process and leave error handling for other processes in order to build a robust system that handles errors internally and does not go down as a whole.

Context. You are developing a distributed control system that consists of several processes and subsystems that need to cooperate to complete tasks.

DATA-CENTRIC ARCHITECTURE or some other asynchronous decoupled architectural design has been utilized so that processes are not using shared memory.

Some subsystems might have safety-critical functionality, but it is possible to move the system to SAFE STATE (i.e. the system is fail-safe type, not fail-operate). The system has dynamic state information from the user inputs and working environment in the process memory, e.g. tool tracking data in the case of a robot manipulator. This state data needs to be recovered after a failure.

The system has a mechanism to supervise and restart the processes. This can be implemented at operating system, programming language or framework level, e.g. with the SERVICE MANAGER.

Problem. How to implement lightweight form of error handling that improves reliability and predictability?

Forces

- *Availability*: The system as a whole should remain available, even if some subsystems or processes experience failures, since degraded functionality is better than no functionality. In case of a fault, only minimal part of the system should be affected. Recovery from failures should happen without human intervention and with minimal downtime.
- *Reliability:* Generation of incorrect outputs should be prevented, otherwise errors may propagate and the system could cause damage to the environment.
- *Safety*: If an error is detected, any functionality using the affected process should be stopped and taken to a safe state in order to prevent and minimize damages.
- *Cost-efficiency*: Design diverse fault tolerance techniques are oversized or impractical for the application, but the system needs to be able to recover from errors.
- *Real-time performance*: Control system needs to react within a certain time-limit; exceeding the time-limit causes a failure.
- *Predictability*: The system should behave in a consistent manner. If the process tries to repair its corrupted state, behavior of the system cannot be predicted, which complicates debugging and verification of reliability. Predictability includes system behavior when a fault is triggered.
- *Recovery*: Because it is impossible to foresee all possible faults, specifications do not cover all possible error situations. Various error situations occur seldom, are difficult to handle and non-trivial to simulate in testing [11]. If the programmers try to implement recovery, they will make ad hoc decisions not based on the specifications (i.e. they cannot know how the error should be handled), possibly causing unwanted and undocumented behavior.

Solution. Make processes crash-safe and fast to recover; flush corrupted state by "crashing" the process instead of writing extensive error handling code.
Commodore 64, DOS machines and other old computers were designed to be shut down by simply turning the power off, essentially crashing the system. On the other hand, if an operating system caches disk data in memory, workstation crash may

corrupt the file system, which is inconvenient and slow to repair. Control system processes and subsystems should also be designed to be easily terminated and recoverable with a simple recovery path if an error is detected, instead of guessing how error recovery should be attempted, possibly corrupting program state further and causing unpredictable behavior.

Therefore, implement error handling by terminating the process that has encountered the error. Only program extended error recovery routines if they are based on the specification or it is self-evident how the error should be handled – otherwise crash the process. However, only the module or process where the error is should be crashed, not the whole system.

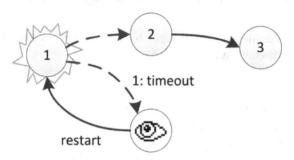

Fig. 4. Process 1 encounters an error and dies, after which it is restarted by the service manager, represented as an eye. If the process 2 detects a deadline overrun, it needs to stop, potentially interrupting process 3, and wait until process 1 is active again before resuming work. Alternatively the process 2 does not notice any deadline overruns and continues working normally.

Processes that have been designed with LET IT CRASH can (1) help to find faults, by making them more visible ("offensive programming"), (2) prevent software degradation with REJUVENATION [11, 14], and (3) be used to implement fault tolerance (recovery from faults). In the final case it is possible to perform recovery without affecting service availability if the recovery process is fast enough. Recovery (and rejuvenation) needs an external entity to initiate the procedure, since the process itself has crashed (see Fig. 4). This pattern focuses mostly on the final case since it is more problematic to implement correctly.

You have a monitoring layer that can supervise and recover processes e.g. by restarting. To have the monitoring layer detect a failure, you may need to implement timeouts or the faulty process must terminate upon encountering an error in order to send a signal for the monitoring layer (parent process knows the liveliness state of its child processes). How the error is detected in the first place is not part of LET IT CRASH, but contract programming or error checks could be used. Abnormal program termination can be forced e.g. by using *abort()* or *raise(SIGSEGV)*. If the monitoring layer has implemented failure detection – based on watchdog, heartbeat, etc. – it can also hard-fail the service using e.g. *kill(pid, SIGTERM)*. This might be necessary if the process is incapable of detecting its own fault.

Error recovery is performed by restarting the process. Therefore, make processes fast and easy to restart in order to minimize service failures and downtime. To keep recovery path simple, use the single responsibility principle, thereby minimizing responsibilities of a single process. If the process encounters an error and crashes, it might be possible to recover from the error without causing deadline misses for other processes and tripping the system to a SAFE STATE. However, if a control loop has a period of e.g. 1 ms and restarting of a process that provides information for the loop takes several milliseconds, control loop execution will be interrupted.

LET IT CRASH does not mean that error handling or exception handling should not be implemented at all. Indeed, sanity checks and error handling are essential for control systems and should be implemented to prepare for exceptional (but expected) circumstances, such as write operation failures or unavailable dependencies. LET IT CRASH, on the other hand, is applicable in situations where the program experiences an unexpected failure and cannot reliably perform its function. This can happen due to programmer errors, complex interaction faults, intermittent faults, etc.

Recovery paths can be tested extensively by terminating the system forcibly every time it needs to be shut down or restarted, instead of letting it run through a normal shutdown process. This forces the system to do a recovery during the startup.

Make processes crash-safe. Processes typically handle three types of state data: dynamic, static, and internal. Internal state is related to current computations and is usually discarded after use. If a process crashes, you must think if you want to recycle its internal state. If you recycle everything you risk hitting the exact same fault again and crashing, so it might be reasonable to recycle only parts of this state. Static state is configuration data that can be easily recovered or read from other processes. Finally, the dynamic state data is generated as the program is executed by reading user inputs, interacting with other processes and environment, etc. Some of it can be computed from other data or read directly from sensors, but rest cannot be reconstructed. This data must be protected by using checkpointing, journaling or some other form of dedicated state store, for example databases and distributed data structures. To implement this, you must know WHAT TO SAVE [6].

Implement a reporting functionality that reports failures so that they do not go unnoticed. Failure information can be forwarded e.g. by using a service manager or supervisors to send NOTIFICATION messages [12].

The corollary to the LET IT CRASH approach is that you must design your software to be ready for processes failing. There is now a possibility that a dependency is not available because it has been crashed and is being restarted. To detect this situation, add timeouts or appropriate QoS policies to interactions between components. If a timeout is triggered, move the system to a SAFE STATE. Normal operation can be resumed when dependencies are back online. A missing dependency is therefore not considered to be an error that would necessitate a crash.

Consequences

+ Enables simple error handling & recovery; avoids complex error handling constructs in code, therefore improving predictability of the system.
+ Cost-effective (lightweight) form of fault tolerance that does not require use of redundancy.
+ Allows error handling to be implemented separately (externally) from the business logic, e.g. with supervisors.
+ Supports recovery from transient faults since a restart is usually enough to handle them.
+ Possible to achieve high availability (for the system as a whole, not necessary for all services provided by the system).
+ Complements other fault tolerant designs such as REDUNDANCY and REJUVENATION.
+ Processes can be updated to new versions on-the-fly, since the old process can be killed and replaced using the normal recovery path.
+ Limits error propagation to other parts of the system (babbling idiot failure) by acting as an ERROR CONTAINMENT BARRIER [6].
+ Errors are less likely to cause the system to perform unpredictable and potentially dangerous or irreversible operations.
+ Finding faults should be easier, since they are made more visible by crashing and reporting.
− Availability of some services provided by the system is lower (when compared to redundant fault tolerance solutions) − on the other hand availability of other unrelated services provided by the system should be unaffected.
− Cannot mitigate persistent faults.
− Processes need additional code to react to missing dependencies (i.e. other services, when waiting for them to come back online).
− Possible performance cost if state needs to be saved to enable recovery.
− Recovery speed is non-deterministic since it depends on how fast the processes can be restarted, loading of saved state, loading of dependencies, system load level, etc

Known uses. Erlang actor model and supervisors (Erlang is used e.g. in Ericsson AXD301 ATM switches) [2]: supervisors are processes that are responsible for starting, stopping and monitoring their child processes. The basic idea of a supervisor is that it should keep its child processes alive by restarting them when necessary [13].

Control system of Curiosity: Mars rovers are highly autonomous vehicles that operate in high-radiation environment, relying on a low-bandwidth, high-latency communication link. A warm reset can be executed by control system when it identifies a problem with one of its operations. On November 7, 2013 Curiosity rover performed a reset of its control software upon encountering an unexpected event (an error in a catalog file) [17]. After the reset, rover entered safe mode, but was able to perform operations and communications as expected and successfully resumed nominal operations mode after the fault had been analyzed.

Related Patterns. ERROR CONTAINMENT BARRIER, NOTIFICATIONS, SAFE STATE, SERVICE MANAGER, REDUNDANCY, WHAT TO SAVE.

MINIMIZE HUMAN INTERVENTION (MHI) is about how the system can process and resolve errors automatically before they become failures [6]. LET IT FAIL could be implemented as part of MHI as a final resort or in case there is no specification for error handling.

Software REJUVENATION is a proactive technique where the system has been designed to be booted periodically. Microrebooting [11] refers to a technique where suspect components are restarted before they fail.

Acknowledgements. Authors would like to thank reviewers and VikingPLoP 2013 participants for the feedback and providing valuable comments, Robert Hanmer for shepherding the paper and VikingPLoP organizers for a great pattern conference. This work was carried out under the EFDA Goal Oriented Training Programme (WP10-GOT-GOTRH) and financial support of TEKES, which are greatly acknowledged. The views and opinions expressed herein do not necessarily reflect those of the European Commission.

Appendix: List of Referenced Patterns

Table 2. Short descriptions of referenced patterns.

Pattern	Pattern intent
BUS ABSTRACTION [7]	Nodes communicate via a message bus. The bus is abstracted so it can be changed easily
ERROR CONTAINMENT BARRIER [6]	System should stop the flow of errors from one part to another by isolating them to a unit of mitigation and initiating error recovery
FAULT OBSERVER [6]	Coordinate reporting to all observers that a fault is present, reported, and recovery actions escalated
HEARTBEAT [6, 7]	Send a status report at regular intervals to let other parts of the system know their status
LEAKY BUCKET COUNTER [6]	Implement a method to ride over transients by keeping a counter that is automatically decremented and incremented by errors
MINIMIZE HUMAN INTERVENTION [6]	System should take care of itself without human intervention
MONITOR [10]	Support many entities of same or similar type. The MANAGER object is designed to keep track of all the entities. In many cases, the MANAGER will also route messages to individual entities
MEDIATOR [9]	Define an object that encapsulates how a set of objects interact. Mediator promotes loose coupling by keeping objects from referring to each other explicitly, and it lets you vary their interaction independently
NOTIFICATIONS [12]	Communicate noteworthy or alarming events and state changes in the system using a dedicated message type

(continued)

Table 2. (*continued*)

Pattern	Pattern intent
PUBLISH/SUBSCRIBE [8]	Define a change propagation infrastructure that allows publishers in a distributed application to disseminate events that convey information that may be of interest to others. Notify subscribers interested in those events whenever such information is published
QUARANTINE [6]	Take steps to isolate faulty unit in order to stop fault propagation
REDUNDANCY [6]	Maximize availability by having alternate hardware or software that can perform the same function
REJUVENATION [11, 14]	Periodically rejuvenate a software item by shutting it down and restarting it
REPLICA MANAGER [15]	Hide communication algorithms from the applications to cope with the possible non-deterministic behaviour of replicas by delaying requests until all replicated nodes make the same request
SAFE STATE [7]	If something potentially harmful occurs, all nodes should enter a predetermined safe state
SERVICE CONFIGURATOR [16]	Decouple the behaviour of services from the point in time at which service implementations are configured into an application or system
SOMEONE IN CHARGE [6]	Every fault tolerance action undertaken by the system should have a clearly identified entity controlling and monitoring the action
START-UP MONITOR [7]	During start-up all devices are started in certain order and with correct delays. Additionally, care is taken that there are no malfunctions
STATIC RESOURCE ALLOCATION [7]	Critical services are always available when all resources are allocated when the system starts
SYSTEM MONITOR [6]	Some errors will only manifest themselves at a system level. Check for them at this level
UNITS OF MITIGATION [6]	Decide what the unit of fault tolerance is
WATCHDOG [6, 7]	Build a special entity to watch over another to make sure that it is still operating well
WHAT TO SAVE [6]	Use checkpoints to save information of global interest to a shared, globally accessibly data storage

References

1. Avizienis, A., Laprie, J.-C., Randell, B., Landwehr, C.: Basic concepts and taxonomy of dependable and secure computing. Trans. Dependable Secure Comput. **1**(1), 11–33 (2004)
2. Armstrong, J.: Making Reliable Distributed Systems in the Presence of Software Errors. Royal Institute of Technology, Stockholm (2003)
3. Dunn, W.: Practical Design of Safety-Critical Computer Systems. Reliability Press, Solvang (2002)
4. Knight, J., Leveson, N.: An experimental evaluation of the assumption of independence in multi-version programming. Trans. Softw. Eng. **12**, 96–109 (1986)

5. Herder, J.: Building a Dependable Operating System: Fault Tolerance in MINIX 3. Vrije Universiteit. USENIX Association, Netherlands (2010)
6. Hanmer, R.: Patterns for Fault Tolerant Software. Wiley, Hoboken (2007)
7. Eloranta, V.-P., Koskinen, J., Leppänen, M., Reijonen, V.: A pattern language for distributed machine control systems. Department of Software Systems, Tampere University of Technology (2010)
8. Buschmann, F., Henney, K., Schmidt, D.: Pattern Oriented Software Architecture: A Pattern Language for Distributed Computing. Wiley, Hoboken (2007)
9. Gamma, E., Helm, R., Johnson, R., Vlissides, J.: Design Patterns: Elements of Reusable Object-Oriented Software. Addison-Wesley, Boston (1995)
10. EventHelix.com Inc.: Manager Design Pattern. http://www.eventhelix.com/realtimemantra/ManagerDesignPattern.htm#.UOQm6kUbR8E. Accessed 2 Jan 2013
11. Candea, G., Fox, A.: Crash-only software. In: Proceedings of HotOS IX: The 9th Workshop on Hot Topics in Operating Systems (2003)
12. Eloranta, V.-P.: Event notification patterns for distributed machine control systems. In: Proceedings of VikingPLoP 2012 Conference. Department of Software Systems, Tampere University of Technology (2012)
13. Erlang/OTP R16A documentation. http://www.erlang.org/doc/. Accessed 13 Feb 2013
14. Hanmer, R.: Software rejuvenation. In: Proceedings of 17th Conference on Pattern Languages of Programs. ACM (2010)
15. Pinho, L., Vasques, F.: Replica management in real-time Ada 95 applications. In: Proceedings of the 9th International Workshop on Real-time Ada. ACM (1999)
16. Jain, P., Schmidt, D.: Dynamically configuring communication services with the service configurator pattern. C++ report, June issue (1997)
17. NASA Jet Propulsion Laboratory: Curiosity Out of Safe Mode. http://www.jpl.nasa.gov/news/news.php?release=2013-330. Accessed 19 Dec 2013

Safety Architecture Pattern System with Security Aspects

Christopher Preschern$^{(\boxtimes)}$, Nermin Kajtazovic, and Christian Kreiner

Institute for Technical Informatics, Graz University of Technology, Graz, Austria
{christopher.preschern,nermin.kajtazovic,christian.kreiner}@tugraz.at

Abstract. This article builds a structured pattern system with safety patterns from literature and presents the safety patterns. The patterns are analyzed regarding their basic safety-related design decisions (safety tactics) and relationships between the patterns are structurally developed based on these safety tactics. To analyze security aspects, the STRIDE security analysis is used to list relevant threats for the patterns. The threats and the safety tactics are represented in Goal Structuring Notation diagrams as part of the patterns to enable security and safety reasoning.

Keywords: Architecture patterns · Safety · Security · Goal structuring notation · STRIDE analysis

1 Introduction

Increasing connectivity of embedded systems makes the influence of security aspects even for safety-critical systems more and more relevant. However, rather often safety experts are not familiar with the field of security.

To provide safety architects with a starting point how to bring security into their system and to provide them with good solutions for safety architectures, we build a safety architecture pattern system[1] including a security analysis for the patterns. We analyze safety patterns for basic design decisions (safety tactics) which are applied in the patterns. Based on the applied safety tactics we find relationships between the patterns. For example, all patterns applying the *Voting* tactic, are likely to be related. Additionally we use the tactics to build a Goal Structuring Notation (GSN) diagram which presents how a pattern achieves its safety goal by applying these tactics. Furthermore, we relate the safety tactics to the IEC 61508 safety certification standard to build a GSN diagram which allows to reason how the overall architecture is related to safety methods described in the standard.

---

[1] A "pattern system" is similar to a "pattern language", but compared to a pattern language it does not claim to be complete (Buschmann et al. 1996). Precise definitions about the difference between pattern collections/systems/languages can be found in (Schumacher 2003).

© Springer Nature Switzerland AG 2019
J. Noble et al. (Eds.): TPLOP IV, LNCS 10600, pp. 22–75, 2019.
https://doi.org/10.1007/978-3-030-14291-9_2

From a security point of view, we analyze all safety patterns with the STRIDE security method. STRIDE results in a list of relevant threats for the pattern which we structurally present in a GSN diagram.

Section 2 provides definitions, basics on safety tactics, GSN, and the STRIDE analysis. Section 3 presents related work on safety patterns, on how to organize safety patterns, and on security analysis of safety systems and patterns in particular. Section 4 integrates an example pattern into our pattern system. Section 5 applies a safety pattern to a case study and Sect. 6 concludes this work. Appendix A presents all the patterns of the safety pattern system and Appendix B presents safety tactics.

2 Basics

2.1 Definitions

Reliability

"A system's reliability is the probability that it will perform without deviations from agreed-upon behavior for a specific period of time." (Hanmer 2007)

Reliability can be measured for a component in isolation and is often expressed by the mean time to failure, where a failure is a deviation from the required behavior of the system. This means that reliability is tightly related to the requirements of the system. If no requirements are assumed or defined, then there can be no failures and any behavior of the system would be reliable (Leveson 2012).

Fault Tolerance

"Fault tolerance means to avoid service failures in the presence of faults." (Avizienis et al. 2004)

Fault tolerance is a way to achieve high reliability of a system by designing it in a way that the system is able to perform its required service even if some parts of the system do not perform correctly (Hanmer 2007).

Safety

"Safety is the freedom of unacceptable risk." (International Electrotechnical Commission 2010)

Safety-critical systems are systems whose malfunctioning poses a threat to human health of even human lives. Safety measures focus on eliminating such risks. Compared to simply minimizing failures, this also includes the prevention of unknown or undefined system behavior which could lead to an accident. Safety cannot be measured for a component in isolation and has to be considered for the overall system and its environment (Leveson 2012).

Therefore safety cannot be achieved by simply taking special safety measures during design or implementation of a system, but safety has to be considered during all stages of system development. For that, safety standards, such as the IEC 61508, propose safety-development-lifecycles describing processes which have to be followed during system development (International Electrotechnical Commission 2010).

Security

> *"A condition that results from the establishment and maintenance of protective measures that enable an enterprise to perform its mission or critical functions despite risks posed by threats to its use of information systems."* (Committee on National Security Systems 2010)

Security copes with protection from unwanted, maliciously caused behavior. Many other definitions of security target the three main goals to be achieved by secure systems: Confidentiality, integrity, and availability (Dasarathy 2013). Just like safety, also security has to be considered during all stages of system development and also for security there exist several development lifecycles, for example the security development lifecycle suggested in (Howard and Lipner 2006).

2.2   Architectural Tactics

Tactics are architectural design decisions which influence and manipulate quality attributes (Bachmann et al. 2003). Compared to design patterns, they describe general concepts or principles and do not describe solutions for a problem in a given context. For example, the *Voting* safety tactic describes the idea how to achieve failure containment by choosing an appropriate output from redundant components. The concrete application of this idea would, for example, be the TRIPLE MODULAR REDUNDANCY pattern which uses the *Voting* tactic to choose for the majority of three redundant subsystem outputs.

It is difficult to keep tactics and patterns apart as there is no clear boarder between the two. For example, (Saridakis 2002) describes different forms of degradation as fault tolerances patterns, whereas (Wu 2003) considers *Degradation* as a safety tactic. (Ryoo et al. 2010) specify some criteria to identify tactics. For a design decision on order to be a tactic, it has to be atomic. This means that it cannot be divided into other multiple tactics, however it can be refined. For example, the *Redundancy* tactic is refined by the *Replication Redundancy* tactic and the *Diverse Redundancy* tactic, but it is not composed of them. Furthermore, (Ryoo et al. 2010) say that tactics focus on a single quality attribute (e.g. safety) and patterns usually affect several quality attributes. However, this criterion does not hold for all tactics described in literature. For example, the *Voting* tactic influences several quality attributes such as safety, availability, or perhaps even performance.

There are also different opinions whether tactics are basic building blocks for design patterns (as in (Kumar and Prabhakar 2010a)) or whether tactics represent the possible design space and can be used as additional design enhancements for certain design patterns (as in (Harrison and Avgeriou 2008)).

In this article we take the list of safety tactics from (Preschern et al. 2013c) and we consider safety tactics as atomic design decisions which represent building blocks for safety architecture patterns. The full list of safety tactics is given in Appendix B and shows the tactic names, a short description of the tactics, and the methods of the IEC 61508 safety standard which can be related to these tactics.

2.3   Goal Structuring Notation

The Goal Structuring Notation (GSN) was developed by (Kelly and Weaver 2004) and is often used in the safety domain to provide a structured argument for the achievement of specific goals. Recently, a standard for GSN was published which contains definitions of the notation and which presents approaches how to use GSN to elaborate a specific goal (Spriggs 2012). GSN can also be used to argue for system security like, for example, in (Cockram and Lautieri 2007). We will use GSN to argue for safety and for security of the presented patterns and we will use the GSN concepts from Fig. 1.

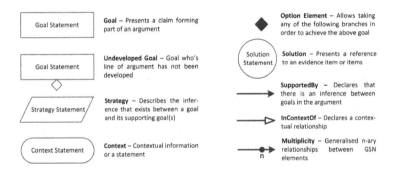

Fig. 1. GSN concepts used in this article, based on (GSN Working Group 2011)

To show how a GSN goal is achieved, it is linked by arrows to an argument (GSN strategies, GSN subgoals) which ends up in the evidence (GSN solutions) supporting the claim that the goal is achieved.

Figure 2 shows an example for the application of GSN. The main goal in the example is that an attacker cannot obtain some confidential data. In the next step, context elements are added which say that the data is locally stored on a computer and transmitted to another computer. The main goal is split up into the subgoals to protect the stored data and the transmitted data. Protecting transmitted data is achieved by transmitting data over a protected TLS channel

(GSN strategy). For this TLS channel, we need evidence that it is reliable. This evidence (GSN solution element) is that the used implementation is robust and proven in use. Protecting stored data is an undeveloped goal which means that the security argument for this subgoal is not yet complete and further arguments have to be included here in order to obtain a complete argument that the overall goal to protect data is achieved. In this example, GSN provides a structured way to show how the rather unspecific goal to protect confidential data is (partially) achieved by specific measures (the TLS channel).

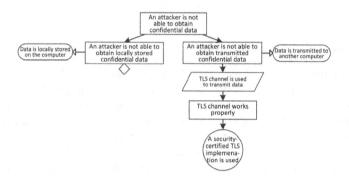

Fig. 2. GSN example showing a security argument

2.4 STRIDE Analysis

In order to build a secure system, it is necessary to first find the relevant threats to the system before finding solutions how to mitigate them. The STRIDE approach is a structured way to find these threats. The STRIDE approach was proposed by Microsoft (Howard and LeBlanc 2003) and is nowadays often used for security engineering. STRIDE is an acronym, where the letters stand for the six threat categories which are analyzed (Spoofing, Tampering, Repudiation, Information Disclosure, Denial of Service (DoS), Elevation of Priviledge (EoP)).

For threat modeling with STRIDE, first a data flow diagram has to be constructed. A data flow diagram shows the interaction between system elements and external elements (e.g. users of the system) by graphically presenting all the data flows (inputs/outputs of elements). All relevant STRIDE threats for each element in the diagram are then listed. The relevant threats for different data flow diagram elements types are given in Table 1.

Figure 3 shows an example data flow diagram. It shows a system which receives some encrypted data, decrypts this data, and stores the data on a harddrive. The STRIDE approach yields the following list of threats for this system by simply going through all elements of the diagram and listing all their relevant threats:

Table 1. STRIDE mapping to data flow diagram element types (Howard and LeBlanc 2003)

Data flow diagram element type	S	T	R	I	D	E
External entity	X		X			
Data flow		X		X	X	
Data store		X	X	X	X	
Process	X	X	X	X	X	X

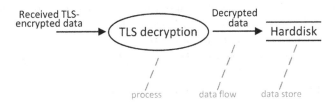

Fig. 3. Example data flow diagram

- Tampering of the encrypted data
- Information disclosure of the encrypted data
- Denial of service of the encrypted data
- Spoofing of the decryption mechanism
- Tampering of the decryption mechanism
- Repudiation of the decryption mechanism
- Information disclosure in the decryption mechanism
- Denial of service of the decryption mechanism
- Elevation of privilege on the decryption mechanism
- Tampering of the decrypted data
- Information disclosure of the decrypted data
- Denial of service of the decrypted data
- Tampering of the harddrive
- Repudiation of the harddrive
- Information disclosure on the harddrive
- Denial of service of the harddrive

The resulting list of threats can further be elaborated by implementing countermeasures for relevant threats and by excluding threats which are not relevant for the specific system. For example, the above mentioned information disclosure threat for the encrypted data is irrelevant if we assume that the attacker does not possess the decryption key.

When all threats are covered, one has a structured security argument. In this article we will use Goal Structuring Notation to present such a structured argument.

3   Related Work

3.1   Safety Patterns

The patterns described in this article are classified as "Safety patterns". Some of the patterns could as well be called "Fault tolerance patterns". In particular, most of the redundancy-based patterns fall into that category. However, several other of the presented patterns focus on protection from unknown hazards and should thus rather be called safety patterns.

We call the patterns in this article "Safety patterns", because they provide a connection to the IEC 61508 safety standard, because the provided known uses mostly target safety applications, and because most of the patterns are based on literature in which these patterns are already called safety patterns.

Table 2 gives an overview of literature presenting safety patterns.

Table 2. Literature which introduces safety-related patterns

Title	Description
(Daniels et al. 1997) *"The Reliable Hybrid Pattern - A Generalized Software Fault Tolerant Design Pattern"*	A pattern which includes several software fault tolerance techniques, such as N-version programming, voting or acceptance tests, is presented. The pattern is presented as a generic architecture which explicitly states decision alternatives, like different kinds of voting mechanisms, in the pattern
(Douglass 1998) *"Safety-Critical System Design"*	The article covers safety architecture patterns such as a protected single channel, or redundant channels. The article further discusses issues and decisions to be made when implementing safety patterns. For example, the article discusses the decision of programming language or the testing issues for safety patterns
(Saridakis 2002) *"A System of Patterns for Fault Tolerance"*	This paper introduces several architectural fault-tolerance patterns like passive and active duplication patterns. The paper further discusses how to group these patterns, for example regarding the failure type they handle or regarding their fault reaction time
(Douglass 2002) *"Real-Time Design Patterns: Robust Scalable Architecture for Real-Time Systems"*	Besides other patterns, this book covers safety-related architecture patterns and also includes much more detailed descriptions of the patterns from (Douglass 1998)
(Grunske 2003) *"Transformational Patterns for the Improvement of Safety Properties in Architectural Specification"*	This paper presents patterns for architectures to increase safety. The patterns are described as architecture transformations which explicitly show the safety architecture before and after the application of the pattern. Some of the presented patterns are closely related to the patterns from (Douglass 2002)

(*continued*)

Table 2. (*continued*)

Title	Description
(Hanmer 2007) *"Patterns for Fault Tolerant Software"*	The book provides a pattern language of fault-tolerance patterns grouped as error detection, error processing, error mitigation, fault treatment, and architectural patterns. A diagram showing the relations between the patterns is provided for each of these categories
(Douglass 2010) *"Design Patterns for Embedded Systems in C"*	The book presents design patterns implemented in C. Some of the patterns such as the protected single channel, or redundant channels are safety-related and are based on (Douglass 2002)
(Armoush 2010) *"Design Patterns for Safety-critical Embedded Systems"*	This PhD thesis introduces new and collects existing safety patterns for embedded systems (mostly based on (Douglass 2002) for hardware and (Pullum 2001) for software patterns). The patterns all include reliability and risk reduction calculations
(Hampton 2012) *"Survey of Safety Architectural Patterns"*	This survey presents the application of the patterns from (Armoush 2010) within a company. The survey shows which of the patterns are often applied in practice and which of the patterns are just rarely applied. Furthermore, some new, rather domain-specific, safety patterns are introduced
(Rauhamäki et al. 2012) *"Architectural Patterns for Functional Safety"*	The paper presents 4 patterns related to general safety architectures. The four presented patterns describe how safety functionality should be separated from non-critical functionality while still keeping the system productive
(Rauhamäki et al. 2013) *"Patterns for Safety and Control System Cooperation"*	The paper presents 3 safety patterns which focus on how a safety system can effectively be integrated into a larger control system
(Rauhamäki and Kuikka 2013) *"Patterns for Control System Safety"*	The paper presents 4 patterns describing how safety functionality can be included into larger control systems
(Douglass 2013) *"Software Design Architecture Patterns for Embedded Systems"*	The book chapter discusses how and why safety pattern should be applied when developing embedded systems. Most of the presented patterns were introduced in (Douglass 1998).

3.2 Organizing Safety Patterns

(Saridakis 2002) presents several fault-tolerance patterns in detail and discusses how they can be related to each other. The patterns are classified according to several criteria: pattern complexity, space requirements, time requirements, failure types which are handled by the pattern, and the pattern aim (error detection, recovery, or masking). (Hanmer 2007) also describes fault-tolerance patterns and presents the patterns and their relationships as a pattern language.

(Armoush 2010) provides in his PhD thesis a comprehensive collection of safety architecture patterns for embedded systems. Most of the patterns are taken from literature and all are presented in a common pattern format. However, the relationships between the patterns are not described in detail. Armoush provides a tool which lists the patterns and provides information about them (e.g. reliability calculations) when selected.

To bridge the gap between the high-level safety pattern descriptions and their actual implementation, (Gawand et al. 2011) represent safety patterns in UML notation. This is also done by (Sarma et al. 2013) with the pattern catalog of (Armoush 2010). This idea was taken further by (Antonino et al. 2012) who introduce a safety-related UML profile to capture architectural safety pattern elements (e.g. voter) and to define rules for them. Based on this idea (Olivera 2012) implements a repository for safety patterns including their UML notation.

3.3   Security Analysis of Design Patterns and Safety Systems

(Yautsiukhin and Scandariato 2008) conduct a STRIDE analysis for a case study and discuss how well several patterns can counter the threats. They use a risk assessment method to rate the threat severity and they assign a value to each pattern describing how well the pattern copes with different threats. With this method the security of different patterns for a system can be quantitatively compared. A similar approach is taken in (Halkidis et al. 2006a,b; Halkidis and Tsantalis 2008). They evaluate the effectiveness of web security patterns against STRIDE attacks by experiments. With these results they suggest patterns for a web system by first conducting a STRIDE analysis for the concrete system and then suggesting the patterns which mitigate the STRIDE attacks best. This work is also done for security patterns in general in (Halkidis et al. 2004), where a mapping between several security patterns and their effectiveness for STRIDE attacks is presented. In (Schaad and Borozdin 2012; Schaad and Garaga 2012), a tool is presented which reports threats for an architecture by automatically applying the STRIDE analysis to an architecture model. As in our approach, the STRIDE analysis is adapted to just include the threats relevant for the specific architecture element types. (Hamid et al. 2010) take another approach with the TERESA project, by applying a model-based approach to integrate design patterns in order to argue about the safety and security of a system. The tool-based process of how to apply the design patterns is described in (Hamid et al. 2013). (Buckley et al. 2011) discuss how to integrate reliability concerns into security systems and vice versa. Furthermore they present two patterns coping with reliability and security.

Unrelated to design patterns, but related to security evaluation of safety systems in general, (Hansen 2009) analyzes a safety-critical automation device and highlights attacks compromising system safety. (Johnson and Yepez 2011a,b) present a combined security and safety risk assessment methodology where security and safety arguments are shown in a GSN diagram. Security threats are analyzed for a case study and the threats are included in an existing safety GSN to obtain a unified assurance case for safety and security. (Nai-Fovino et al. 2009) present a method to integrate security reasoning into fault trees. They discuss how to analyze the risk of security aspects in order to integrate their probabilities consistently into the fault tree notation. This idea is further elaborated in (Steiner and Liggesmeyer 2013) where a safety and security analysis is performed based on component fault trees. A similar approach is taken by (Ugljesa and Wacker 2011) to integrate security considerations into the error probability calculation of a 2oo4 architecture[2]. A detailed security analysis with security enhancements for the 1oo2 architecture is shown in (Preschern et al. 2012a). (Yampolskiy et al. 2012) present an extension of data flow diagrams which allows analyzing an architecture for STRIDE attacks as well as for safety.

4 Safety Pattern System

This section explains with an example (the HOMOGENOUS DUPLEX PATTERN) how to include a safety architecture pattern into our pattern system. We explain the applied pattern format and we describe how to bring a safety pattern into this format (which includes building GSN diagrams for safety and security). Furthermore, we describe how to find the relationships to other patterns. An overview of this described approach is shown in Fig. 4. This approach was applied for all the safety patterns presented in Appendix A.

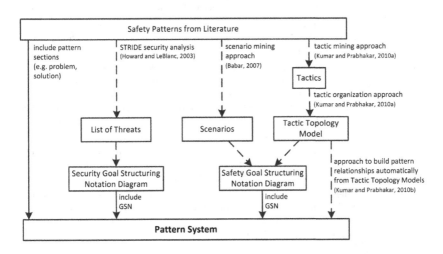

Fig. 4. Applied approach to build the pattern system

---

[2] The 2oo4 architecture is a special version of the M-OUT-OF-N PATTERN which is explained in Appendix A.

4.1 Pattern Format

We use the pattern format presented by (Babar 2007) for all our safety architecture patterns. The pattern format explicitly provides architectural information
like relevant scenarios with the aim to aid architecture design and evaluation
processes. Table 3 shows which sections the pattern format contains and where
we got the information for these sections from.

Table 3. Applied pattern format

Section	What it contains and where the contents comes from
Pattern Name	The pattern name is taken from existing patterns - most of which come from (Armoush 2010)
Pattern Type	Classification into hardware/software and fail-safe/fail-over. We classify these pattern types during the process of building up the pattern language
Also Known As	Other names for the pattern used in literature
Context	The contents of this section comes from existing patterns and was structurally adapted to fit our pattern system
Problem	The contents of this section comes from existing patterns and was structurally adapted to fit our pattern system
Forces	The contents of this section comes from existing patterns (mostly from (Grunske 2003)) and was structurally adapted to fit our pattern system
Solution	The solution is shortly described in a few sentences and the structure of the safety architecture is shown in a diagram. Most of the diagrams are based on (Armoush 2010; Douglass 2002)
Safety GSN	This section contains a Goal Structuring Notation (GSN) diagram which relates the main safety aim of the pattern to the architectural design decisions which were taken to achieve this aim. The GSN diagram is based on information about the usage of basic architectural design decisions (safety tactics) which are applied in the pattern
Security GSN	This section contains a Goal Structuring Notation (GSN) diagram with the main goal to maintain safety also in case of attacks. The STRIDE method is used to identify threats for the pattern and the GSN diagram structurally presents relevant threats
Consequences	The consequences are split into a part containing general consequences and a part explicitly covering quality-attribute related consequences (e.g. consequences on safety or security). Information about consequences mostly comes from the safety patterns from (Armoush 2010; Grunske 2003)
General Scenarios	This section contains scenarios of the system which can, for example, be used during architecture evaluations. The information of the scenarios is also needed to build the safety GSN diagrams
Known Uses	This section presents known uses for the patterns. We added this information by searching for literature which applies the pattern. We just included patterns for which we could find at least three known uses
Credits	References to previous work on the pattern

4.2 Elaborating Pattern Sections

The following pattern sections of the presented safety patterns are based on safety patterns from literature: **Pattern Name, Also Known As, Context, Problem, Forces, Solution, Consequences**. Most of the information is mainly based on (Armoush 2010) and is further elaborated by using other literature on similar safety patterns. This means we consider several patterns from literature, gather all information, and bring it into our format to be consistent.

For example, (Armoush 2010) describes the HOMOGENOUS REDUNDANCY PATTERN, which is also described by (Douglass 2002; Grunske 2003). We take the pattern from (Armoush 2010) as a starting point and include more detailed information about the **Solution** from (Douglass 2002) and about the **Forces** from (Grunske 2003).

We added the **Known Uses** section to the safety patterns by searching for examples in literature which apply the patterns. We just included safety patterns for which we could at least find three known uses. We also added the **Credits** section to state where we obtained the pattern information from.

The following section describes how we construct the **Safety GSN** and how we obtain **General Scenarios** for the patterns. Section 4.5 then shows how we construct the **Security GSN**.

4.3 Developing the Safety GSN

In this section we construct the safety GSN diagram for the HOMOGENOUS DUPLEX PATTERN based on safety tactics applied by this pattern.

Mining Patterns for Safety Tactics
The HOMOGENOUS DUPLEX PATTERN is mentioned in literature by (Douglass 2002; Grunske 2003; Armoush 2010). We studied all three descriptions of the pattern to find text passages which indicate the usage of general safety-related architectural design decisions (safety tactics). We do this as proposed by (Kumar and Prabhakar 2010a), where tactics are mined from GoF and POSA patterns to find relationships between patterns which use similar tactics. We apply the same method to find relationships between safety architecture patterns.

As proposed by (Kumar and Prabhakar 2010a), we construct a table of pattern text passages and corresponding tactics that this text passage relates to. For example, the HOMOGENOUS DUPLEX PATTERN pattern in (Armoush 2010) says: *"The system consists of two identical modules"* This indicates that the pattern applies the *Replication Redundancy* safety tactic[3].

Table 4 shows the table with the pattern text passages and also shows the tactics which we found in the HOMOGENOUS DUPLEX PATTERN. The tactics are: *Replication Redundancy, Override*, and *Condition Monitoring*.

Building a Structured Tactic Representation
With the gathered tactics we construct a *Tactic Topology Model* which is also part of the method described by (Kumar and Prabhakar 2010a). First, one has to

---

[3] A list of all safety tactics is available in Appendix B.

Table 4. Mining Tactics of the HOMOGENOUS DUPLEX PATTERN

Abstract Section		
Core Intent		**Tactic**
It is a hardware pattern that is used to increase the safety and reliability of the system by providing a replication of the same module (Modular redundancy).		Replication Redundancy
Problem Section		
Problem	**Elaboration of Problem (scenario)**	**Tactic**
Make the system continue operating in the presence of a fault	The system is fully operational even in case of a single channel failure.	Replication Redundancy
	A single channel random fault does not lead to a system failure.	Override
	The system can detect a fault in a single channel.	
Solution Section		
Solution Description		**Tactic**
The system consists of two identical modules; a primary (active) module and secondary (standby). *Test by redundant hardware*		Replication Redundancy
There is a fault detection unit that monitors the primary module and switches to the secondary module when a fault appears in the primary. *Fault detection and diagnosis (Comparator and Acceptance Test)*		Override
This method performs a check on the two channels by checking for input valid data within a given range and by checking the output signals from the two modules.		Condition Monitoring
Consequences Section		
Consequence Description		**Tactic**
When a fault is detected in the primary channel, the switch circuit switches over to the secondary channel		Override
Implementation Section		
Implementation Description		**Tactic**
To implement this pattern, the computational channel should be duplicated		Replication Redundancy

think about the main goal of the pattern. According to (Kumar and Prabhakar 2010a), the main tactics which achieve this goal are usually related to the **Intent** or the **Problem** section of the pattern. In the Tactic Topology Model, these main tactics are connected to the patterns' goal with arrows. Further explanation about this connection is given in textual form next to the arrow. The tactics can bring up new goals which have to be achieved by additional tactics - these are also added with arrows and a textual description. In that way, a structured graph containing the patterns' tactics is constructed.

Figure 5 shows the Tactic Topology Model for the HOMOGENOUS DUPLEX PATTERN. The main goal in the Tactic Topology Model for the pattern is identified as *"Continue operation even in case of random faults"*. The two tactics directly connected to this goal are *Replication Redundancy* and *Override*, because they are mentioned in the **Core Intent** or **Problem** section of the pattern (see Table 4). An additional goal that has to be fulfilled is to detect when the *Override* tactic should switch to the backup channel. Therefore, the *Condition Monitoring* tactic is connected to the *Override* tactic.

We use the Tactic Topology Models to structurally establish relationships in our pattern system (this is explained in Sect. 4.4). Apart from that, the Tactic Topology Models are just intermediate results used to build GSN diagrams and are not included in the patterns. All Tactic Topology Models for the presented safety patterns can be found in (Preschern et al. 2013b).

Fig. 5. Tactic topology model for the HOMOGENOUS DUPLEX PATTERN

Constructing the Safety GSN

Based on the Tactic Topology Model, we construct the safety GSN diagram. The GSN diagram contains the tactics from the Tactic Topology Model and they additionally contain general scenarios which are mined from the pattern descriptions. This scenario mining is done as proposed in (Babar 2007) by searching the **Problem** and **Solution** statements for safety-related scenarios. The scenarios found for the HOMOGENOUS DUPLEX PATTERN are shown in Table 4 under **"Problem Section"**.

All our safety GSNs start with the main goal to maintain safety. This main goal is split up into subgoals based on the scenarios which we obtained from the patterns. If the scenarios are independent from each other, then they are put on the same level in the GSN. If a scenario depends on another scenario (as it is the case for the HOMOGENOUS DUPLEX PATTERN), then it is modeled as a subgoal of the scenario it depends on. The tactics which are necessary to achieve a GSN goal are put below this (sub-)goal as a GSN strategy which has the title of the tactic and which contains additional information (taken from the textual description of the Tactic Topology Model arrow connections). GSN context elements are added if information of the pattern's context section is relevant for the GSN goals.

Figure 6 shows the GSN diagram of the HOMOGENOUS DUPLEX PATTERN pattern. We can see that it consists of all the tactics of the Tactic Topology Model from Fig. 5 and of the scenarios of the HOMOGENOUS DUPLEX PATTERN from Table 4.

4.4   Finding Pattern Relationships

To obtain the relationships between the patterns, we use the approach presented by (Kumar and Prabhakar 2010b). They interpret Tactic Topology Models as directed graphs, compare these graphs, and define a mapping between formal graph predicates and pattern relationships. For example, if the Tactic Topology Models of two different patterns are equal, then (Kumar and Prabhakar 2010b) say that these patterns are similar. Table 5 shows all kinds of considered pattern relationships and the corresponding graph predicates. To find all relationships in a pattern system, every pattern's Tactic Topology Model has to be compared to the Tactic Topology Models of all other patterns and every such Tactic Topology Model pair has to be checked for all the predicates described in Table 5.

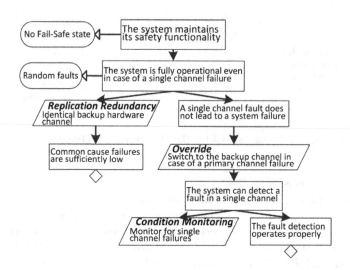

Fig. 6. GSN diagram of the HOMOGENOUS DUPLEX PATTERN

Table 5. Description of pattern relationships (slightly modified from (Kumar and Prabhakar 2010b)) and explanation of the predicates

Relation-ship	Description	Tactic Topology Model predicate
is an alternative	Patterns A and B solve the same problem, but propose different solutions.	$SourceNode(A) = SourceNode(B)$ **AND** $Graph(A) \neq Graph(B)$
uses	A sub-problem of pattern A is similar to the problem addressed by pattern B.	$Graph(A) \supset Graph(B)$
refines	Pattern B provides a more detailed solution than pattern A.	$SourceNode(A) = SourceNode(B)$ **AND** $Graph(A) \subset Graph(B)$
specializes	The solution of pattern B is a special case of the solution of pattern A. *Example: Pattern B specializes pattern A if they have the same graph structure, but pattern B uses a refined tactic where pattern A uses a more general tactic (e.g. B uses Replication Redundancy where A uses Redundancy).*	$Graph(A) \subset GeneralizedGraph(B)$
is similar	Patterns A and B provide the same solution to a similar problem *Example: Pattern B is similar to pattern A if they have the same graph structure and use two related refined tactics. E.g. A uses Replication Redundancy and B uses Diverse Redundancy*	$GeneralizedGraph(A) = GeneralizedGraph(B)$

Explanation for the predicates	*Graph(X):*	The Tactic Topology Model interpreted as a graph including all boxes (graph nodes) and arrows (graph transitions) from the Tactic Topology Model.
	SourceNode(X):	The box in the Tactic Topology Model to which no arrow points.
	GeneralizedGraph(X):	The graph of the Tactic Topology Model in which all tactics are substituted by their more generalized versions, if available. For example, *Replication Redundancy* would be substituted by the more general *Redundancy* tactic.
	X = Y:	Graph or node X is exactly the same as Y.
	X ⊂ Y:	Graph X is part of graph Y.

We applied this approach to our safety patterns to structurally build the relationships in our pattern system. We built the Tactic Topology Models as described in Sect. 4.3 for all our patterns. Then we compared each Tactic Topology Models with one another and checked for the predicates defined in Table 5. This delivers us the pattern relationships for our pattern system.

Figure 7 shows our safety patterns and their relationships which we obtained with the described approach. We can see that the approach to find pattern relationships worked out quite well. All the relationships between the patterns seem to be comprehensible. For example, according to the relationships obtained through the Tactic Topology Model comparison, the HOMOGENOUS DUPLEX PATTERN is a specialization of the M-OUT-OF-N-D PATTERN and is similar to the HETEROGENOUS DUPLEX PATTERN which is both reasonable.

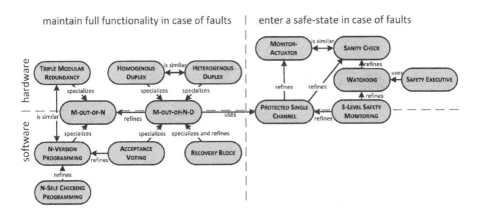

Fig. 7. Safety architecture pattern system

To not overload the the pattern-relationship representation, we did not explicitly annotate the *is alternative* relationships, but instead grouped patterns which are alternatives to one another into the group of patterns trying to maintain a safe-state in case of faults and the group of patterns providing full system functionality in case of faults. Additionally, we divided the patterns into software and hardware patterns as already suggested by (Armoush 2010). However, the classification of software and hardware patterns is not very strict. Some of the patterns are intended for either software or hardware, but could also be implemented for the other. For example, the WATCHDOG pattern is a hardware pattern, but could also be realized in software by a timer which monitors the execution of another program. The group a pattern belongs to is stated in the **Pattern Type** section. All patterns from Fig. 7 are presented in Appendix A.

4.5   Developing the Security GSN

In this section we apply the STRIDE analysis to the HOMOGENOUS DUPLEX PATTERN to obtain a GSN security representation. More detailed information about this approach can be found in (Preschern et al. 2013d).

Getting the Data Flow Diagram

The covered safety architecture patterns each provide a diagram which shows the hardware and software elements of the pattern. These diagrams can be used as data flow diagrams in the STRIDE analysis, because the diagrams all explicitly display the interactions and data flows between the different hardware or software elements of the pattern.

Figure 8 shows such a diagram for the HOMOGENOUS DUPLEX PATTERN. The system gets input data and processes that input data with redundant channels which provide output data. A fault-detector and a switch component decide which of the channel outputs is used.

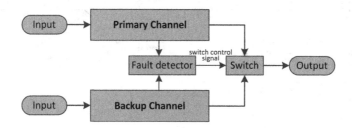

Fig. 8. HOMOGENOUS DUPLEX PATTERN architecture

Applying the STRIDE Analysis

By using an adapted STRIDE approach, we analyze the pattern diagrams to list the security threats for each of the patterns.

We just require two element types for the STRIDE analysis: *Data Flows* and *Processing Elements*. For both types, we omit the threats Repudiation and Information Disclosure, because they do not directly influence the safety functionality of a system. Both threats might by relevant when combined with attacks related to other threats. For example, one might obtain passwords (Information Disclosure) for a safety-critical system and then be able to log in to the system and turn it off. Still, the action of logging in and turning the system off implies the exploitation of other threats (in this case Elevation of privilege). Therefore it is sufficient for our purpose to not consider Repudiation and Information Disclosure, because they can just become safety-critical when combined with other threats which we do consider.

Furthermore, for the *Processing Elements*, we omit the Tampering and Denial of Service threats, because an attacker usually has no access to processing elements which perform safety-critical functionality. Therefore, the attacker needs to elevate his privileges before starting a tampering or denial of service attack on a processing element.

Our resulting relevant threats for the pattern diagram element types are shown in Table 6.

Table 6. STRIDE mapping to safety pattern element types

DFD element type	Symbol	S	T	R	I	D	E
Data Flow	⟶		X			X	
Processing Element	▭	X					X

With this mapping of relevant threats, we go through each element of the HOMOGENOUS DUPLEX PATTERN to obtain a list of security threats. We did not consider the identical *Primary Channel* and *Secondary Channel* separately, but we just cover a *Single Channel* which can be either of them. For the HOMOGE-NOUS DUPLEX PATTERN we get the following list of threats:

- Tampering of *Single Channel* input data
- DoS of *Single Channel* input data
- Spoofing of *Single Channel*
- EoP on *Single Channel*
- Tampering of *Single Channel* output data
- DoS of *Single Channel* output data
- Tampering of *Fault Detector* input data
- DoS of *Fault Detector* input data
- Spoofing of *Fault Detector*
- EoP on *Fault Detector*
- Tampering of *Fault Detector* output data
- DoS of *Fault Detector* output data
- Spoofing of *Switch*
- EoP on *Switch*
- Tampering of *Switch* output data
- DoS of *Switch* output data

From this list of threats it is not very easy to grasp important threats, because some of the listed threats do not even pose a direct threat to safety. For example, the *DoS of Fault Detector output data* threat itself cannot bring the system into a safety-critical state, because as long as both channels work properly, it does not matter which channel output is selected. Therefore, this threat is not as relevant as for example the *DoS of Switch output data* threat which can bring the system into a safety-critical state in any case.

Constructing the Security GSN

Based on the list of threats for a pattern, we develop a GSN diagram to argue that attacks cannot affect system safety. The security GSN diagram for the HOMOGENOUS DUPLEX PATTERN is shown in Fig. 9.

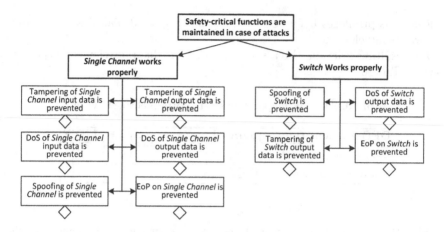

Fig. 9. Homogenous Duplex Pattern security GSN

Each security GSN starts with the main aim that "Safety-critical functions are maintained in case of attacks". Next, all threats are added which can bring the system into a safety-critical state. Threats are represented as undeveloped GSN goals in form of: "Threat X is prevented". If the pattern is applied, these undeveloped goals have to be further developed to obtain a complete security argument (evidence that the goals are achieved has to be provided).

An example for a threat in the GSN diagram of the Homogenous Duplex Pattern is "Tampering of Switch output data". If someone mounts an attack related to this threat, the attacker can produce arbitrary system output data which violates system safety. Therefore, the threat is safety-critical and is directly added to the GSN diagram as "Tampering of Switch output data is prevented" GSN goal[4].

After all safety-critical threats are included in the GSN diagram, all the remaining threats (which by themselves cannot bring the system into a safety-critical state) are considered. Any combination of these threats is also added to the GSN diagram if it can affect system safety (combinations are notated in the diagram with the *GSN Option Element*, however none are present for the Homogenous Duplex Pattern).

The remaining threats are not directly relevant for the safety functionality of the system and are therefore not included in the GSN diagram. For example, in the Homogenous Duplex Pattern there are threats related to the Fault Detector unit. None of the threats related to the Fault Detector are included in the GSN diagram, because if an attacker has full control of the Fault Detector, he can just influence which of the two channels is actually used for the system output. However, if both channels work properly this is not safety-critical. Still,

---

[4] Actually the threat is added after the "Switch works properly" GSN goal. This goal is just introduced to make the GSN diagram easier to read and it changes nothing about the semantics of the diagram.

with an attack on the Fault Detector, an attacker can disable the systems' safety measures, because switching to the redundant channel in case of failure would not work anymore. However, we do not consider such threats, because they are much less critical (they require a targeted attack and a fault in the system) than the ones included in the GSN.

5   Pattern Application - Case Study

In this section we describe the application of the HOMOGENOUS DUPLEX PATTERN in an industrial case study. We apply the pattern and use the safety and security GSN diagrams to argue for the system's safety and security. An overview of this process is shown in Fig. 10.

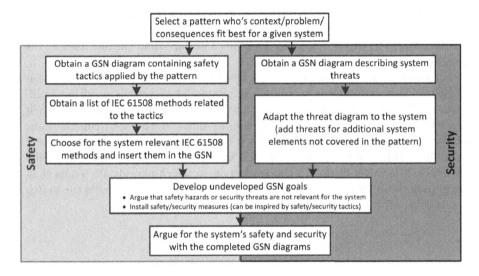

Fig. 10. Building a safety/security argument based on a pattern

According to the definitions in Sect. 2.1, one has to consider safety and security during all stages of system development and not just during design or implementation. This means that the sole application of the patterns provided in this article does by itself not make a system safe or secure, because not all stages of a system development lifecycle are considered. However, applying the proposed patterns helps with part of the challenges faced with during safety and security development, because the patterns provide safety design guidance as well as GSN arguments why safety or security goals are being achieved.

In the industrial case study, the patterns were applied to help during the design, implementation, and verification phases of the IEC 61508 safety lifecycle. For other lifecycle stages, such as the safety analysis for example, the processes described in the IEC 61508 standard were followed.

5.1 System Description

A controller for a hydro-power plant is developed. The controller unit has to maintain safety-critical functions such as controlling the turbine speed and shutting down the system if an overvoltage is detected. Failing to maintain these functions can result in damage of the equipment and even human injuries. Sensors are connected to a merging unit which is a separate controller collecting sensor data and transmitting this data to the hydro-power plant controller via Ethernet. Based on the sensor input, the hydro-power plant controller has to control actuators which are hardwired to the controller. The controller is connected to the local hydro-power plant network to be able to receive firmware updates. However, this is a different Ethernet interface than the one used by the merging unit.

For this system, the HOMOGENOUS DUPLEX PATTERN (see Appendix A) is applied to protect from hardware failures. Figure 11 shows the resulting architecture. The system consists of two main CPUs which are supplied with their own set of sensor data from different merging units. Both CPUs run the same software to compute outputs for the actuators. A separate switch component determines which output is actually used for the actuators. The switch usually takes CPU1, however, if the watchdog component which periodically sends challenges to both CPUs detects that one CPU does not work, it instructs the switch to take the output of the other CPU.

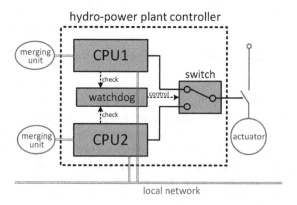

Fig. 11. Hydro-power plant controller architecture

5.2   Safety Argument

From the HOMOGENOUS DUPLEX PATTERN we obtain the basis for the safety GSN diagram which was already shown in Fig. 6. From this diagram we can see that the pattern applies the *Replication Redundancy*, the *Override*, and the *Condition Monitoring* tactics. Table 7 shows the related IEC 61508 methods for these tactics (taken from Appendix B). Thus, when applying a pattern, one gets a list of relevant IEC 61508 conform methods for the specific architecture. From this list, a safety architect now has to choose which of the suggested IEC 61508 methods are appropriate for the specific system.

Table 7. Tactics and IEC 61508 methods used by the HOMOGENOUS DUPLEX PATTERN

Tactics	Related IEC 61508 methods	
Replication Redundancy	A.2.1 Test by redundant hardware	✓
	A.2.5 Monitored redundancy	
	A.3.5 Reciprocal comparison by software	
	A.4.5 Block replication	
	A.6.3 Multi-channel output	
	A.6.5 Input comparison/Voting	
	A.7.3 Complete hardware redundancy	✓
	A.7.5 Transmission redundancy	
Override	A.1.3 Comparator	✓
	A.1.5 Idle current principle	
	A.8.1 Overvoltage protection with safety shut-off	
	A.8.3 Power-down with safety shut-off	
Condition Monitoring	A.1.1 Failure detection by online monitoring	✓
	A.6.4 Monitored output	
	A.8.2 Voltage control	
	A.9.1 Watch dog with separate time base without time-window	
	A.9.2 Watch dog with separate time base and time-window	
	A.9.3 Logical monitoring of program sequence	
	A.9.4 Temporal and logical program sequence monitoring	
	A.9.5 Temporal monitoring with on-line check	✓
	A.12.1 Reference sensor	
	A.13.1 Monitoring	

In our case study, the methods from Table 7 which are marked with a tick were chosen. These methods are then included in the GSN diagram instead of the general tactics. Furthermore, additional information can be added to the GSN diagram if the safety argument is not complete. For example, all undeveloped goals have to be developed which means that they have to be linked to evidence which suggests that the goal is fulfilled. Figure 12 shows the resulting GSN diagram (additionally added elements are presented in orange, dashed lines). The GSN shows how the high level safety goal can be achieved by the actually applies methods suggested by the IEC 61508 safety standard.

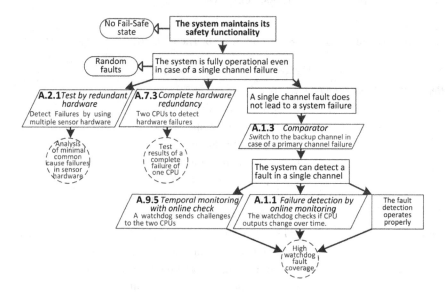

Fig. 12. Hydro-power plant controller safety GSN diagram

5.3 Security Argument

To develop a security argument, we start with the security GSN diagram provided by the pattern and complete all the undeveloped goals. For all the undeveloped goals we either argue why the goal is not relevant or what measures are applied to handle the threat. An example for not relevant threats are any threats to the switch element, because the switch element for the hydro-power plant architecture is hardwired to the other elements and not accessible for an attacker. An example for measures against a threat is related to the *"EoP on Single Channel is prevented"* goal. To detect some attacks related to this threat, a runtime-integrity-checker is used to detect malware on the CPUs. Figure 13 shows the complete security GSN diagram for the hydro-power plant architecture. Additionally added elements in the GSN are marked with blue, dashed lines. This GSN shows how the high level goal that the safety functionality cannot be influenced by attacks is achieved by specific measures and arguments.

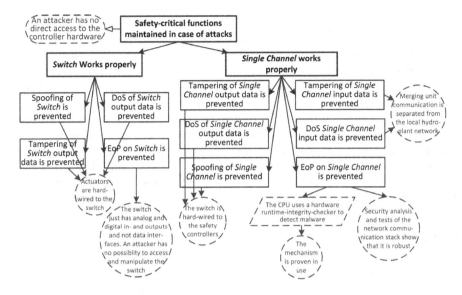

Fig. 13. Hydro-power plant controller security GSN diagram

5.4 Discussion

With the application of the safety pattern we get a blueprint for a safety and for a security GSN diagram.

- For safety, system architects get the benefit, that they are provided with suggestions for IEC 61508 methods. Additionally the safety GSN provides a way to argue how the main goal to keep the system safe can be achieved by implementing the IEC 61508 methods. (Preschern et al. 2013a) evaluates the quality of IEC 61508 method suggestion by comparing the pattern suggestions to real-life safety projects.
- For security, system architects get the benefit that on the one hand they are introduced to a security analysis technique and on the other hand that they are already provided with a security GSN diagram for the pattern which they can use and extend to argue for system security. To implement security methods in order to mitigate the threats in the GSN diagram, (Preschern et al. 2012b) provides a list of general methods in form of security tactics.

For both, the safety and security GSN, it is always difficult to say whether the arguments provided are enough to argue that the main goal is achieved.

- For the safety GSN we use relevant scenarios from the patterns. (Wu 2007) argues that if a GSN contains all relevant scenarios for the main goal, the argument is sufficiently complete.
- For the security GSN we use STRIDE to include all relevant threats in the GSN.

To make sure that the constructed GSNs include all safety and security aspects of an architecture, other relevant scenarios could be included into the safety GSN and additional elements of the architecture which are not included in the patterns have to be analyzed with STRIDE for the security GSN. Thus, the provided GSNs can be used as a basis for safety and security reasoning, but they have to be adapted or extended for specific architectures, especially, if compared to the pattern additional elements are present. However, just constructing the GSNs does not by itself lead to a safety and secure system, but can just be seen as part of the safety and security engineering. Further measures to be taken can be found in safety development lifecycles such as (International Electrotechnical Commission 2010) or security development lifecycles such as (Howard and Lipner 2006).

6   Conclusion

This article presented a system of safety architecture patterns which contain a security analysis. A detailed explanation how these patterns can be constructed was given and a case study applying one of the patterns was shown.

The provided patterns can be used by system architects to develop safety-critical architectures and to additionally see how to apply security analysis methods. This has the benefit that the patterns provide a starting point how to analyze and argue for system security. From a safety point of view the patterns bring the advantage that they provide a way to reason about system safety. They additionally provide suggestion for IEC 61508 methods as a starting point for safety architects to see which methods of the safety standard are relevant for the chosen architecture.

For future work, further patterns could be included to the pattern system. It would be interesting to see if the approach to find pattern relationships with Tactic Topology Models also works for other safety patterns. As well it would be interesting to see if the approach to find pattern relationships can also be applied to other domains such as security patterns. Furthermore, it would be interesting to apply the safety patterns including the safety and security GSNs in other real-life projects to be able to better discuss the benefits and shortcomings of the patterns.

With the presented patterns we want to give safety architects guidance for efficiently constructing well-proven architectures and we hope to increase the security awareness in the safety domain.

A   Security Enhanced Safety Pattern System

The patterns in our safety pattern system are mostly taken from (Armoush 2010), because these patterns already provide a comprehensive collection of other patterns in literature and they focus on rather large-scale architectural design decisions which is the main focus of our pattern system. We included all but one of Armoush's patterns. We excluded one pattern (RECOVERY BLOCK WITH BACKUP VOTING), because we could not find any known uses for it. Additionally to Armoush's patterns we included the M-OUT-OF-N and the M-OUT-OF-N-D pattern, which are based on architectures described in the IEC 61508 safety standard. For each of the patterns from Fig. 7, we here present the full pattern.

Pattern Name	HOMOGENOUS DUPLEX PATTERN	Pattern Type	hardware, failover
AlsoKnownAs	Homogeneous Redundancy Pattern, Standby-Spare Pattern, Dynamic Redundancy Pattern, Two-Channel Redundancy Pattern, 1oo2D Pattern		
Context	A safety-critical application without a fail-safe state has potentially many random and few systematic faults.		
Problem	How to design a system which continues operating even in the presence of a fault in one of the system components		
Forces	- the system cannot shut down because it has no safe state - development costs should not increase - safety standard requires high fault coverage for single-point of failure components - high availability requires hardware platforms to be maintained at the runtime		
Solution	The system consists of a *Primary Channel* (active) and a *Secondary Channel* (backup) which are two identical hardware modules. A *Fault detector* monitors the channels and controls a *Switch* to select the *Backup Channel* in case of a *Primary Channel* failure. 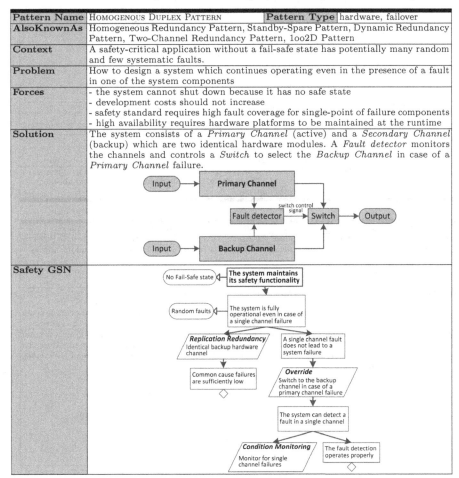		
Safety GSN			

Security GSN	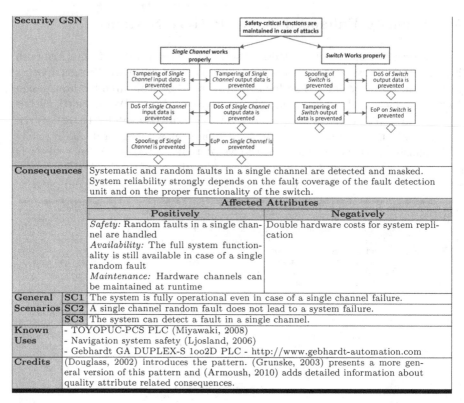
Consequences	Systematic and random faults in a single channel are detected and masked. System reliability strongly depends on the fault coverage of the fault detection unit and on the proper functionality of the switch.

Affected Attributes	
Positively	Negatively
Safety: Random faults in a single channel are handled *Availability:* The full system functionality is still available in case of a single random fault *Maintenance:* Hardware channels can be maintained at runtime	Double hardware costs for system replication

General Scenarios	SC1	The system is fully operational even in case of a single channel failure.
	SC2	A single channel random fault does not lead to a system failure.
	SC3	The system can detect a fault in a single channel.
Known Uses		- TOYOPUC-PCS PLC (Miyawaki, 2008) - Navigation system safety (Ljosland, 2006) - Gebhardt GA DUPLEX-S 1oo2D PLC - http://www.gebhardt-automation.com
Credits		(Douglass, 2002) introduces the pattern. (Grunske, 2003) presents a more general version of this pattern and (Armoush, 2010) adds detailed information about quality attribute related consequences.

Pattern Name	HETEROGENOUS DUPLEX PATTERN	Pattern Type	hardware, failover
AlsoKnownAs	Heterogenous Redundancy Pattern, Diverse Redundancy Pattern, 1oo2D Pattern		
Context	A safety-critical application without a fail-safe state has many random and systematic faults.		
Problem	How to design a system which continues operating even in the presence of a fault in one of the system components		
Forces	- the system cannot shut down because it has no safe state - high safety certification levels require handling of systematic faults - safety standard requires high fault coverage for single-point of failure components - high availability requires hardware platforms to be maintained at the runtime		
Solution	The system consists of a *Primary Channel* (active) and a *Secondary Channel* (backup) which are two diverse hardware modules. A *Fault detector* monitors the channels and controls a *Switch* to select the *Backup Channel* in case of a *Primary Channel* failure. 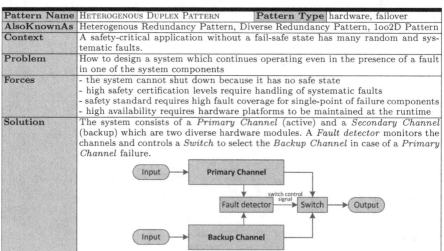		

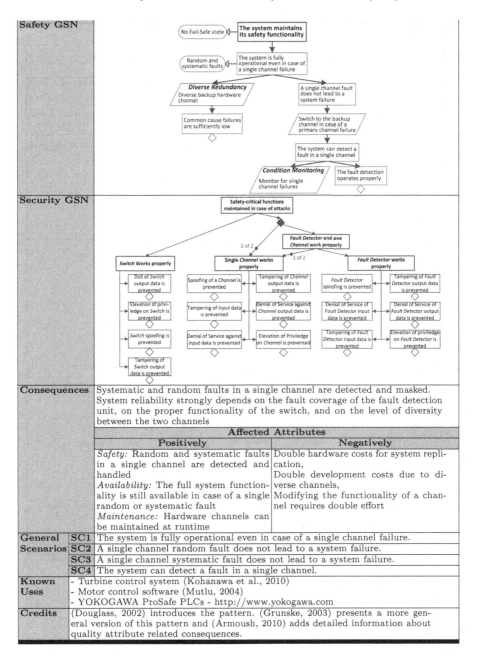

Safety GSN	
Security GSN	

Consequences	Systematic and random faults in a single channel are detected and masked. System reliability strongly depends on the fault coverage of the fault detection unit, on the proper functionality of the switch, and on the level of diversity between the two channels

Affected Attributes	
Positively	Negatively
Safety: Random and systematic faults in a single channel are detected and handled	Double hardware costs for system replication,
Availability: The full system functionality is still available in case of a single random or systematic fault	Double development costs due to diverse channels,
Maintenance: Hardware channels can be maintained at runtime	Modifying the functionality of a channel requires double effort

General Scenarios	SC1	The system is fully operational even in case of a single channel failure.
	SC2	A single channel random fault does not lead to a system failure.
	SC3	A single channel systematic fault does not lead to a system failure.
	SC4	The system can detect a fault in a single channel.

Known Uses	- Turbine control system (Kohanawa et al., 2010) - Motor control software (Mutlu, 2004) - YOKOGAWA ProSafe PLCs - http://www.yokogawa.com
Credits	(Douglass, 2002) introduces the pattern. (Grunske, 2003) presents a more general version of this pattern and (Armoush, 2010) adds detailed information about quality attribute related consequences.

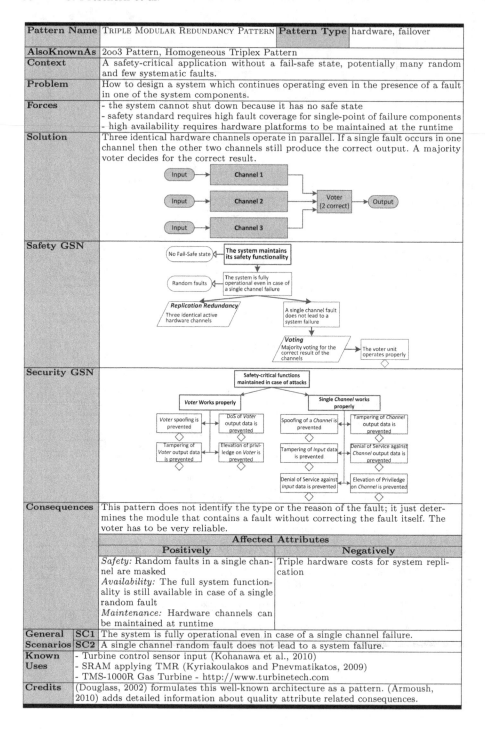

Pattern Name	TRIPLE MODULAR REDUNDANCY PATTERN	Pattern Type	hardware, failover
AlsoKnownAs	2oo3 Pattern, Homogeneous Triplex Pattern		
Context	A safety-critical application without a fail-safe state, potentially many random and few systematic faults.		
Problem	How to design a system which continues operating even in the presence of a fault in one of the system components.		
Forces	- the system cannot shut down because it has no safe state - safety standard requires high fault coverage for single-point of failure components - high availability requires hardware platforms to be maintained at the runtime		
Solution	Three identical hardware channels operate in parallel. If a single fault occurs in one channel then the other two channels still produce the correct output. A majority voter decides for the correct result.		
Safety GSN			
Security GSN			
Consequences	This pattern does not identify the type or the reason of the fault; it just determines the module that contains a fault without correcting the fault itself. The voter has to be very reliable.		

Affected Attributes	
Positively	**Negatively**
Safety: Random faults in a single channel are masked *Availability:* The full system functionality is still available in case of a single random fault *Maintenance:* Hardware channels can be maintained at runtime	Triple hardware costs for system replication

General	SC1	The system is fully operational even in case of a single channel failure.
Scenarios	SC2	A single channel random fault does not lead to a system failure.
Known Uses		- Turbine control sensor input (Kohanawa et al., 2010) - SRAM applying TMR (Kyriakoulakos and Pnevmatikatos, 2009) - TMS-1000R Gas Turbine - http://www.turbinetech.com
Credits		(Douglass, 2002) formulates this well-known architecture as a pattern. (Armoush, 2010) adds detailed information about quality attribute related consequences.

Pattern Name	M-OUT-OF-N PATTERN	Pattern Type	hard/software, failover
AlsoKnownAs	M/N Parallel Redundancy Pattern, MooN Pattern		
Context	A safety-critical application without a fail-safe state has potentially many random and few or many systematic faults.		
Problem	How to design a system which continues operating even in the presence of faults in one or more of the system components.		
Forces	- the system cannot shut down because it has no safe state - high safety certification levels require handling of systematic faults - safety standard requires high fault coverage for single-point of failure components - high availability requires hardware platforms to be maintained at the runtime		
Solution	N identical or diverse channels (software or hardware) operate in parallel. If a fault occurs in one or more channels then the other channels still produce the correct output. A voter decides for the result given by at least M channels. Other voting mechanisms than majority voting can be used as well. For example, in the 1oo2 architecture, the voting element usually decides for the more reliable channel or for the safer output state.		

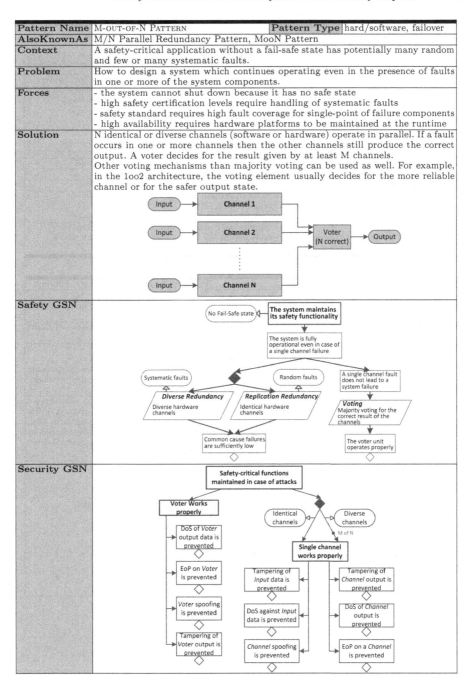

Consequences	This pattern does not identify the type or the reason of the fault; it just determines the module that contains a fault without correcting the fault itself. To achieve high reliability, the voter has to be very reliable.

	Affected Attributes	
	Positively	**Negatively**
	Safety: Random faults (and systematic faults with *Diverse Redundancy*) are masked *Availability:* The full system functionality is still available in case of a single fault *Maintenance:* Hardware channels can be maintained at runtime	Multiple hardware costs for system replication and multiple development costs if diverse channels are used

General	SC1	The system is fully operational even in case of failures in N-M channels.
Scenarios	SC2	M-N Single channel random faults do not lead to a system failure.
	SC3	M-N Single channel systematic faults do not lead to a system failure.

Known Uses	- 1oo2 Architecture for LHC detectors (Vergara-Fernandez and Denz, 2002) - Steering system controller (Börcsök et al., 2011) - Netherlocks safety lock - http://halmapr.com/news/netherlocks/tag/3oo4/
Credits	(Grunske, 2003) describes this pattern and calls it MULTI-CHANNEL-REDUNDANCY WITH VOTING. (Armoush, 2010) adds detailed information about quality attribute related consequences.

Pattern Name	M-OUT-OF-N-D PATTERN		Pattern Type	hard/software, failover
AlsoKnownAs	MooN-D Pattern			
Context	A safety-critical application without a fail-safe state has potentially many random and few or many systematic faults.			
Problem	How to design a system which continues operating even in the presence of faults in one ore more of the system components.			
Forces	- the system cannot shut down because it has no safe state - high safety certification levels require handling of systematic faults - safety standard requires high fault coverage for single-point of failure components - due to these high availability requirements the hardware platforms must be maintained at the runtime of the system			
Solution	N identical or diverse channels operate in parallel. If a fault occurs in one or more of the channels then the other channels still produce the correct output. A *Voter* decides for the result given by at least M channels. Other voting mechanisms than majority voting can be used as well. Additionally, the *Voter* can be influenced by a diagnostic check implemented within the channels. For example, a channel could be excluded from the vote if its diagnostic check fails. 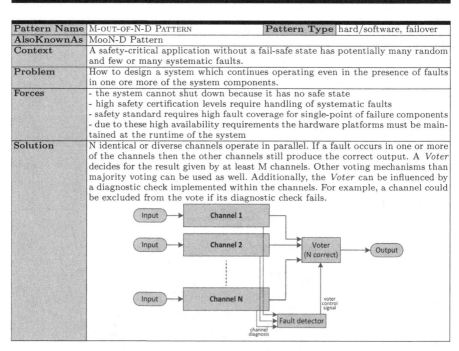			

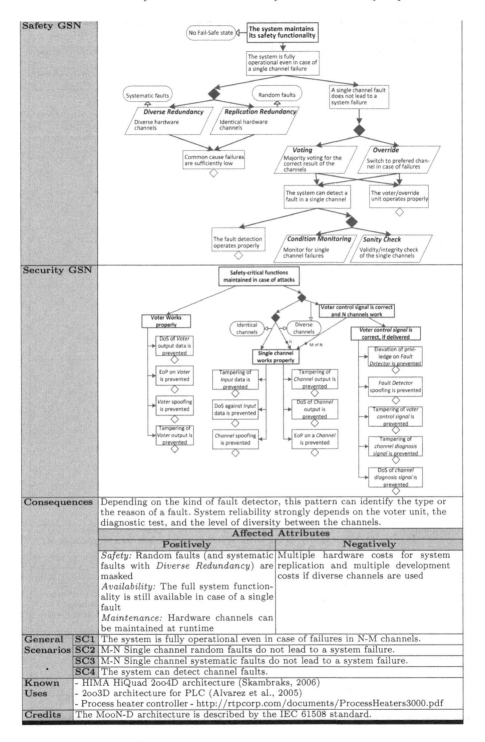

Safety GSN	

| Security GSN | |

Consequences	Depending on the kind of fault detector, this pattern can identify the type or the reason of a fault. System reliability strongly depends on the voter unit, the diagnostic test, and the level of diversity between the channels.

Affected Attributes	
Positively	**Negatively**
Safety: Random faults (and systematic faults with *Diverse Redundancy*) are masked	Multiple hardware costs for system replication and multiple development costs if diverse channels are used
Availability: The full system functionality is still available in case of a single fault	
Maintenance: Hardware channels can be maintained at runtime	

General	SC1	The system is fully operational even in case of failures in N-M channels.
Scenarios	SC2	M-N Single channel random faults do not lead to a system failure.
.	SC3	M-N Single channel systematic faults do not lead to a system failure.
	SC4	The system can detect channel faults.
Known Uses		- HIMA HiQuad 2oo4D architecture (Skambraks, 2006) - 2oo3D architecture for PLC (Alvarez et al., 2005) - Process heater controller - http://rtpcorp.com/documents/ProcessHeaters3000.pdf
Credits		The MooN-D architecture is described by the IEC 61508 standard.

Pattern Name	N-Version Programming Pattern		Pattern Type	software, failover
AlsoKnownAs	-			
Context	A safety-critical software without a fail-safe state which probably contains software faults.			
Problem	How to design a system which continues operating even in the presence of software faults.			
Forces	- software often contains faults - high safety certification levels require handling of systematic faults - safety standard requires high fault coverage for single-point of failure components			
Solution	N software versions are developed independently from the same specification. The outputs of these software versions are sent to the *Voter* which determines the best output.			

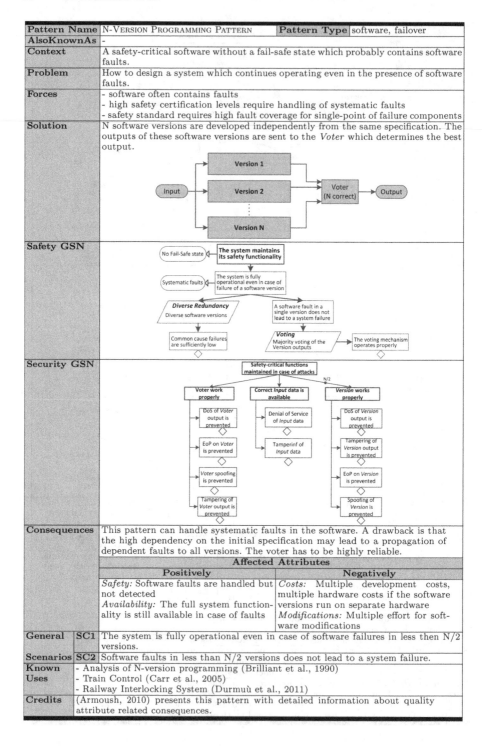

Safety GSN	
Security GSN	
Consequences	This pattern can handle systematic faults in the software. A drawback is that the high dependency on the initial specification may lead to a propagation of dependent faults to all versions. The voter has to be highly reliable.

Affected Attributes	
Positively	**Negatively**
Safety: Software faults are handled but not detected *Availability:* The full system functionality is still available in case of faults	*Costs:* Multiple development costs, multiple hardware costs if the software versions run on separate hardware *Modifications:* Multiple effort for software modifications

General	SC1	The system is fully operational even in case of software failures in less then N/2 versions.
Scenarios	SC2	Software faults in less than N/2 versions does not lead to a system failure.
Known Uses		- Analysis of N-version programming (Brilliant et al., 1990) - Train Control (Carr et al., 2005) - Railway Interlocking System (Durmuù et al., 2011)
Credits		(Armoush, 2010) presents this pattern with detailed information about quality attribute related consequences.

Pattern Name	ACCEPTANCE VOTING PATTERN		Pattern Type	software, failover
AlsoKnownAs	-			
Context	A safety-critical software without a fail-safe state which probably contains software faults.			
Problem	How to design a system which continues operating even in the presence of software faults.			
Forces	- software often contains faults - high safety certification levels require handling of systematic faults - safety standard requires high fault coverage for single-point of failure components			
Solution	N software versions and one acceptance test are developed independently from the same initial specification. The outputs of these versions are checked by one *Acceptance Test* and valid outputs are sent to a *Voter* which determines the best output.			
	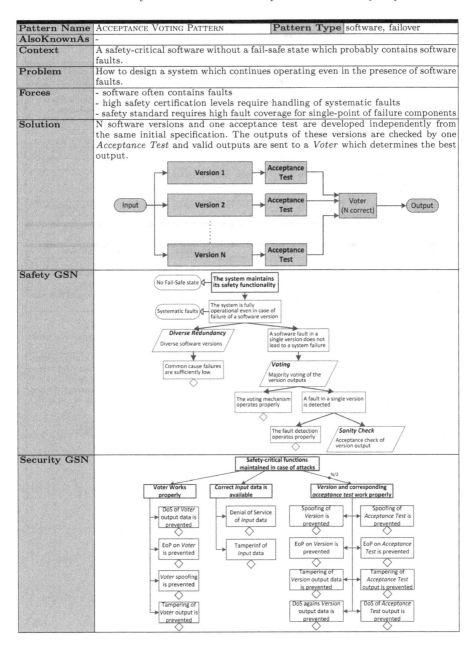			
Safety GSN				
Security GSN				

Consequences	This pattern can handle systematic faults in the software. A drawback is that the high dependency on the initial specification may lead to a propagation of dependent faults to all versions. The acceptance test has to be very reliable and ideally runs in a separate component.

Affected Attributes	
Positively	**Negatively**
Safety: Software faults are handled and probably detected *Availability:* The full system functionality is still available in case of faults	*Costs:* Multiple development costs, multiple hardware costs if the software versions run on separate hardware *Modifications:* Multiple effort for software modifications

General Scenarios	SC1	The system is fully operational even in case of failures in less than N/2 versions.
	SC2	Failures in N/2 software versions do not lead to a system failure.
	SC3	Faults in software versions are detected.
Known Uses	- Dependable web services (Nourani and Azgomi, 2009) - Protected C++ Dispatcher (Borchert et al., 2012) - Fault-tolerant middleware (Kim, 1998)	
Credits	(Armoush, 2010) presents this pattern with detailed information about quality attribute related consequences.	

Pattern Name	Recovery Block Pattern	Pattern Type	software, failover
AlsoKnownAs	-		
Context	A safety-critical software without a fail-safe state which probably contains software faults. There is much time to run the safety-critical software available.		
Problem	How to design a system which continues operating even in the presence of software faults.		
Forces	- software often contains faults - high safety certification levels require handling of systematic faults - safety standard requires high fault coverage for single-point of failure components - no additional processing hardware or processing time is available		
Solution	N software versions are developed independently from the same initial specification. Only a single version is executed at a time. After the execution of *Version 1*, an *Acceptance Test* is executed to check if the software output is reasonable. If the *Acceptance Test* is passed, then the outcome is considered as correct. Otherwise, the system state is restored to its original state and an alternate version is invoked. 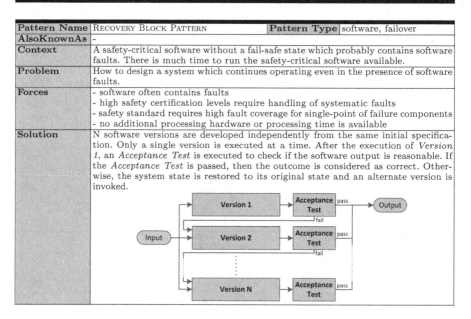		

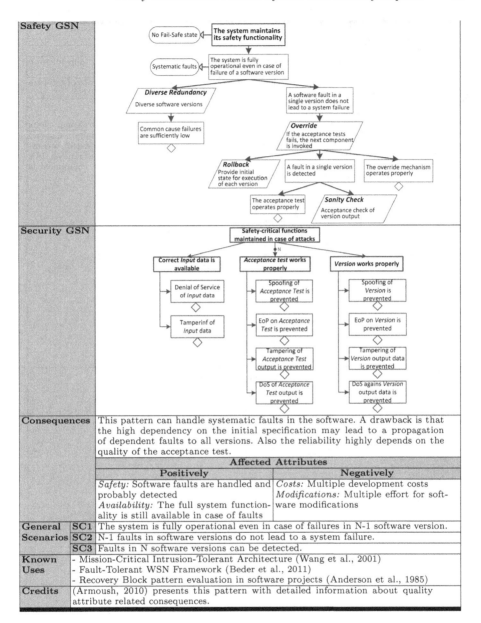

		This pattern can handle systematic faults in the software. A drawback is that the high dependency on the initial specification may lead to a propagation of dependent faults to all versions. Also the reliability highly depends on the quality of the acceptance test.	
Consequences			
		Affected Attributes	
		Positively	**Negatively**
		Safety: Software faults are handled and probably detected
Availability: The full system functionality is still available in case of faults	*Costs:* Multiple development costs
Modifications: Multiple effort for software modifications
General Scenarios	SC1	The system is fully operational even in case of failures in N-1 software version.	
	SC2	N-1 faults in software versions do not lead to a system failure.	
	SC3	Faults in N software versions can be detected.	
Known Uses		- Mission-Critical Intrusion-Tolerant Architecture (Wang et al., 2001)
- Fault-Tolerant WSN Framework (Beder et al., 2011)
- Recovery Block pattern evaluation in software projects (Anderson et al., 1985)	
Credits		(Armoush, 2010) presents this pattern with detailed information about quality attribute related consequences.	

Pattern Name	N-Self Checking Programming Pattern	Pattern Type	software, failover
AlsoKnownAs	-		
Context	A safety-critical software without a fail-safe state which probably contains software faults.		
Problem	How to design a system which continues operating even in the presence of software faults.		
Forces	- software often contains faults - high safety certification levels require handling of systematic faults - safety standard requires high fault coverage for single-point of failure components		
Solution	N>=4 software versions are developed independently from the same initial specification. The versions are arranged in pairs of two as components. Within a component, the results of the two versions are compared to detect mismatches. If a component fails due to different results from its versions, the next component is invoked to start delivering the required functionality. 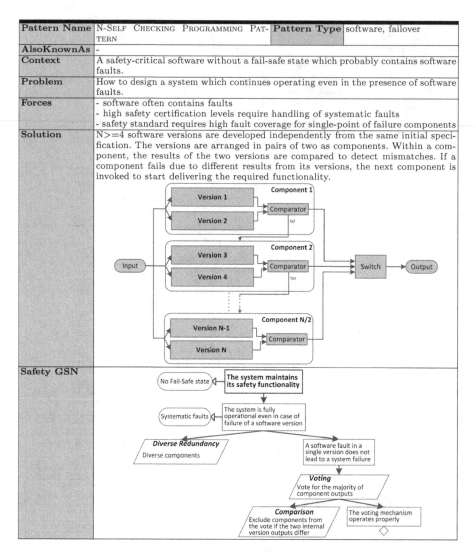		
Safety GSN			

Security GSN	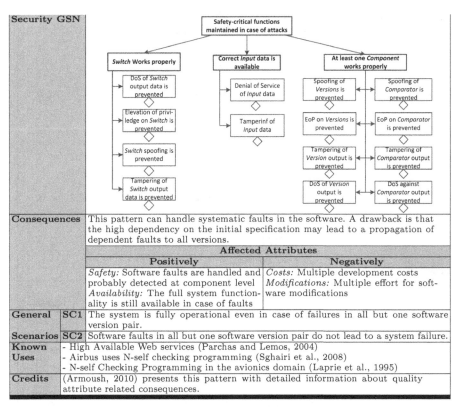
Consequences	This pattern can handle systematic faults in the software. A drawback is that the high dependency on the initial specification may lead to a propagation of dependent faults to all versions.

Affected Attributes	
Positively	**Negatively**
Safety: Software faults are handled and probably detected at component level *Availability:* The full system functionality is still available in case of faults	*Costs:* Multiple development costs *Modifications:* Multiple effort for software modifications

General	SC1	The system is fully operational even in case of failures in all but one software version pair.
Scenarios	SC2	Software faults in all but one software version pair do not lead to a system failure.
Known Uses		- High Available Web services (Parchas and Lemos, 2004) - Airbus uses N-self checking programming (Sghairi et al., 2008) - N-self Checking Programming in the avionics domain (Laprie et al., 1995)
Credits		(Armoush, 2010) presents this pattern with detailed information about quality attribute related consequences.

Pattern Name	SAFETY EXECUTIVE PATTERN	Pattern Type	hardware, fail-safe
AlsoKnownAs	Safety Kernel Pattern, Shadow-Pattern, Simplex-Pattern		
Context	A system with a complex fail-safe state should maintain its safety functionality even in case of faults.		
Problem	How to check if a fail-safe state should be entered and how to maintain it.		
Forces	- Full redundancy solutions are expensive - An unavailable component cannot tell that it is unavailable - Complex fail-safe state		
Solution	The *Primary Channel* performs all the required functionality. An optional *Fail-Safe Channel* executes just the safety-critical functionality. A *Watchdog* detects faults in the *Primary Channel* and notifies the *Safety Executive* component which coordinates all safety-measures required to shut down the system or to switch over to the *Fail-Safe* processing channel. 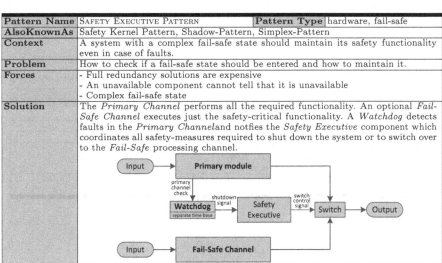		

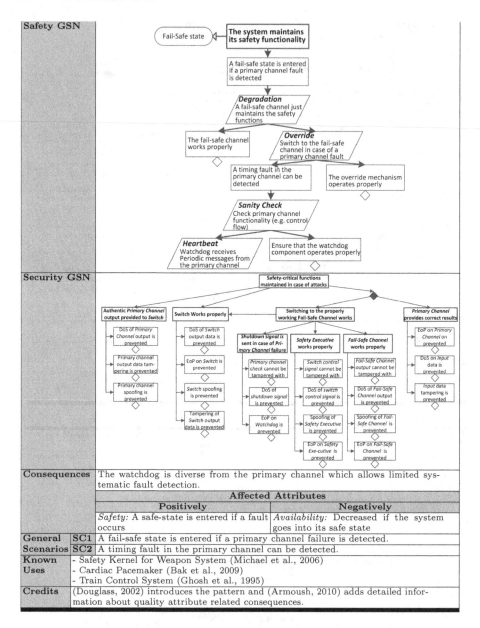

Safety GSN	

Security GSN	

Consequences	The watchdog is diverse from the primary channel which allows limited systematic fault detection.

Affected Attributes		
Positively	**Negatively**	
Safety: A safe-state is entered if a fault occurs	*Availability:* Decreased if the system goes into its safe state	

General	SC1	A fail-safe state is entered if a primary channel failure is detected.
Scenarios	SC2	A timing fault in the primary channel can be detected.

Known Uses	- Safety Kernel for Weapon System (Michael et al., 2006) - Cardiac Pacemaker (Bak et al., 2009) - Train Control System (Ghosh et al., 1995)

Credits	(Douglass, 2002) introduces the pattern and (Armoush, 2010) adds detailed information about quality attribute related consequences.

Pattern Name	SANITY CHECK PATTERN		Pattern Type	hardware, fail-safe
AlsoKnownAs	-			
Context	A safety-critical system with a fail-safe state and low availability requirements.			
Problem	Find an appropriate mechanism to detect failures or errors that can lead to known hazards.			
Forces	- The set of relevant hazards is often known for a specific application domain - Full redundancy solutions are expensive			
Solution	A separate *Sanity Channel* monitors the correct operation of the *Primary Channel*. If the *Primary Channel* output deviates too much from the expected result, then the *Sanity Channel* shuts the system down. 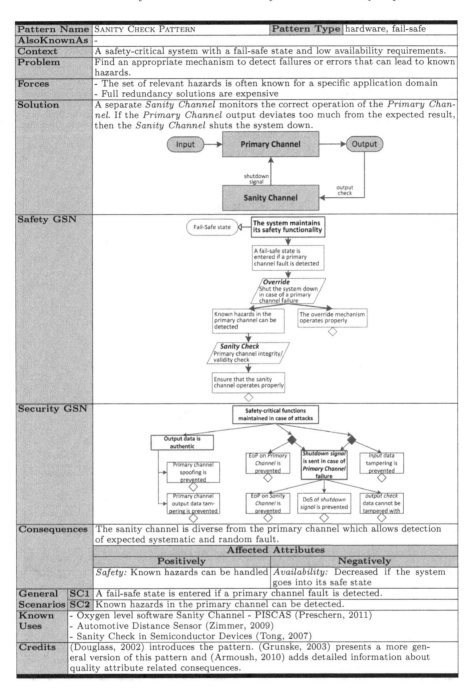			
Safety GSN				
Security GSN				
Consequences	The sanity channel is diverse from the primary channel which allows detection of expected systematic and random fault.			

Affected Attributes	
Positively	**Negatively**
Safety: Known hazards can be handled	*Availability:* Decreased if the system goes into its safe state

General	SC1	A fail-safe state is entered if a primary channel fault is detected.
Scenarios	SC2	Known hazards in the primary channel can be detected.
Known Uses		- Oxygen level software Sanity Channel - PISCAS (Preschern, 2011) - Automotive Distance Sensor (Zimmer, 2009) - Sanity Check in Semiconductor Devices (Tong, 2007)
Credits		(Douglass, 2002) introduces the pattern. (Grunske, 2003) presents a more general version of this pattern and (Armoush, 2010) adds detailed information about quality attribute related consequences.

Pattern Name	MONITOR-ACTUATOR PATTERN	Pattern Type	hardware, fail-safe
AlsoKnownAs	-		
Context	A safety-critical system with a fail-safe state and with low availability requirements.		
Problem	Find an appropriate mechanism to detect failures or errors.		
Forces	- Full redundancy solutions are expensive		
Solution	A separate, diverse and compared to the *Primery Channel* simpler mechanism monitors the correct operation of the *Primary Channel*. The *Monitor Channel* computes reference values from the inputs and compares them to the *Primary Channel* output. If the value deviates too much from the expected result, then the *Monitor Channel* shuts the system down.		

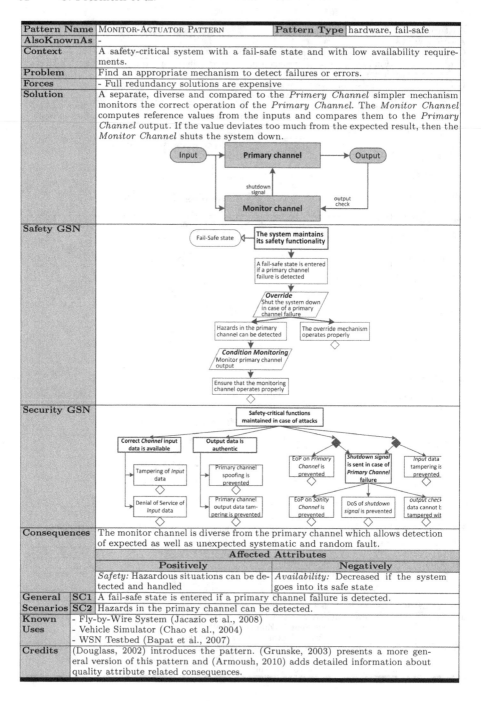

Safety GSN	
Security GSN	
Consequences	The monitor channel is diverse from the primary channel which allows detection of expected as well as unexpected systematic and random fault.

Affected Attributes	
Positively	**Negatively**
Safety: Hazardous situations can be detected and handled	*Availability:* Decreased if the system goes into its safe state

General	SC1	A fail-safe state is entered if a primary channel failure is detected.
Scenarios	SC2	Hazards in the primary channel can be detected.
Known Uses		- Fly-by-Wire System (Jacazio et al., 2008) - Vehicle Simulator (Chao et al., 2004) - WSN Testbed (Bapat et al., 2007)
Credits		(Douglass, 2002) introduces the pattern. (Grunske, 2003) presents a more general version of this pattern and (Armoush, 2010) adds detailed information about quality attribute related consequences.

Pattern Name	WATCHDOG PATTERN	Pattern Type	hardware, fail-safe
AlsoKnownAs	Watchdog Timer, Watchdog Processor, Hardware Watchdog Pattern		
Context	A system provides a timing-critical safety functionality.		
Problem	How to make sure that the internal computational processing is proceeding properly and timely.		
Forces	- Full redundancy solutions are expensive - An unavailable component cannot tell that it is unavailable		
Solution	A separate *Watchdog* component receives liveness messages (which could require complex calculations) from the *Primary Channel*. If the *Watchdog* does not receive the expected messages, it will initiate a corrective action such as a shutdown signal. 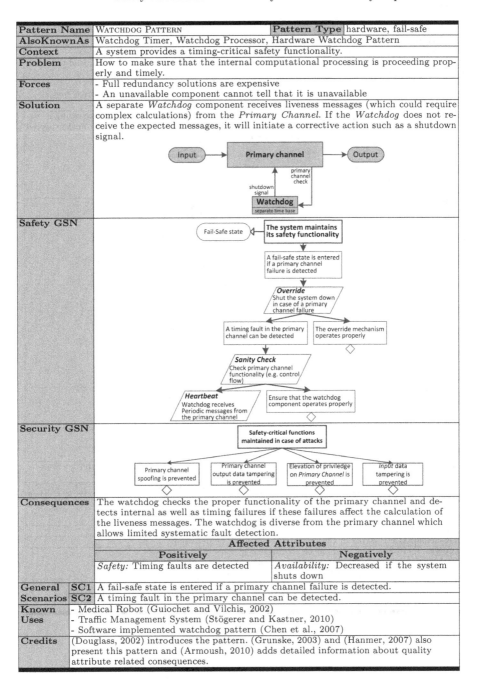		
Safety GSN			
Security GSN			
Consequences	The watchdog checks the proper functionality of the primary channel and detects internal as well as timing failures if these failures affect the calculation of the liveness messages. The watchdog is diverse from the primary channel which allows limited systematic fault detection.		

Affected Attributes	
Positively	**Negatively**
Safety: Timing faults are detected	*Availability:* Decreased if the system shuts down

General	SC1	A fail-safe state is entered if a primary channel failure is detected.
Scenarios	**SC2**	A timing fault in the primary channel can be detected.
Known Uses		- Medical Robot (Guiochet and Vilchis, 2002) - Traffic Management System (Stögerer and Kastner, 2010) - Software implemented watchdog pattern (Chen et al., 2007)
Credits		(Douglass, 2002) introduces the pattern. (Grunske, 2003) and (Hanmer, 2007) also present this pattern and (Armoush, 2010) adds detailed information about quality attribute related consequences.

Pattern Name	PROTECTED SINGLE CHANNEL	Pattern Type	hard/software, fail-safe

AlsoKnownAs	Safety Kernel Pattern, Shadow-Pattern, Simplex-Pattern
Context	A system with a fail-safe state and with low availability requirements.
Problem	Find an appropriate mechanism to handle failures or errors that can lead to known hazards.
Forces	- Full redundancy solutions are expensive - Components are so complex that we cannot assume them to be error free - Not any additional hardware components can be introduced
Solution	The input data of the *Primary Channel* is monitored and checked regarding its validity (e.g range checks) and the output is monitored and checked against expected outputs (e.g. again range checks).

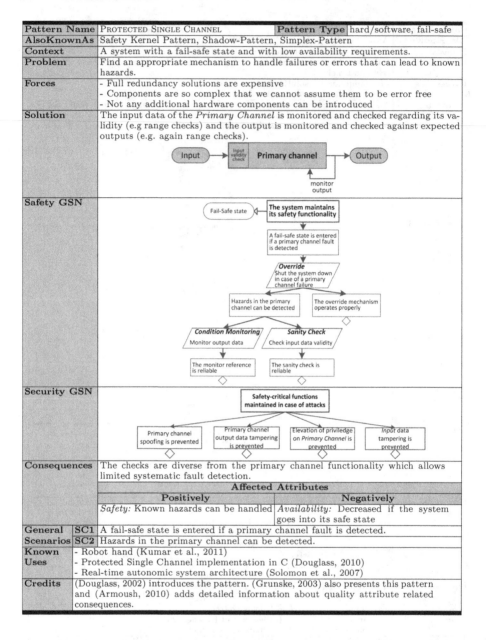

Consequences	The checks are diverse from the primary channel functionality which allows limited systematic fault detection.

Affected Attributes	
Positively	**Negatively**
Safety: Known hazards can be handled	*Availability:* Decreased if the system goes into its safe state

General	**SC1**	A fail-safe state is entered if a primary channel fault is detected.
Scenarios	**SC2**	Hazards in the primary channel can be detected.

Known Uses	- Robot hand (Kumar et al., 2011) - Protected Single Channel implementation in C (Douglass, 2010) - Real-time autonomic system architecture (Solomon et al., 2007)
Credits	(Douglass, 2002) introduces the pattern. (Grunske, 2003) also presents this pattern and (Armoush, 2010) adds detailed information about quality attribute related consequences.

Pattern Name	3-LEVEL SAFETY MONITORING	Pattern Type	hard/software, fail-safe
AlsoKnownAs	Safety Kernel Pattern, Shadow-Pattern, Simplex-Pattern		
Context	A system with a fail-safe state and with low availability requirements		
Problem	Find an appropriate mechanism to handle failures or errors that can lead to known hazards.		
Forces	- Full redundancy solutions are expensive - Components are so complex that we cannot assume them to be error free		
Solution	Divide the system into 3 layers: - The *Actuation Layer* performs the system functionality - The *Monitoring Layer* monitors the *Actuation Layer* and forces a fail-safe state if values deviate too much from references - The *Control Layer* checks the system hardware and sends messages to a *Watchdog* component which can shut the system down		

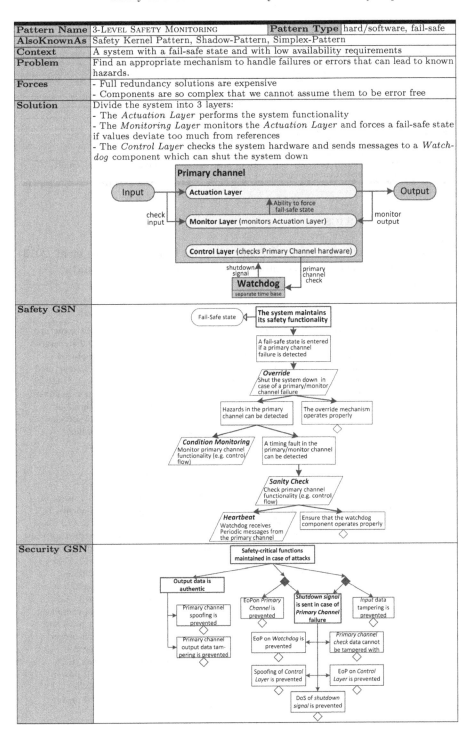

Safety GSN	
Security GSN	

Consequences	The pattern is not applicable for systems with high availability requirements. The checks are diverse from the primary channel which allows limited systematic fault detection.	
	Affected Attributes	
	Positively	**Negatively**
	Safety: Known hazards can be handled	*Availability:* Decreased if the system goes into its safe state
General Scenarios	SC1	A fail-safe state is entered if a primary channel failure is detected.
	SC2	Hazards in the primary channel can be detected.
	SC3	A timing fault in the primary/monitor channel can be detected.
Known Uses	- E-Gas unit to control motor vehicle drive power (Bederna and Zeller, 1999) - Standardized E-Gas concept (EGAS, Arbeitskreis, 2006) - Yokogawa ProSafe-RS PLC (Emori and Kawakami, 2005)	
Credits	(Armoush, 2010) presents this pattern with detailed information about quality attribute related consequences.	

B   Safety Tactics

This section presents the full list of safety tactics from (Preschern et al. 2013) (where a more detailed explanation about safety tactics can be found).

Tactic	Aim	Description	IEC 61508 methods
Simplicity	Avoid failures through keeping the system as simple as possible	*Simplicity* reduces the system complexity. It includes structuring methods or cutting unnecessary functionality and organizes system elements or reduces them to their core safety functionality, thus, eliminating hazards. An example for the application of the *Simplicity* tactic is an emergency stop switch system which is usually kept as simple as possible	IEC 61508-7: B.2.1 structured specification, B.3.2 structured design, C.2.7 structured programming, E.3 structured description method, C.4.2 programming language subset, C.4.2 limit asynchronous constructs, E.5.13 software complexity controller
Substitution	Avoid failures though usage of more reliable components	Components or methods are replaced by other components or methods one has higher confidence in. For hardware and software this can mean usage of existing components which are well-proven in the safety domain	IEC 61508-7: B.3.3 usage of well-proven components, B.5.4 field experience, C.2.10 usage of well-proven/verified software elements, E.20 application of validated soft-cores, E.35 application of validated hard-cores, E.41 usage of well-tried circuits, C.4.3 certified tools and compilers, C.4.4 well-proven tools and compilers, E.4 well-proven tools, E.42 well-proven production process, E.28 application of well-proven synthesis tools, E.29 application of well-proven libraries

Tactic	Aim	Description	IEC 61508 methods
Sanity Check (Checking)	Detection of implausible system outputs or states	The *Sanity Check* tactic checks whether a system state or value remains within a valid range which can be defined in the system specification or which is based on knowledge about the internal structure or nature of the system. An example for a *Sanity Check* is a stuck-at fault RAM-test which checks the proper functionality of the memory during system runtime. The test is based on the understanding of the memory behavior (if we write data to the memory, we should later on be able to read the same data). Faults are detected if the memory behaves differently	A.1.2 monitoring relay contacts, A.2.7 analog signal monitoring, A.3.1–A.3.3 self-tests, A.4.1–A.4.4 checksums, A.5.1–A.5.5 RAM-Tests, A.6.1 test pattern, A.7.1 one-bit hardware redundancy, A.7.2 multi-bit hardware redundancy, A.7.4 inspection using test patterns, A.9 temporal and logical program monitoring, C.3.3 assertion programming, C.5.3 interface checking, C.4.1 strong typed programming language
Condition Monitoring (Checking)	Detect deviations from the intended system outputs or states	*Condition Monitoring* checks whether a system value remains within a reasonable range compared to a more reliable, but usually less accurate, reference value. The reference value is computed at runtime by a redundant part in the implementation which can be based on system input values and is not pre-known from the specification (like it would be the case for *Sanity Check*). An example for *Condition Monitoring* is a system which has to be time-synchronized via the Internet and which checks if the synchronized time is feasible by comparing it to an internal clock	IEC 61508-7: A.1.1 failure detection by online monitoring, A.6.4 monitored outputs, A.8.2 voltage control, A.9 temporal and logical program monitoring, A.12.1 reference sensor, A.13.1 monitoring
Comparison	Detection of discrepancies of redundant system outputs	*Comparison* tests if the outputs of fully redundant subsystems are equal in order to detect failures. The *Comparison* tactic usually implies the usage of a redundancy tactic. An example for the application of the *Comparison* tactic is a dual-core processor running in lock-step mode. The processor runs the same software on both cores and compares their outputs after each cycle	IEC 61508-7: A.1.3 comparator, A.6.5 input comparison/voting

Tactic	Aim	Description	IEC 61508 methods
Diverse Redundancy (Redundancy)	Introduction of a redundant system which allows detection or masking of failures in the specification or implementation as well as random hardware failures	*Diverse Redundancy* can be applied to the specification or to the implementation level. In a system using *Diverse Redundancy* on the implementation level, redundant components use different implementations which were developed independently from the same specification. *Diverse Redundancy* on a specification level goes one step further and additionally requires that even the requirement specifications for the redundant components have to be set up by individual teams	IEC 61508-7: A.7.6 information redundancy, A.13.2 cross-monitoring of multiple actuators, B.1.4 diverse hardware, C.4.4 diverse programming
Replication Redundancy (Redundancy)	Introduction of a redundant systems which allows detection or masking of random hardware failures (not systematic failures)	*Replication Redundancy* means introduction of a redundant system of the same implementation. The redundant systems maintain the same functionality, use identical hardware, and run the same software implementation. An example for *Replication Redundancy* is the RAID1 data storage technology	IEC 61508-7: A.2.1 tests by redundant hardware, A.2.5 monitored redundancy, A.3.5 reciprocal comparison by software, A.4.5 block replication, A.6.3 multi-channel output, A.7.3 complete hardware redundancy, A.7.5 transmission redundancy
Repair (Recovery)	Bring a failed system back to a state of full functionality	The full system functionality is manually or automatically restored if a system failure occurs	IEC 61508-7: C.3.9 error correction, C.3.10 dynamic reconfiguration
Degradation (Recovery)	*Degradation* brings a system with an error into a state with reduced functionality in which the system still maintains the core safety functions	*Degradation* systems define a core safety functionality. The systems maintain this safety functionality and additional non-critical functions. In case of an error, the system falls back into a degraded mode in which it just maintains the core safety functionality. An example where the *Degradation* tactic is often applied are automation systems. These systems control safety-critical processes and often visualize these processes in a GUI. If the system has too few resources (e.g. processing time), then the system stops the GUI service and just focuses on its core functionality to control the safety-critical processes	IEC 61508-7: A.8 voltage supply error handling, C.3.8 degraded function limitation

Tactic	Aim	Description	IEC 61508 methods
Voting (Masking)	Mask the failure of a subsystem so that the failure does not propagate to other systems	*Voting* makes a failure transparent. The tactic does not try to repair the failure, but it hides the failure through choosing a correct result from redundant subsystems. It decides for the majority of the output values	IEC 61508-7: A.1.4 voter, A.6.5 input comparison/voting
Override (Masking)	Mask the failure of a subsystem so that the failure does not propagate to other systems	The *Override* tactic forces the system output to a safe state. For example, if we have a system which is in a safe state when shut off, we can apply the *Override* tactic to shut off the system if we have doubt about the system output (e.g. if an output validity check fails). In this scenario overriding the system output with a safe output value decreases the availability of the system. Another form of the *Override* tactic, which does not decrease the availability and is closely related to the *Voting* tactic, chooses the output of redundant subsystems by preferring one subsystem or one output state over another	IEC 61508: Fail-Safe Principle, A.1.3 comparator
Barrier	Protect a subsystem from influences or influencing other subsystems	The *Barrier* tactic provides a mechanism to protect from unintentional influences between subsystems. To apply *Barrier*, the interfaces between subsystems have to be analyzed and specified. These interfaces are controlled at runtime by a trustworthy component (the *Barrier*) which often is an already existing reliable mechanism. An example for a *Barrier* is a memory protection unit which controls and restricts the communication between different tasks	IEC 61508-7: A.11 separation of energy lines from information lines, B.1.3 separation of safety functions from non-safety functions, B.3.4 modularization, C.2.8 information hiding/ encapsulation, C.2.9 modular approach, E.12 modularization, C.3.11 time-triggered architecture

Appendix References

ALVAREZ, Jacobo et al. (2005). Safe PLD-based programmable controllers. In: *International Conference on Field Programmable Logic and Applications.* IEEE, 559–562.
ANDERSON, T. et al. (1985). Software Fault Tolerance: An Evaluation. IEEE *Transactions on Software Engineering* SE-11, 12, 1502–1510.

ARMOUSH, Ashraf (2010). Design patterns for safety-critical embedded systems. PhD thesis. RWTH Aachen University.

BAK, Stanley et al. (Apr. 2009). The System-Level Simplex Architecture for Improved Real-Time Embedded System Safety. In: *2009 15th IEEE Real-Time and Embedded Technology and Applications Symposium*. IEEE, 99–107.

BAPAT, Sandip et al. (2007). Chowkidar: A Health Monitor for Wireless Sensor Network Testbeds. In: *3rd International Conference on Testbeds and Research Infrastructure for the Development of Networks and Communities (TridentCom)*. IEEE.

BEDER, Delano M., Jo Ueyama, and Marcos L. Chaim (Dec. 2011). A generic policy-free framework for fault-tolerant systems: Experiments on WSNs. In: *2011 IEEE 2nd International Conference on Networked Embedded Systems for Enterprise Applications*. IEEE, 1–7.

BEDERNA, F. and T. Zeller (1999). *Method and arrangement for controlling the drive unit of a vehicle.*

BORCHERT, Christoph, Horst Schirmeier, and Olaf Spinczyk (2012). Protecting the Dynamic Dispatch in C ++ by Dependability Aspects. In: *1st GI Workshop on Software-Based Methods for Robust Embedded Systems (SOBRES'12)*.

BÖRCSÖK, Josef et al. (2011). High-Availability Controller Concept for Steering Systems: The Degradable Safety Controller. In: Proceedings of the 2nd international conference on Circuits, Systems, Communications & Computers, 220–228. isbn: 9781618040565.

BRILLIANT, S.S., J.C. Knight, and N.G. Leveson (1990). Analysis of faults in an N-version software experiment. *IEEE Transactions on Software Engineering* 16, 2, 238–247.

CARR, D.W. et al. (2005). An Open On-Board CBTC Controller Based on N-Version Programming. In: *International Conference on Computational Intelligence for Modelling, Control and Automation and International Conference on Intelligent Agents, Web Technologies and Internet Commerce (CIMCA-IAWTIC'06)*. Vol. 1. IEEE, 834–839.

CHAO, H.C., T.W. Pearce, and M.J.D. Hayes (2004). Use of the HLA in a Real-Time Multi-Vehicle Simulator. In: *The Canadian Society of Mechanical Engineering Forum*, 1–10.

CHEN, Xi et al. (2007). Application of Software Watchdog as a Dependability Software Service for Automotive Safety Relevant Systems. In: *37th International Conference on Dependable Systems and Networks (DSN)*. IEEE.

DOUGLASS, Bruce Powel (2002). *Real-Time Design Patterns: Robust Scalable Architecture for Real- Time Systems*. Pearson.

DOUGLASS, Bruce Powel (2010). *Design Patterns for Embedded Systems in C*. Elsevier.

DURMUÚ, Mustafa Seçkin et al. (2011). A New Voting Strategy in Diverse Programming for Railway Interlocking Systems. In: *International Conference on Transportation, Mechanical, and Electrical Engineering (TMEE)*. IEEE, 723–726.

EGAS, Arbeitskreis (2006). *Standardisiertes E-Gas-Ueberwachungskonzept fuer Motorsteuerungen von Otto- und Dieselmotoren.*

EMORI, Toshiyuki and Shigehito Kawakami (2005). Safety technologies incorporated in the safety control system. *Yokogawa Technical Report* 40, 4, 43–46.

GHOSH, A.K. et al. (1995). A distributed safety-critical system for real-time train control. In: *21st Annual Conference on IEEE Industrial Electronics.* Vol. 2. IEEE, 760–767.

GRUNSKE, Lars (2003). Transformational Patterns for the Improvement of Safety Properties in Architectural Specification. In: *Proceedings of The Second Nordic Conference on Pattern Languages of Programs (VikingPLoP).*

GUIOCHET, J. and A. Vilchis (2002). Safety Analysis of a Medical Robot for Tele-echography. In: *2nd IARP IEEE/RAS joint workshop on Technical Challenge for Dependable Robots in Human Environments.* IEEE, 217–227.

HANMER, Robert S. (2007). *Patterns for Fault Tolerant Software.* Wiley.

JACAZIO, G., P. Serena Guinzio, and M. Sorli (2008). A dual-duplex electro-hydraulic system for the fly-by-wire control of a helicopter main rotor. In: *26th International Congress of the Aeronautical Sciences*, 1–9.

KIM, K H Kane (1998). ROAFTS : A Middleware Architecture for Real-time Object-oriented Adaptive Fault Tolerance Support. In: *3rd International High-Assurance Systems Engineering Symposium.* IEEE.

KOHANAWA, Akihiko, Masami Hasegawa, and Shigeharu Kanamori (2010). Safety Control Solutions Protecting Onsite Safety. *Fuji Electric Group* 56, 1.

KUMAR, S Phani, P. Seetha Ramaiah, and V. Khanaa (2011). Architectural patterns to design software safety based safety-critical systems. In: *Proceedings of the 2011 International Conference on Communication, Computing & Security - ICCCS '11.* ACM Press, 620.

KYRIAKOULAKOS, Konstantinos and Dionisios N. Pnevmatikatos (2009). A novel SRAM-based FPGA architecture for efficient TMR fault tolerance support. In: *19th International Conference on Field Programmable Logic and Applications (FPL).* IEEE.

LAPRIE, J.C. et al. (1995). Architectural Issues in Software Fault Tolerance. In: *Software Fault Tolerance.* Wiley, 47–80.

LJOSLAND, Ingvar (2006). BUCS : Patterns and Robustness A Navigation System Case Study.

MICHAEL, J Bret, Anil Nerode, and Duminda Wijesekera (2006). On the Provision of Safety Assurance via Safety Kernels for Modern Weapon Systems. In: *DTIC Science & Technology*, 102–105.

MIYAWAKI, Nii (2008). Study of Machine Safety Control. *JTEKT Engineering Journal* 1004E, 119–124.

MUTLU, Ahmet (2004). DC Motor Speed Controller Software.

NOURANI, Esmaeil and Mohammad Abdollahi Azgomi (Dec. 2009). A design pattern for dependable web services using design diversity techniques and WS-BPEL. In: *2009 International Conference on Innovations in Information Technology (IIT).* IEEE, 325–329.

PARCHAS, E. and R. de Lemos (2004). An architectural approach for improving availability in Web services. In: *Third Workshop on Architecting Dependable Systems (WADS).* IET.

PRESCHERN, Christopher (2011). PISCAS: Pisciculture Automation System Product Line. MA thesis. Graz University of Technology.

PRESCHERN, Christopher, Nermin Kajtazovic, and Christian Kreiner (2013). Catalog of Safety Tactics in the light of the IEC 61508 Safety Lifecycle. In: *VikingPLoP*.

SGHAIRI, M. et al. (2008). Challenges in Building Fault-Tolerant Flight Control System for a Civil Aircraft. *IAENG International Journal of Computer Science* 35, 4, 495–499.

SKAMBRAKS, Martin (Sept. 2006). An Architecture for Runtime State Restoration after Transient Hardware-Faults in Redundant Real-Time Systems. In: *Conference on Emerging Technologies and Factory Automation*. IEEE, 78–85.

SOLOMON, Bogdan et al. (May 2007). Towards a Real-Time Reference Architecture for Autonomic Systems. In: *International Workshop on Software Engineering for Adaptive and Self-Managing Systems (SEAMS '07)*. IEEE.

STÖGERER, Christoph and Wolfgang Kastner (2010). Distributed Monitoring for Component-based Traffic Management Systems. In: *Conference on Emerging Technologies and Factory Automation (ETFA)*. IEEE.

TONG, Adams N. (2007). Fabrication of deep-submicron complementary metal-oxide semiconductor devices. PhD thesis. University of Notre Dame.

VERGARA-FERNANDEZ, Antonio and Reiner Denz (2002). Reliability Analysis for the quench detection in the LHC machine. In: *8th European Particle Accelerator Conference*, 2445–2447.

WANG, Feiyi et al. (2001). SITAR : A Scalable Intrusion-Tolerant Architecture for Distributed Services. In: *Foundations of Intrusion Tolerant Systems (OASIS'03)*. June. IEEE, 5–6.

ZIMMER, Marcel (2009). Prototypische Implementierung und Evaluation von Sicherheitsmustern in eingebetteten Systemen. MA thesis. Technische Universität Kaiserslautern.

References

Antonino, P.O., Keuler, T., Antonino, P.: Towards an approach to represent safety patterns. In: The Seventh International Conference on Software Engineering Advances (ICSEA), pp. 228–237 (2012)

Armoush, A.: Design patterns for safety-critical embedded systems. Ph.D. thesis. RWTH Aachen University (2010)

Avizienis, A., et al.: Basic concepts and taxonomy of dependable and secure computing. IEEE Trans. Dependable Secure Comput. **1**, 1 (2004)

Babar, M.A.: Improving the reuse of pattern-based knowledge in software architecting. In: EuroPLoP, Lero, Ireland, pp. 7–11 (2007)

Bachmann, F., Bass, L., Klein, M.: Deriving architectural tactics: a step toward methodical architectural design. Techncial report, March, Carnegie Mellon Software Engineering Institute (2003)

Buckley, I., Fernandez, E.B., Larrondo-Petrie, M.M.: Patterns combining reliability and security. In: The Third International Conferences on Pervasive Patterns and Applications, PATTERNS 2011 (2011)

Buschmann, F., et al.: Pattern-Oriented Software Architecture: A System of Patterns. Wiley, Hoboken (1996)

Cockram, T.J., Lautieri, S.R.: Combining security and safety principle in practice. In: 2nd Institution of Engineering and Technology International Conference on System Safety, pp. 159–164. IEEE (2007)

Committee on National Security Systems: National Information Assurance Glossary. CNSS Instruction No. 4009 (2010)

Daniels, F., Kim, K., Vouk, M.A.: The reliable hybrid pattern a generalized software fault tolerant design pattern. In: European Conference on Pattern Language of Programs (EuroPLoP), pp. 1–9 (1997)

Dasarathy, B.: Cyber security definitions and academic landscape. In: NPSMA Workshop (2013)

Douglass, B.P.: Safety-critical systems design. Electron. Eng. **70**, 862 (1998)

Douglass, B.P.: Real-Time Design Patterns: Robust Scalable Architecture for Real-Time Systems. Pearson, London (2002)

Douglass, B.P.: Design Patterns for Embedded Systems in C. Elsevier, Amsterdam (2010)

Douglass, B.P.: Software design architecture patterns for embedded systems, chap. In: Software Engineering for Embedded Systems. Elsevier (2013)

Gawand, H., Mundada, R.S., Swaminathan, P.: Design patterns to implement safety and fault tolerance. Int. J. Comput. Appl. **18**(2), 6–13 (2011)

Grunske, L.: Transformational patterns for the improvement of safety properties in architectural specification. In: Proceedings of The Second Nordic Conference on Pattern Languages of Programs (VikingPLoP) (2003)

GSN Working Group: GSN Community Standard Version 1 (2011). http://www.goalstructuringnotation.info/

Halkidis, S.T., Chatzigeorgiou, A., Stephanides, G.: A qualitative evaluation of security patterns. In: Lopez, J., Qing, S., Okamoto, E. (eds.) ICICS 2004. LNCS, vol. 3269, pp. 132–144. Springer, Heidelberg (2004). https://doi.org/10.1007/978-3-540-30191-2_11

Halkidis, S., Chatzigeorgiou, A., Stephanides, G.: A qualitative analysis of software security patterns. Comput. Secur. **25**(5), 379–392 (2006a)

Halkidis, S.T., Chatzigeorgiou, A., Stephanides, G.: Quantitative evaluation of systems with security patterns using a fuzzy approach. In: Meersman, R., Tari, Z., Herrero, P. (eds.) OTM 2006. LNCS, vol. 4277, pp. 554–564. Springer, Heidelberg (2006b). https://doi.org/10.1007/11915034_79

Halkidis, S., Tsantalis, N., et al.: Architectural risk analysis of software systems based on security patterns. IEEE Trans. Dependable Secure Comput. **5**(3), 129–142 (2008)

Hamid, B., Desnos, N., et al.: Model-based security and dependability patterns in RCES - the TERESA approach. In: Proceedings of the International Workshop on Security and Dependability for Resource Constrained Embedded Systems - S&D4RCES 2010. ACM Press (2010)

Hamid, B., Geisel, J., Ziani, A., Bruel, J.-M., Perez, J.: Model-driven engineering for trusted embedded systems based on security and dependability patterns. In: Khendek, F., Toeroe, M., Gherbi, A., Reed, R. (eds.) SDL 2013. LNCS, vol. 7916, pp. 72–90. Springer, Heidelberg (2013). https://doi.org/10.1007/978-3-642-38911-5_5

Hampton, P.: Survey of safety architectural patterns. In: Dale, C., Anderson, T. (eds.) Achieving Systems Safety, pp. 137–158. Springer, London (2012). https://doi.org/10.1007/978-1-4471-2494-8_11

Hanmer, R.S.: Patterns for Fault Tolerant Software. Wiley, Hoboken (2007)

Hansen, K.: Security attack analysis of safety systems. In: IEEE Conference on Emerging Technologies and Factory Automation, pp. 1–4, September 2009

Harrison, N.B., Avgeriou, P.: Incorporating fault tolerance tactics in software architecture patterns. In: Proceedings of the 2008 RISE/EFTS Joint International Workshop on Software Engineering for Resilient Systems - SERENE 2008. ACM Press (2008)

Howard, M., LeBlanc, D.: Writing Secure Code. Microsoft Press (2003)

Howard, M., Lipner, S.: The Security Development Lifecycle. Microsoft Press (2006)

International Electrotechnical Commission: IEC 61508, Functional Safety of Electrical/ Electronic/ Programmable Electronic Safety Related Systems (2010)

Johnson, C., Yepez, A.: Cyber security threats to safety-critical space-based infrastructures. In: Proceedings of the Fifth Conference of the International Association for the Advancement of Space Safety, no. 1 (2011a)

Johnson, C., Yepez, A.: Mapping the impact of security threats on safety-critical global navigation satellite systems. In: Proceedings of the 29th International Systems Safety Society, no. 1. International Systems Safety Society (2011b)

Kelly, T., Weaver, R.: The goal structuring notation, a safety argument notation. In: Proceedings of the Dependable Systems and Networks Conference (2004)

Kumar, K., Prabhakar, T.V.: Design decision topology model for pattern relationship analysis. In: 1st Asian Conference on Pattern Languages of Programs (AsianPLoP 2010) (2010a)

Kumar, K., Prabhakar, T.V.: Pattern-oriented knowledge model for architecture design. In: 17th Conference on Pattern Languages of Programs (PLoP) (2010b)

Leveson, N.G.: Engineering a Safer World. MIT Press, Cambridge (2012)

Nai-Fovino, I., Masera, M., De-Cian, A.: Integrating cyber attacks within fault trees. Reliab. Eng. Syst. Saf. **94**(9), 1394–1402 (2009)

Olivera, A.R.: Taim: a safety pattern repository. B.Sc. thesis. Federal University of Rio Grande do sul (2012)

Preschern, C., Kajtazovic, N., Kreiner, C.: Built-in security enhancements for the 1oo2 safety architecture. In: International Conference on Cyber Technology in Automation, Control, and Intelligent Systems (CYBER), pp. 103–108. IEEE (2012a)

Preschern, C., Kajtazovic, N., Kreiner, C.: Catalog of security tactics linked to common criteria requirements. In: 19th Conference on Pattern Languages of Programs (PLoP) (2012b)

Preschern, C., Kajtazovic, N., Kreiner, C.: Applying and evaluating architectural IEC 61508 safety patterns. In: 5th International Conference on Software Technology and Engineering (ICSTE) (2013a)

Preschern, C., Kajtazovic, N., Kreiner, C.: Building a safety architecture pattern system. In: 18th European Conference on Pattern Languages of Programs (EuroPLoP) (2013b)

Preschern, C., Kajtazovic, N., Kreiner, C.: Catalog of safety tactics in the light of the IEC 61508 safety lifecycle. In: VikingPLoP (2013c)

Preschern, C., Kajtazovic, N., Kreiner, C.: Security analysis of safety patterns. In: 20th Conference on Pattern Languages of Programs (PLoP) (2013d)

Pullum, L.: Software Fault Tolerance Techniques and Implementation. Artech House, Norwood (2001)

Rauhamäki, J., Kuikka, S.: Patterns for control system safety. In: 18th European Conference on Pattern Languages of Programs (VikingPLoP) (2013)

Rauhamäki, J., Vepsäläinen, T., Kuikka, S.: Architectural patterns for functional safety. In: Nordic Conference on Pattern Languages of Programs (VikingPLoP) (2012)

Rauhamäki, J., Vepsäläinen, T., Kuikka, S.: Patterns for safety and control system cooperation. In: Nordic Conference on Pattern Languages of Programs (VikingPLoP) (2013)

Ryoo, J., Laplante, P., Kazman, R.: A methodology for mining security tactics from security patterns. In: 2010 43rd Hawaii International Conference on System Sciences, pp. 1–5. IEEE (2010)

Saridakis, T.: A system of patterns for fault tolerance. In: EuroPLoP (2002)

Sarma, U.V.R., Rampelli, S., Premchand, P.: A catalog of architectural design patterns for safety-critical real-time systems. Int. J. Eng. Res. Appl. **3**(1), 125–131 (2013)

Schaad, A., Borozdin, M.: TAM2: automated threat analysis. In: Proceedings of the 27th Annual ACM Symposium on Applied Computing, pp. 1103–1108. ACM (2012)

Schaad, A., Garaga, A.: Automating architectural security analysis. In: Proceedings of the 17th ACM Symposium on Access Control Models and Technologies, pp. 131–132. ACM (2012)

Schumacher, M.: Security Engineering with Patterns. LNCS, vol. 2754. Springer, Heidelberg (2003). https://doi.org/10.1007/b11930

Spriggs, J.: GSN—The Goal Structuring Notation: A Structured Approach to Presenting Arguments. Springer, London (2012). https://doi.org/10.1007/978-1-4471-2312-5

Steiner, M., Liggesmeyer, P.: Combination of safety and security analysis - finding security problems that threaten the safety of a system. In: Workshop on Dependable Embedded and Cyberphysical Systems - Held at the 32nd International Conference on Computer Safety, Reliability and Security (2013). https://hal.archives-ouvertes.fr/file/index/docid/848604/filename/7_-_main.pdf

Ugljesa, E., Wacker, H.: Modeling security aspects in safety environment. In: 7th International Conference on Electrical and Electronics Engineering, pp. 46–50 (2011)

Wu, W.: Safety tactics for software architecture design. MA thesis. The University of York (2003)

Wu, W.: Architectural reasoning for safety-critical software applications. Ph.D. thesis. University of York (2007)

Yampolskiy, M., et al.: Systematic analysis of cyber-attacks on CPS-evaluating applicability of DFD-based approach. In: 5th International Symposium on Resilient Control Systems, pp. 55–62. IEEE, August 2012

Yautsiukhin, A., Scandariato, R.: Towards a quantitative assessment of security in software architectures. In: 13th Nordic Workshop on Secure IT Systems (NordSec) (2008)

An Open Source Pattern Language

Christoph Hannebauer$^{(\boxtimes)}$ and Volker Gruhn

University of Duisburg-Essen, Schützenbahn 70, 45127 Essen, Germany
{christoph.hannebauer,volker.gruhn}@uni-due.de
http://se.wiwi.uni-due.de

Abstract. This article presents an overview about the current state of research on Open Source Software (OSS) patterns. Currently, there are 40 published OSS patterns. The article argues that 35 of these OSS patterns are unique and categorizes them in eight categories. Two additional types of relationships complement this categorization. The categorization and the relationships shed light on the pattern language aspect of OSS patterns.

1 Introduction

Researchers have observed and described different characteristics of software development in Open Source Software (OSS) projects [1,2] and their communities [3,4]. However, the definition of Open Source from the Open Source Initiative (OSI) [5] and the definition of Free Software from the Free Software Foundation (FSF) [6] depend only on the license used for the project and not on the development style. Therefore, development methods differ strongly between OSS projects.

The pattern approach introduced by Alexander allows the description of individual parts of a method, independently from other parts and still showing their interrelations [7]. Kelly suggested that this pattern approach may be applicable to OSS development, and that the best practices of running OSS projects may constitute its own OSS pattern language [8]. In fact, several authors picked up the idea and wrote down OSS patterns that they had observed in practice and drawn from literature [9–21].

Currently, there are 40 OSS patterns described in 13 monographs. Although patterns are supposed to facilitate the reader's understanding of a domain, it is difficult to gain an overview of this large number of patterns distributed in several publications, with no apparent order in these OSS patterns.

The goal of this paper is to give a concise overview of all OSS patterns and thereby serve as a guideline that helps readers to find the OSS patterns relevant for their situation.

As part of this endeavor, the OSS patterns have been categorized into eight categories. Additionally, some OSS patterns are similar and it turned out that they describe different aspects of the same problem and solution. These OSS patterns have been combined. Resulting OSS patterns, whether unchanged or

© Springer Nature Switzerland AG 2019
J. Noble et al. (Eds.): TPLOP IV, LNCS 10600, pp. 76–99, 2019.
https://doi.org/10.1007/978-3-030-14291-9_3

combined, are described as thumbnails according to the PROBLEM/SOLUTION SUMMARY PATTERN of the pattern language for pattern writing [22].

OSS patterns currently stand mostly on their own, as current research did not put much emphasis on the relationship between patterns, especially between patterns of different authors. Partly, this is due to the publication order of patterns, as obviously a work can only reference previously published patterns. Sometimes earlier OSS patterns rest upon later OSS patterns, possibly without the authors' knowledge, and these relations have yet to be revealed. Thus, we also identified relationships between OSS patterns.

1.1 Classification of OSS Patterns

Each of the eight OSS pattern categories has its own section. A category section starts with a summary of the patterns in the category as described in the PATTERN LANGUAGE SUMMARY PATTERN [22]. This summary introduces the patterns as a whole and describes their relations. A diagram known as pattern map visualizes the patterns in the category. Section 1.3 describes the pattern maps of this paper in more detail. The remainder of each section contains thumbnails of all patterns in the category.

According to the PROBLEM/SOLUTION SUMMARY PATTERN [22], thumbnails of patterns present patterns in a strongly abbreviated form, limited to the name of the pattern, the problem that the pattern tackles, and the main idea of the solution. The thumbnail of a pattern gives a basic idea of the pattern, but it is insufficient for its implementation. In this study, thumbnails of patterns additionally include an icon symbolizing each OSS pattern. Readers interested in a specific OSS pattern should read the cited source containing the full OSS pattern.

Some OSS patterns described in this study have been published in multiple papers by different names, sometimes by different authors. The original publications do not explicitly state that these OSS patterns are refinements of previously published OSS patterns. In fact, at least in some cases the authors of refined OSS patterns have not been aware that the refined OSS patterns resemble previously published OSS patterns. Indeed, these different versions of the same OSS pattern differ in emphasis and highlight slightly different aspects of the OSS pattern. A hard proof that these OSS patterns are the same is impossible and therefore up to discussion. Consequentially, thumbnails of these deduplicated OSS patterns additionally contain a deduplication section with arguments showing why the different variants represent the same OSS pattern.

1.2 Related Work on Pattern Languages and Pattern Maps

Alexander explains that patterns cannot stand on their own, but have relations constituting a pattern language [7]. Alexander et al. [23] present their architectural pattern language in order of application size, starting with the structure of countries and regions and ending with specific arrangements of interiors in a house. In this pattern language, each pattern usually relies on more specific patterns that come later in the pattern language.

A diagram that visualizes a pattern language, especially the classification of patterns and their relationships, is called a pattern map. Alexander et al. [23] do not use a pattern map. Other authors have no common let alone standardized notation for pattern maps. Hence, authors of pattern languages focusing on software development teams and organizations varied in their use of pattern maps and similar visualizations of pattern languages.

In the following, we present a short survey of related work about pattern languages and the different kinds of pattern maps. This lays the groundwork for structuring and visualizing the OSS pattern language.

Pattern languages can be seen as graphs, with patterns being nodes that have edges to the patterns required or useful for their implementation. This graph structure is a common technique used for pattern maps.

For example, Fowler [24] shows pattern names in a figure with arrows between two patterns when the first influences the second. Furthermore, the patterns' x-axis positions designate their complexity. Their positions on the y-axis show to which of two major categories they belong. In contrast, Cunningham [25] uses the position of the pattern name in the diagram to indicate who (first dimension) implements the pattern on which type of work (second dimension). Again, related patterns are connected, although only with a line instead of an arrow. Cunningham explains that a relationship means that after application of a pattern, the related pattern may be applicable. These connections seem similar to Alexander's interpretation of pattern relationships [7]. Coplien and Harrison [26] described this notion in more detail: Every project applies pattern after pattern in any order that the pattern relations allow. Each such series of pattern applications is called a sequence. They use example sequences to illustrate the use of their pattern languages.

Notably, Weir [27] and Roberts and Johnson [28] used a different approach to visualize patterns: Each pattern spans a time frame on the chronological x-axis, indicating in which phases of the design process it is applicable. Hannebauer et al. also applied this to a set of OSS patterns [10].

Another type of pattern map can be seen in different works from Kelly [8,29]. These pattern maps categorize the patterns into families and lead the readers with questions to applicable patterns.

Previous work on OSS patterns also frequently visualized OSS patterns as nodes in directed graphs [10,11,13,14,16–19]. This often implied a chronological order or order of dependency, but also included more complex relationships. In some cases, edges included labels to denote their meanings. However, as explained before, previous work referenced OSS patterns from other works only rarely. Consequently, it is unclear how patterns of different works relate to each other. This work tries to address this gap and give an overview over the OSS pattern language as a whole.

There is a pattern language about writing patterns including a section on pattern languages [22]. The pattern COMMON PROBLEMS HIGHLIGHTED

PATTERN [22] of this pattern language describes the case where multiple different patterns solve the same problem. Thus, these patterns are alternatives and at most one of them should be used at once. Ratzka connects alternative patterns in his pattern map with an arrow with two heads [30, p. 123].

Where applicable, the pattern language on writing patterns has been used as a guide for the OSS pattern language. As discussed above, two types of relationships stand out in the related work: First, a pattern may depend on another pattern. Second, implementation of a pattern may exclude implementation of another pattern. We identified these types of relationships between OSS patterns by two means:

1. The original publications of OSS patterns described related patterns, most of which are OSS patterns. We evaluated whether these patterns constitute one of the two relationships described above.
2. Especially for pairs of OSS patterns of different authors, we compared descriptions of OSS patterns, and whether these implied any kind of relationship.

In both cases, we explained the rationale for the relationship in the text at the beginning of each category section.

1.3   Pattern Maps for the OSS Pattern Language

Figure 1 shows an example of a pattern map as used in this paper. A pattern is represented as a rectangle containing a pattern symbol and a pattern name in small caps. In the example, PATTERN A is a pattern with a symbol shaped like an A.

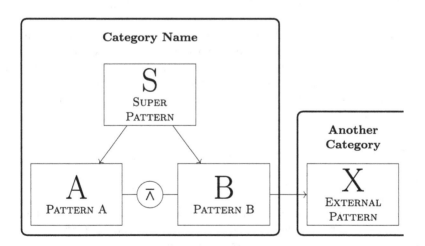

Fig. 1. Example pattern map

The pattern maps in this paper were limited to the two types of relationship identified in the related work to keep them simple and understandable. The first type of relationship are alternatives that exclude each other. PATTERN A and PATTERN B are alternatives, indicated by a line with a circled $\overline{\wedge}$. At most one of the two or more alternatives can be implemented.

The second type of relationship is indicated by arrows, like the ones from SUPER PATTERN to PATTERN A and from SUPER PATTERN to PATTERN B. Arrows indicate that the starting pattern uses or requires the ending pattern. In this example, when choosing to implement SUPER PATTERN, it is also advisable or required to implement PATTERN A and/or PATTERN B. Whether it is strictly required or only sensible depends on the specific pattern combination and is not visible in the pattern maps.

In some cases, one of multiple alternatives must be implemented, for example because another pattern requires this. The example in Fig. 1 might mean that SUPER PATTERN requires either PATTERN A or PATTERN B, but this is not clear from the pattern map alone and readers would have to look at the patterns in detail.

All OSS patterns were unambiguously categorized to one of eight categories. In the pattern maps, a box for each category surrounds all patterns of that category and the box contains the category name in boldface. Each category has its own color that fills the category box (not shown in Fig. 1). Besides the categorization, pattern positions have no further meaning, although more specialized patterns tend to be placed lower or more on the right in the figures.

The pattern map for each category section shows all OSS patterns that belong to this category and also each other OSS pattern that they depend on. EXTERNAL PATTERN is an example of such a pattern belonging to Another Category. However, for the sake of conciseness, dependencies are included only in one direction: The pattern maps do not show patterns that depend on patterns of the current category, but only patterns with arrows *from* the current category. In the example, there might be ANOTHER EXTERNAL PATTERN depending on PATTERN A, but it is not shown because no pattern of the current category depends on this ANOTHER EXTERNAL PATTERN. Patterns in other categories also have their respective category boxes. These category boxes are open on one side to indicate that there are other patterns not shown in the pattern map belonging to the category.

1.4   Overview of All OSS Patterns

Figures 2 and 3 are the two parts of a pattern map including all OSS patterns collected in this study.

Figure 2 contains organizational OSS patterns. Organizational OSS patterns are especially interesting for commercial companies, as the OSS patterns in the category *Revenue from OSS* provide methods to earn money with an OSS project. OSS patterns in the category *Licensing* help to choose a licensing model for an OSS project that fits the purposes of its maintainer. While this covers the power over the source code from a copyright perspective, OSS patterns in

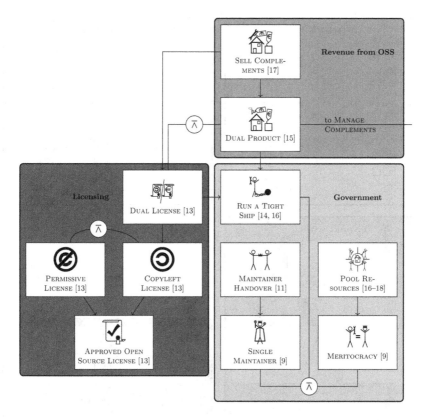

Fig. 2. Pattern map for organizational OSS patterns

the category *Government* focus on social aspects and help to channel the power over the OSS project's community.

Figure 3 contains performance OSS patterns: how can a project improve its software development using OSS? The category *New Developers* contain OSS patterns that help new developers onboard the OSS project and become code contributors. These OSS patterns rely on those in other categories; the category *Architecture* comprises of OSS patterns that help create a program and organizational architecture to enable code contributions and help to have components with which to earn money. OSS patterns in the category *User Community* describe how to attract new users and how to activate them for contributions. The OSS patterns in the category *Project Gestation* help to start a new OSS project from scratch or based on a closed source project.

The category *Code from Other OSS Projects* contains the only OSS patterns that can also be used in closed-source software development projects. All other OSS patterns target maintainers of OSS projects.

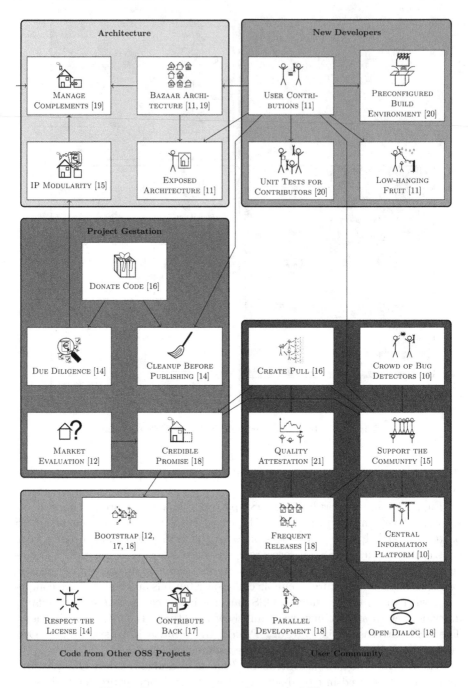

Fig. 3. Pattern map for performance OSS patterns

2   Revenue from OSS

Commercial maintainers of OSS projects need a business model to generate revenue from an OSS project. Figure 4 shows the main OSS pattern SELL COMPLEMENTS and its dependencies. There are multiple ways to SELL COMPLEMENTS for the OSS application, one of which is a DUAL PRODUCT: One basic version is free and another extended version must be paid for. In this case, maintainers must have IP MODULARITY in their architecture to separate free from paid modules. Another possibility is a DUAL LICENSE. In both cases, maintainers RUN A TIGHT SHIP to use external contributions for their commercial products.

Sell Complements [17]
Problem: How do you monetize an OSS product?
Solution: Sell products or services (such as hardware or support) that complement the OSS product.

Dual Product [15]
Problem: You want to entice commercial users to pay for an OSS product.
Solution: Keep parts of the OSS project closed, and sell a commercial version of the product with exclusive features.

3   Project Gestation

The OSS patterns in this section help to start a new OSS project. Figure 5 shows the five OSS patterns and their relations. DONATE CODE is the core pattern if the new OSS project founds on an internal closed source project. The two related OSS patterns CLEANUP BEFORE PUBLISHING and DUE DILIGENCE describe preparation steps before publishing that help being successful and prevent legal problems in the project, respectively.

IP MODULARITY helps to deal with those parts of the code that shall not be published after DUE DILIGENCE.

The two OSS patterns MARKET EVALUATION and CREDIBLE PROMISE do not require a previous closed source project and may also be used to start an OSS project from scratch. MARKET EVALUATION explains how OSS facilitates the production of what Ries calls a Minimum Viable Product (MVP) [31]. This first software version should show a CREDIBLE PROMISE to attract early adopters.

BOOTSTRAP helps to build the core features for CREDIBLE PROMISE. SUPPORT THE COMMUNITY attracts a user base from which to recruit developers with the CREDIBLE PROMISE.

Market Evaluation [12]
Problem: How to facilitate interest in your software, determine if it is the right product and attract the early adopters, and cross the chasm and get the market majority to adopt your product?
Solution: Establish a beach head by releasing your component from the start as OSS.

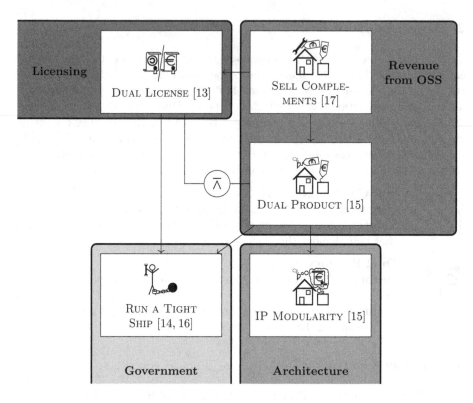

Fig. 4. Pattern map for revenue from OSS

Credible Promise [18]
Problem: How do you mobilize developers to contribute to your project?
Solution: Build a critical mass of functionality early in your project that demonstrates that the project is doable and has merit.

Donate Code [16]
Problem: How do you extend the lifespan of your proprietary code?
Solution: Relinquish control over the code by releasing it under a flexible OSS license that allows others to build on it easily.

Cleanup Before Publishing [14]
Problem: How to prepare the publication of a component as OSS in a way that attracts and not discourages acceptance and contributions and prevents problems with intellectual property?
Solution: Cleanup the structure, source, documentation, and supporting material of your project material before you publish it.

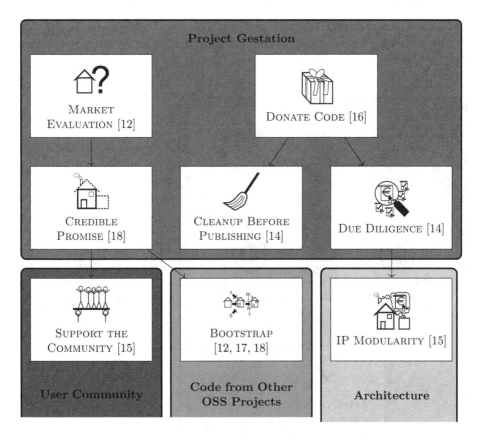

Fig. 5. Patterns in the category Project Gestation

Due Diligence [14]
Problem: How to reduce the risk of being attacked because of claimed
intellectual property violations like copyright, patent, trade secrets, or
license violations?
Solution: Check for copied or otherwise integrated code, intellectual
property, or patented technology. Ensure that the reuse complies with
licenses and regulations.

4   Licensing

The FSF as well as the OSI define Free Software and Open Source by their
licenses [5,6]. Figure 6 shows OSS patterns that help to choose the right license
for an OSS project. While an APPROVED OPEN SOURCE LICENSE is generally
recommended, this still leaves the choice open between a PERMISSIVE LICENSE
and a COPYLEFT LICENSE. The latter allows the combination with a commercial
license in the DUAL LICENSE model. Notably, the pattern DUAL LICENSE does

not cover any combination of two licenses, but of two specific kinds. In fact, PERMISSIVE LICENSE and COPYLEFT LICENSE are exclusive alternatives and therefore cannot be combined in a reasonable way.

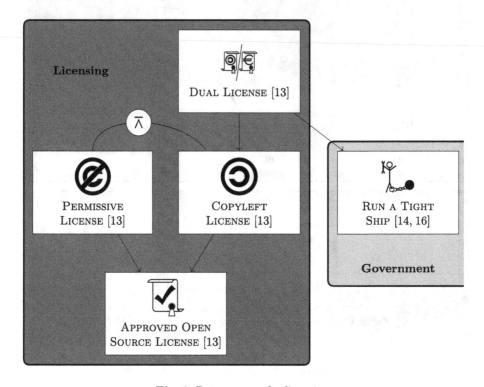

Fig. 6. Pattern map for licensing

External contributors must assign copyright to the maintainer for the DUAL LICENSE model. Therefore, the maintainer must RUN A TIGHT SHIP in the OSS project or not accept external contributions at all.

Not depicted in Fig. 6 is the relationship to RESPECT THE LICENSE. No license for a composite OSS project is compatible with all possible OSS licenses for OSS components, no matter if the license of the composite OSS project is a COPYLEFT LICENSE or a PERMISSIVE LICENSE. Therefore, there is no specific dependency of one the OSS patterns in this category to RESPECT THE LICENSE.

Dual License [13]
Problem: How to encourage people to pay for your OSS component?
Solution: Release your software component with two (or more) licenses.

Copyleft License [13] (also known as RECIPROCAL LICENSE [13])
Problem: How do you choose the type of OSS license so that it
supports your business model?
Solution: Choose a license which requires derived or combined works
to be released under the identical license.

Permissive License [13]
Problem: How do you choose the type of OSS license so that it
supports your business model?
Solution: Publish your component under a license which permits
distribution with modifications without enforcing the publication of
the source.

Approved Open Source License [13]
Problem: How to choose the OSS license for your component?
Solution: Use an existing OSS license which best fits your needs.

5   Government

OSS licenses ensure that there is no legal owner of the software who has the
exclusive rights to decide how to develop the OSS component. Nevertheless, there
is usually a community around any OSS component with a social hierarchy. The
core developers and maintainers rank highest in this hierarchy and decide about
the direction of the OSS project [3]. The OSS project's power model determines
who these maintainers are. Figure 7 shows OSS patterns describing these power
models. SINGLE MAINTAINER and MERITOCRACY are very common basic models
that exclude each other, with only special exceptions. When organizations RUN
A TIGHT SHIP on OSS projects, the locus of power is outside the OSS project's
volunteer community; therefore, in this case the volunteer community is usually
smaller than in other forms of government and it is more suited if there are
enough paid contributors.

A SINGLE MAINTAINER may transfer power over an OSS project to a succes-
sor with a MAINTAINER HANDOVER. When multiple companies want to POOL
RESOURCES, they typically use a MERITOCRACY to direct the corresponding
OSS project.

In addition to the OSS patterns in this category, DONATE CODE handles who
has power over a software development project: Publishing closed sources under
an OSS license allows others to take advantage of the previously closed source
code in their own projects. However, DONATE CODE deals primarily with legal
power, as do the OSS patterns in Sect. 4, and not with the social power in OSS
projects as the OSS patterns in this section.

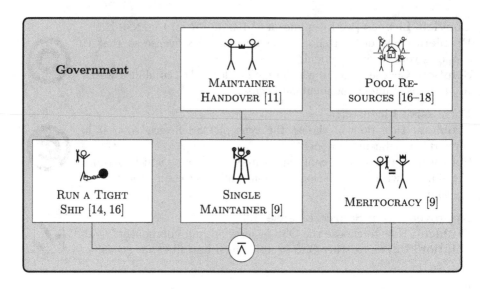

Fig. 7. Pattern map for government

Run a Tight Ship [16] (also known as CONTRIBUTOR AGREE-
MENT [14])
Problem: How do you keep control of the project's direction?
Solution: Maintain full ownership of the code.
De-duplication: The solution of RUN A TIGHT SHIP [16] describes
two alternatives for its realization: Either write all source code yourself or let all external contributors transfer the rights to you. The latter possibility specifically refers to CONTRIBUTOR AGREEMENT [14]
by its previous name ASSIGN COPYRIGHT. Writing all source code
yourself can be seen as a special case of CONTRIBUTOR AGREEMENT
in which no external contributors exist. This special case is not very
interesting for a pattern on OSS, so it does not deserve a pattern on
its own.

Consequences, examples, as well as related patterns for the two OSS patterns
intersect to a high degree, further substantiating their equivalence. However,
CONTRIBUTOR AGREEMENT generally puts more emphasis on legal aspects of
the pattern, while RUN A TIGHT SHIP emphasizes how to keep the power over the
OSS project. Each pattern can hardly exist without the other, making them two
aspects of the same OSS pattern. It should be noted that is formally possible
for an OSS project to RUN A TIGHT SHIP without requiring CONTRIBUTOR
AGREEMENTS: The contributors retain their copyright and must give permission
for licensing decisions. This is not a best practice, though, and therefore not the
core idea of RUN A TIGHT SHIP.

Maintainer Handover [11]
Problem: How can the development pace be kept when the project
is about to lose its maintainer?
Solution: Appoint a new maintainer if you do not want to continue
maintaining the OSS project.

Pool Resources [17] (also known as NO SINGLE VENDOR IN
CHARGE [17], ONE SOLUTION [18], GOOD ENOUGH [18], and FOUN-
DATION [16])
Problem: How do you attract other companies to contribute to an
OSS project that you have created?
Solution: Pool resources with other companies to jointly develop a
common stack of OSS assets that the companies can all build on to
develop their individual products.

De-duplication: In its earliest description, the pattern already has two names,
ONE SOLUTION and GOOD ENOUGH [18]. This pattern helps to decide which
parts of a product should be kept closed and which parts should be offered as
OSS. This has the advantage that externals contribute to the OSS parts. POOL
RESOURCES [17] goes one step further and specifies that likely candidates for
these externals are competitors, as they most likely have the same use cases
and therefore need the same components for their software. The same paper
shortly mentions NO SINGLE VENDOR IN CHARGE [17], which was published
later as FOUNDATION [16]. The pattern FOUNDATION is specific about the legal
framework when implementing POOL RESOURCES and the two papers depict
them as two separate patterns, with POOL RESOURCES being applicable after
FOUNDATION.

We see them as a single OSS pattern because neither can exist without the
other: It is useless to have a FOUNDATION maintain an OSS project in the sense
of the pattern if there are no external contributors who POOL RESOURCES
with the FOUNDATION. As described above, the papers themselves describe
already a dependency in the other direction: It is unlikely that competitors POOL
RESOURCES with you if you remain in control over the source code. One way to
release control is a FOUNDATION. Alternatives are code repositories without legal
form like GitHub organizations [32], but they may resemble FOUNDATIONS in
their organizational structure. All three versions of the pattern include Eclipse as
an implementation example, further supporting that the three versions describe
different aspects of the same OSS pattern instead of separate OSS patterns.

Single Maintainer [9] (also known as BENEVOLENT DICTATOR [9])
Problem: How can an OSS project quickly create an organizational
structure to enable community contributions?
Solution: Concentrate all power in the project in the hands of one
capable individual.

Meritocracy [9]
Problem: How should key decisions of the project be made such that the maximum number of developers identify with the decisions?
Solution: The more a person contributes to the project, the more influence is granted to that person.

6   New Developers

Figure 8 shows the patterns of this section. The success of an OSS project depends on its ability to attract new developers and let them deliver source code as USER CONTRIBUTIONS. There are three other, more specific OSS patterns in this category, which help to get USER CONTRIBUTIONS. Each tackles a specific contribution barrier and presents a technique to lower it. Specifically, PRECONFIGURED BUILD ENVIRONMENT lets newcomers skip the sometimes cumbersome setup of the development environment. UNIT TESTS FOR CONTRIBUTORS allow newcomers to test their modifications before they publish them. LOW-HANGING FRUIT reduce the essential difficulty of a contribution, allowing newcomers to choose a problem suiting their abilities.

Both a BAZAAR ARCHITECTURE and an EXPOSED ARCHITECTURE help developers to integrate new features into the software and therefore foster USER CONTRIBUTIONS. Similarly, CLEANUP BEFORE PUBLISHING reduces the work required for a modification. Some developers go through a phase of being active users before they become developers [3, 33]. As SUPPORT THE COMMUNITY helps to grow an active user base, it also helps to recruit developers and gain USER CONTRIBUTIONS.

User Contributions [11]
Problem: The growing number of users correlates with a growing number of expectations, which the existing contributors cannot fulfill.
Solution: Treat your users as co-developers and have them satisfy the users' demand.

Preconfigured Build Environment [20]
Problem: Joining developers get stuck when setting up the build environment.
Solution: Provide a Virtual Machine with a preconfigured build environment.

Unit Tests for Contributors [20]
Problem: Joining developers hold back their patches as they are afraid to introduce new bugs.
Solution: Provide easy access to unit tests even for prospective developers.

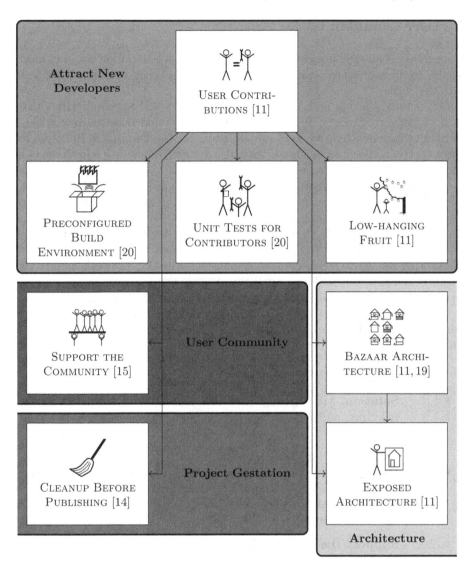

Fig. 8. Pattern map for new developers

 Low-hanging Fruit [11]
Problem: Newcomers do not join the project because there is too much to learn before they could be helpful.
Solution: Mark easy development tasks as such and save them for beginners.

7   User Community

The success of an OSS project depends on its users [34], but OSS projects must be able to draw on their capital of users [35]. Figure 9 shows patterns that help with this goal.

Attracting users via both QUALITY ATTESTATION and SUPPORT THE COMMUNITY helps to CREATE PULL for the OSS project and thereby grow a large and active community. New OSS project may also use CREDIBLE PROMISE to CREATE PULL. Because of Linus's Law [1], a large community can work as a CROWD OF BUG DETECTORS.

Possible ways to SUPPORT THE COMMUNITY are an OPEN DIALOG, a CENTRAL INFORMATION PLATFORM, and FREQUENT RELEASES. An EXPOSED ARCHITECTURE can be one element of an OPEN DIALOG. For FREQUENT RELEASES, it is advisable to use PARALLEL DEVELOPMENT to separate stable from unstable releases.

Another way to attract users is to demonstrate the OSS project's quality via QUALITY ATTESTATION. These QUALITY ATTESTATIONS must always refer to recent releases to be useful, so a requirement is FREQUENT RELEASES.

Patterns that distinctively support source code contributions are excluded from this category because of their distinguished importance for the OSS project. This type of pattern is treated separately in Sect. 6.

Create Pull [16]
Problem: How do you market your OSS product?
Solution: Make it easy to access your product and leverage distributors, partners, as well as community members to market your product.

Crowd of Bug Detectors [10]
Problem: Developers do not fix some of the bugs because they occur only seldom or never in their environments.
Solution: Take bug reports seriously and encourage your users to file bug reports.

Support the Community [15]
Problem: You need to build a healthy community around your project.
Solution: Support the community without expecting an immediate return. It's all about respect and building legitimacy, one step at a time.

Quality Attestation [21]
Problem: Developers and technical users abstain from the OSS project, because they do not want to depend on or be associated with a component of unknown quality.
Solution: Measure your software quality and visualize current results publicly.

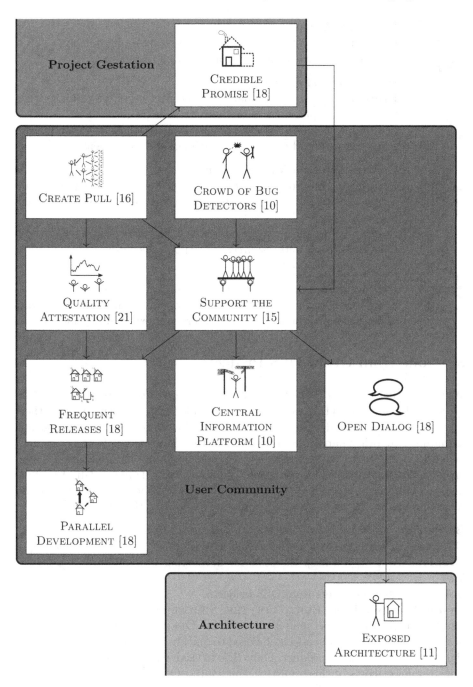

Fig. 9. Pattern map for User Community

Frequent Releases [18]
Problem: How do you move an OSS project along quickly?
Solution: Release code in small, quick increments.

Parallel Development [18]
Problem: How do you balance the need of users for stability with the need to explore new directions for your project?
Solution: Maintain separate release streams, those with the official stable releases and others for experimental development.

Central Information Platform [10]
Problem: The project provides different kinds of development and support resources to its users, but a user has to find the right system for every task.
Solution: Provide a central information platform that describes and links to all tools and resources that the project uses.

Open Dialog [18]
Problem: How do you engage others in your project?
Solution: Conduct the project in the open, maintaining a two-way dialog with project participants (users and external developers).

8   Code from Other OSS Projects

While the other patterns in the OSS pattern language target maintainers of OSS projects, the patterns in this section are not specific to maintainers. Instead, they target general software development projects that want to use OSS components maintained by other parties. Figure 10 shows the three OSS patterns and their dependencies: BOOTSTRAP describes how to quickly build an application based on OSS components. When using OSS components, RESPECT THE LICENSE helps to avoid legal problems, and CONTRIBUTE BACK shows the advantages of returning modifications on the OSS components back to their projects.

Bootstrap [17] (also known as BUILD ON THE SHOULDERS OF OTHERS [18], BUILDING ON OPEN SOURCE [12])
Problem: How do you keep the costs for developing your product low?
Solution: Integrate assets from OSS projects.
De-duplication: Both BUILD ON THE SHOULDERS OF OTH-ERS [18], BOOTSTRAP [17], and BUILDING ON OPEN SOURCE [12] describe how OSS components can be used to quickly develop an initial version of a software product. Only BOOTSTRAP explicitly mentions the lower costs of this approach, but BUILD ON THE SHOULDERS OF OTHERS also talks about cost savings in its opening text. BOOTSTRAP refers to BUILD ON THE SHOULDERS OF OTHERS, so a difference seems to be intended, but it did not become clear from the pattern texts. BUILDING ON OPEN SOURCE argues for the reduced

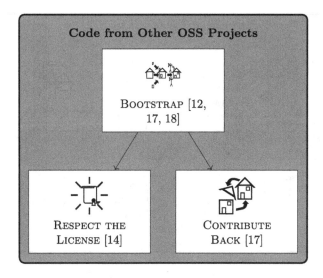

Fig. 10. Pattern map for code from other OSS projects

costs of a failure, and adds the additional aspect of potentially changing OSS components for commercial components once the product turns out to be a success.

Respect the License [14]
Problem: How to prevent problems with licensing after your product is released?
Solution: Check Licenses of OSS components you use starting early in the development process.

Contribute Back [17]
Problem: How do you keep aligned with the OSS project?
Solution: Contribute non-core modifications back to the OSS project.

9   Architecture

The OSS patterns in this section describe how to divide the software into modules and how to manage the resulting architecture. Parnas argues that a system should be composed of modules each of which represent one design decision [36]. This applies to OSS as well as closed-source software. Both types of project may face the same technical issues and must therefore make similar design decisions. In this regard, their ideal architecture should be similar. However, there are also organizational reasons for design decision and some of these are specific for OSS projects. The OSS patterns in this section help to create an architecture that encapsulates these types of design decisions. Figure 11 shows the OSS patterns and their relationships.

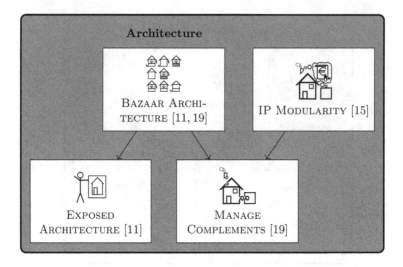

Fig. 11. Pattern map for architecture

A BAZAAR ARCHITECTURE allows easy integration of contributions from the community, but it requires to carefully MANAGE COMPLEMENTS submitted to the OSS project. Contributors see in the EXPOSED ARCHITECTURE where to integrate their contributions. If the OSS project requires the architectural separation of components that are not available as OSS, i.e. IP MODULARITY, the OSS project must also MANAGE COMPLEMENTS to ensure contributions do not affect the separated components.

 Bazaar Architecture [10] (also known as MODULAR ARCHITECTURE [19])

Problem: It is hard for newcomers to add innovative features when these have not been anticipated and require modifications of the architecture.

Solution: Plan the architecture of your software as a flat hierarchy of optional modules.

De-duplication: Both BAZAAR ARCHITECTURE [10] and MODULAR ARCHITECTURE [19] explain that changes to the software may require knowledge not only about the changed part of the source code, but also about related parts of the source code. With more dependencies, contributors have to acquire more knowledge about the code before they can change something. For both patterns, the solution is an improved modularization. BAZAAR ARCHITECTURE argues for a flat dependency tree while MODULAR ARCHITECTURE describes techniques to refactor modules with many dependencies. Thus, the patterns differ in their specific implementation, but the problem and the general method of creating an "architecture for participation" [19,37] is the same. Notably, both patterns include UNIX and Mozilla as examples, but this is no evidence for their equivalence: The specific subsystems and events in Mozilla and UNIX used as examples are disjoint.

Exposed Architecture [11]
Problem: Developers will not add features to the project when they
do not know where to add their code.
Solution: Publish the program's architecture.

Manage Complements [19]
Problem: How to extend the code while maintaining the architectural integrity of the overall system?
Solution: Establish a contribution process, set guidelines and provide a development toolkit to manage complement development.

IP Modularity [15]
Problem: You need to manage open and closed components of a
dual product.
Solution: Align intellectual property (IP) with product architecture.

10 Conclusion

This article analyzed the overall structure of OSS patterns as of the current state of research. This analysis tried to achieve two goals.

First, a classification of all published OSS patterns into eight categories helps readers to get a high-level overview of OSS patterns. Duplicate OSS patterns have been merged and 35 unique OSS patterns have been identified.

Second, besides the association of OSS patterns in the same category, two additional types of relationships between OSS patterns have been introduced and identified between some of the OSS patterns. These relationships constitute a pattern language among OSS patterns.

Future research should try to identify OSS patterns that fill gaps in the proposed OSS pattern language. Newly identified OSS patterns can be classified into the proposed eight categories.

Acknowledgements. We thank Firas Zaidan for his feedback from his analyses of OSS projects. We also thank the anonymous reviewers from TPLOP for their comments to earlier versions of this article.

References

1. Raymond, E.S.: The Cathedral and the Bazaar, 1st edn. O'Reilly & Associates Inc., Sebastopol (1999)
2. Gacek, C., Arief, B.: The many meanings of open source. IEEE Softw. **21**, 34–40 (2004)
3. Ye, Y., Kishida, K.: Toward an understanding of the motivation of open source software developers. In: 2003 Proceedings of the 25th International Conference on Software Engineering, pp. 419–429, May 2003

4. Krishnamurthy, S.: Cave or community? An empirical examination of 100 mature open source projects. In: Social Science Research Network Working Paper Series, vol. 7, no. 6, June 2002
5. Open Source Initiative: The open source definition (2004). http://www.opensource. org/docs/osd. Accessed 14 March 2012
6. Free Software Foundation: The free software definition (2015). http://www.gnu. org/philosophy/free-sw.html. Accessed 14 Sept 2015
7. Alexander, C.: The Timeless Way of Building. Oxford University Press, Oxford (1979)
8. Kelly, A.: Patterns for technology companies. In: Proceedings of the 11th European Conference on Pattern Languages of Programs (2006)
9. Hannebauer, C., Link, C., Gruhn, V.: Patterns for the distribution of power in FLOSS projects. In: Proceedings of the 19th European Conference on Pattern Languages of Programs, EuroPLoP 2014, pp. 35:1–35:7. ACM, New York (2014)
10. Hannebauer, C., Wolff-Marting, V., Gruhn, V.: Contributor-interaction patterns in FLOSS development. In: EuroPLoP 2011, July 2011
11. Hannebauer, C., Wolff-Marting, V., Gruhn, V.: Towards a pattern language for FLOSS development. In: Proceedings of the 2010 Conference on Pattern Languages of Programs. Hillside Group, ACM, New York (2010)
12. Link, C.: Patterns for the commercial use of open source: economic aspects and case studies. In: EuroPLoP 2012. Number Version 398 (2012)
13. Link, C.: Patterns for the commercial use of open source: license patterns. In: EuroPLoP 2011 (2011). Number Version 331
14. Link, C.: Patterns for the commercial use of open source: legal and licensing aspects. In: Proceedings of the 15th European Conference on Pattern Languages of Programs, EuroPLoP 2010, pp. 7:1–7:10. ACM, New York (2010)
15. Weiss, M.: The business of open source: missing patterns. In: Proceedings of the 20th European Conference on Pattern Languages of Programs (2015)
16. Weiss, M.: Profiting even more from open source. In: Proceedings of the 16th European Conference on Pattern Languages of Programs, EuroPLoP 2011, pp. 1:1–1:7. ACM, New York (2011)
17. Weiss, M.: Profiting from open source. In: Proceedings of the 15th European Conference on Pattern Languages of Programs, EuroPLoP 2010, pp. 5:1–5:8. ACM, New York (2010)
18. Weiss, M.: Performance of open source projects. In: 14th Annual European Conference on Pattern Languages of Programming (2009)
19. Weiss, M., Noori, N.: Enabling contributions in open source projects. In: EuroPLoP 2013 (2013)
20. Wolff-Marting, V., Hannebauer, C., Gruhn, V.: Patterns for tearing down contribution barriers to FLOSS projects. In: Proceedings of the 12th SoMeT, September 2013
21. Zaidan, F., Hannebauer, C., Gruhn, V.: Quality attestation: an open source pattern. In: Proceedings of the 21st European Conference on Pattern Languages of Programs, EuroPlop 2016, pp. 2:1–2:7. ACM, New York (2016)
22. Meszaros, G., Doble, J.: A pattern language for pattern writing. In: Martin, R., Riehle, D., Buschmann, F. (eds.) Pattern Languages of Program Design. Software Patterns Series, vol. 3, pp. 529–574. Addison-Wesley (1998)
23. Alexander, C., Ishikawa, S., Silverstein, M., Jacobson, M., Fiksdahl-King, I., Angel, S.: A Pattern Language. Oxford University Press, New York (1977)

24. Fowler, M.: Accountability and organizational structures. In: Vlissides, J.M., Coplien, J.O., Kerth, N.L. (eds.) Pattern Languages of Program Design, vol. 2, pp. 353–370. Addison Wesley (1996)

25. Cunningham, W.: EPISODES: a pattern language of competitive development. In: Vlissides, J.M., Coplien, J.O., Kerth, N.L. (eds.) Pattern Languages of Program Design, vol. 2, pp. 371–388. Addison Wesley (1996)

26. Coplien, J.O., Harrison, N.B.: Organizational Patterns of Agile Software Development. Pearson Prentice Hall, Upper Saddle River (2005)

27. Weir, C.: Patterns for designing in teams. In: Martin, R., Riehle, D., Buschmann, F. (eds.) Pattern Languages of Program Design. Software Patterns Series, vol. 3, pp. 487–501. Addison-Wesley (1998)

28. Roberts, D., Johnson, R.: Patterns for evolving frameworks. In: Martin, R., Riehle, D., Buschmann, F. (eds.) Pattern Languages of Program Design. Software Patterns Series, vol. 3, pp. 471–486. Addison-Wesley (1998)

29. Kelly, A.: More patterns for software companies product development. In: Proceedings of the 12th European Conference on Pattern Languages of Programs (2007)

30. Ratzka, A.: User interface patterns for multimodal interaction. In: Noble, J., Johnson, R., Zdun, U., Wallingford, E. (eds.) Transactions on Pattern Languages of Programming III. LNCS, vol. 7840, pp. 111–167. Springer, Heidelberg (2013). https://doi.org/10.1007/978-3-642-38676-3_4

31. Ries, E.: The Lean Startup. Crown Business, New York (2011)

32. Neath, K.: Introducing organizations. Github Blog, June 2010. https://github.com/blog/674-introducing-organizations. Accessed 30 Oct 2015

33. Herraiz, I., Robles, G., Amor, J.J., Romera, T., González Barahona, J.M.: The processes of joining in global distributed software projects. In: Proceedings of the 2006 International Workshop on Global Software Development for the Practitioner, GSD 2006, pp. 27–33. ACM, New York (2006)

34. Xu, J., Gao, Y., Christley, S., Madey, G.: A topological analysis of the open souce software development community. In: 2005 Proceedings of the 38th Annual Hawaii International Conference on System Sciences, HICSS 2005, p. 198a, January 2005

35. Capiluppi, A., Michlmayr, M.: From the cathedral to the bazaar: an empirical study of the lifecycle of volunteer community projects. In: Feller, J., Fitzgerald, B., Scacchi, W., Sillitti, A. (eds.) OSS 2007. ITIFIP, vol. 234, pp. 31–44. Springer, Boston, MA (2007). https://doi.org/10.1007/978-0-387-72486-7_3

36. Parnas, D.L.: On the criteria to be used in decomposing systems into modules. Commun. ACM **15**, 1053–1058 (1972)

37. MacCormack, A., Rusnak, J., Baldwin, C.Y.: Exploring the structure of complex software designs: an empirical study of open source and proprietary code. Manag. Sci. **52**(7), 1015–1030 (2006)

Patterns for Functional Safety System Development

Jari Rauhamäki[✉]

Department of Automation Science and Engineering,
Tampere University of Technology, P.O. Box 692, 33101 Tampere, Finland
jari.rauhamaki@tut.fi

Abstract. Functional safety is involved in many machines, processes, and systems to mitigate risks by reducing the likelihood of the occurrence or the severity of the consequences of a hazard. The development of functional safety systems realising safety functions is typically directed by laws and standards, which set requirements on the development process and design of the system. In addition, functional safety systems often operate in a context, in which other control entities also affect the operation of the system under control. In this article, nine patterns considering the design and development functional safety systems, in terms of their architecture and co-operation with other controlling entities, are presented. The purpose of the patterns is to support the designers of functional safety systems to cope with the mentioned aspects.

Keywords: Safety function · Safety-related · Control · Architecture · Pattern

1 Introduction

Safety is a property of machines and systems that is constantly gaining more importance in many industrial sectors including industrial control and machinery control applications. Safety is required by laws and regulations and demanded by customers. Consequently, vendors are required to offer safe and safety certified products. As compatibility with safety regulations and standards is increasingly demanded, a cost-effective safety system design process gives an edge to a vendor.

In this article, a set of design patterns for functional safety system design and development, and co-operation with a control system is presented. The patterns consider structures, roles, principles, and approaches applied in functional safety systems. A design pattern approach can help to simplify the design process and provide a comprehensible view to the safety systems. Before the actual patterns, an overview of related work, functional safety systems, relations between the patterns, and a context of a running example, applied throughout the patterns in this article, is provided.

1.1 Related Work

Design patterns are popular in the field of software engineering and a lot of patterns have been published in the domain. These patterns for software development consider, for instance, object-orientated software [1, 2], pattern-orientated software architecture

© Springer Nature Switzerland AG 2019
J. Noble et al. (Eds.): TPLOP IV, LNCS 10600, pp. 100–138, 2020.
https://doi.org/10.1007/978-3-030-14291-9_4

[3, 4], enterprise applications [5, 6], and service-orientated architecture [7]. Some of the ideas presented in these works could be applicable in safety system development, but it is likely that the patterns are not dedicated to safety system development in the first place.

Fortunately to safety and control system developers, patterns more related to the safety systems have been proposed and documented although not in as large quantities as for software engineering. A pattern language by Eloranta et al. [8] considers the development of distributed control systems. The main focus in the language work lies in control systems, but there are connections to safety and safety systems, too.

Fault tolerance and reliability are closely related topics to and can be seen as desired properties of functional safety systems. In this article, fault tolerance and reliability aspects are not considered. It is assumed, for example, that a sensor element provides correct output. Therefore, it is encouraged to apply suitable fault tolerance and reliability measures if needed. Patterns and pattern languages by, among others, Hanmer [9], Douglass [10], Armoush [11], Alho and Rauhamäki [12], and Preschern et al. [13] consider safety primarily from redundancy and reliability viewpoints and can help to identify and mitigate the effect of errors in elements in a functional safety system.

The patterns presented in this article do not directly consider the development process of functional safety systems as such, but focus on the design decisions, structure, and functionality of such systems. Instead, work by Koskinen et al. [14] focus on the development process of functional safety systems especially in the context of IEC 61508-3.

In addition to previously mentioned aspects, real-time and control system and engineering aspects can be seen related to the patterns considering functional safety systems discussed in this article. Real-time aspect has been considered from a pattern viewpoint by, among others, Douglass [15], Gomaa [16], and Zalewski [17], whereas patterns considering control engineering have been proposed by, among others, Pont [18] and Sans and Zalewski [19].

1.2 Functional Safety Systems

The patterns described in this paper focus on functional safety systems. Before we can define a functional safety system, we need to define *safety* in general. IEC 61508 [20] (in part 4) states that safety is "freedom from unacceptable risk". A *safety-related system* can now be defined as a system that "implements the required safety functions necessary to achieve or maintain a safe state for the EUC (Equipment Under Control)" and "is intended to achieve, on its own or with other safety-related systems, the necessary level of safety integrity for the implementation of the required safety functions." [20]. Thus, a safety-related system reduces the risk of an undesired event to an acceptable level by affecting the operation of a system. A safety-related system may reduce the risk by reducing either the probability or the consequences of the hazard, which are the factors of the risk. In this article, the term functional safety system refers to a safety-related system for uniformity reasons.

1.3   Functional Safety System Development

Typically, functional safety systems are developed to be compliant with standards, which regulate the devices and machines of the considered domain. In such a case, a safety system must take into account the requirements proposed by the standards. For instance, IEC 61508 [20] is a generic standard for the development of functional safety systems whereas EN ISO 13849-1 [21] is focused on the safety of machinery applications. The standards define a set of methods and techniques to be used in the development process. In addition, the standards define requirements considering the structure and the operation of the system as well as the development process. IEC 61508, for instance, defines a process, including recommended techniques and methods, specifying how a safety system should be developed. In contrast, domain specific standards are typically more concerned with the safety functionality of the system. That is, what kind of safety functions the system under development must implement. These safety functions include, among others, emergency power off and a shutdown if people enter working area.

The amount of requirements and constraints introduced by standards, laws and regulations related to the development of safety systems is considerably large. Development of a safety system is a somewhat bureaucratic and burdensome process due to various techniques and methods required to be used together with a high level of documentation. The patterns presented in this paper try to ease the burden and help to bridge a gap considering safety system development in the context of the architecture and the generic principles applied in functional safety systems. The patterns present and provide solutions to some of the problems encountered in the development of functional safety systems, which need to co-exist with a control system. In this context, a control system is responsible for handling the normal control operations of the system under control, whereas the main purpose of a functional safety system is to mitigate risks.

1.4   Background of the Patterns

This article presents nine patterns related to the development of functional safety systems in machine and industrial process control applications. According to a number of interviews with professionals in the industrial control domain, the solutions the patterns are known in the industry and utilized in the industrial control systems in either or both of machinery and industrial process control domains. The interviews were mainly conducted during 2015 as a part of a research project focusing on functional safety systems in the domain of machinery [22]. During the project, new known uses for the patterns were acquired. In addition, literature sources have been used to provide additional known uses for the patterns.

The patterns are a part of a larger pattern language, which have been compiled in 2011–2016. Some of the patterns of the language have been published in VikingPLoP and EuroPLoP conferences. The patterns presented in this article originate from VikingPLoP 2012 and 2013. The rationale to revisit the patterns is additional knowledge and known uses obtained since their original publication. The patterns have been updated and enhanced by, for instance, providing a running example through all the patterns.

1.5   Pattern Relations

In this section, the pattern language part formed by the patterns presented in this article is described. The patterns in this article do not constitute a pattern language in terms of a morphologically complete solution space with no unaddressed gaps as suggested by Hanmer [9, p. xiii]. However, the presented patterns form a network where they build on each other, elaborate a design in a particular way, respond to specific forces, and enable different paths through the network, which are, according to Buschmann et al. [23, p. 13], properties of a pattern language. Therefore, the patterns are referred to as a pattern language in this article. Although the patterns relate to and build on each other, one does not necessarily need to apply all the patterns of the language when designing a functional safety system. Instead, the patterns can also be used as standalone solutions, but the idea of the SEPARATED SAFETY pattern lies behind the other patterns.

Relations between the patterns are depicted in Fig. 1. In the figure, arrows illustrate a typical order of usage of the pattern (solid line arrows). That is, when a pattern is applied, the patterns it points at can be considered as subsequent patterns. The relations presented in Fig. 1 has been compiled according to information given in the pattern descriptions, especially in the related patterns sections. Notice, the patterns located within the control system override block indicate alternative solutions to a similar problem. The patterns indicated with dashed outline are not presented in this paper.

SEPARATED SAFETY, is considered as a root pattern of this part of the language. It is typically applied first and it builds ground for the other patterns. SEPARATED SAFETY suggests separating safety and control systems from each other so that the requirements considering the safety system would not restrict the development of the control system. When a safety system is a separate entity of system control, complex corrective functions can be implemented in a control system, as suggested in PRODUCTIVE SAFETY, and the safety system can, if applicable, be implemented without self-developed application software using a HARDWIRED SAFETY approach.

When a safety system is separated from a control system, the safety system has to be able to override the control system so that a SAFE STATE can be taken when necessary. This is realized in control system override patterns, which suggest alternative approaches to implement the override functionality. Especially in a case of override situation, a safety system should inform a control system that changes have occurred in the system under control. Taking the approach even further, a safety system could force actuators controlled by the control system into a safe state alongside the actuators controlled by the safety system. These approaches are introduced in CONTROL SYSTEM NOTIFICATION and CO-OPERATIVE SAFETY RELATED ACTUATION patterns respectively. To reduce the amount of hardware in the system, a SHARED SAFETY ACTUATOR approach can be applied.

For the convenience of the reader, Table 1 below provides short descriptions (aka. patlets) of the patterns that are discussed and referenced in this article.

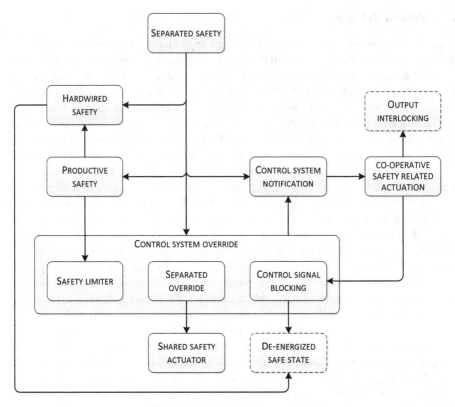

Fig. 1. Relations of the patterns

Table 1. Pattern patlets, aka. Short descriptions of the patterns.

Pattern	Patlet
CONTROL SIGNAL BLOCKING	A safety system needs to have the ability to drive the system under control or the process variable of interest into a SAFE STATE regardless of the operations of a control system. Therefore, override a control signal produced by a control system with a suitable blocking device controlled by a safety system
CONTROL SYSTEM NOTIFICATION	The operation of a control system is disturbed when a safety system overrides or restricts the operation of the control system, which may cause the unexpected behaviour of the control system. Therefore, make a control system aware of the state changes of a safety system so that the control system can react accordingly
CO-OPERATIVE SAFETY RELATED ACTUATION	How to increase the consistency between the operation of a safety system and a control system during situations where the safety system overrides the control system partly or completely? Let a safety system drive a control system into a safe state whenever a safe state needs to be obtained (according to the safety system)

(*continued*)

Table 1. (*continued*)

Pattern	Patlet
DE-ENERGIZED SAFE STATE	"Power supply for the safety system and the control system as well as the system under control cannot be guaranteed, which might inflict a hazardous state during blackout or power loss in (part of the) safety system. Therefore, design the safety system (and control system as well if applicable) to take the safe state when power is lost" [24]
HARDWIRED SAFETY	Development of safety-related application software is costly and provides no real benefit in the context of the considered safety function. Therefore, use a hardware-based safety system instead of application software to implement the safety functionality
OUTPUT INTERLOCKING	Implementing protective functions in control algorithms makes the control algorithms complex. Therefore, use an interlock element alongside each control actuator output in the control system [24]
PRODUCTIVE SAFETY	A system under control should be kept in an operational region for as long as possible to avoid the activation of safety functionality while the functionality of a safety system should be kept minimal in comparison to control functionality. Therefore, implement corrective functions in a control system and use the simplest approach for the safety system functionality
SAFE STATE	"When the control system tries to control a part of the machine that is malfunctioning, the machine may respond in an unpredictable way. Consequently the machine may harm the operator, machine or surroundings. These kinds of situations should not take place." [8] Therefore, "design a safe state that can be entered if the control system encounters a malfunction that cannot be handled autonomously. The safe state is such that it prevents the machine from causing harm. The safe state is device and functionality dependent and is not necessarily the same as the unpowered state" [8]
SAFETY LIMITER	A safety system needs to have the ability to drive a system under control or a process variable of interest into a SAFE STATE regardless of the operations of a control system. Therefore, let the safety system manipulate the control signal before directing the control signal to the actuator.
SEPARATED OVERRIDE	A safety system needs to have the ability to drive the system under control or one of its process variables into a SAFE STATE regardless of the operations of a control system. Therefore, use separate actuators for safety and control systems
SEPARATED SAFETY	Designing a whole control system according to safety standards is a costly, bureaucratic, and slow process. Therefore, divide and separate the system control functionality into two separate entities: a control system and a safety system
SHARED SAFETY ACTUATOR	Providing each subsystem with a dedicated safety actuator when the same input variable is used by multiple subsystems increases the number of needed safety actuators in the system. Therefore, use a shared safety actuator for all the subsystems

1.6   Running Example

The patterns presented in this article share a running example considering control and operation of hydraulic cylinders. Hydraulic systems and cylinders are used in various machinery applications especially when large forces are needed. Hydraulic cylinders are actuators that transfer hydraulic pressure and flow into a linear motion, which can be used to drive and operate, for instance, moving parts of cranes, aerial work platforms, press brakes, and excavators as applied in [25–27] and [28] for example.

In this running example, hydraulic cylinders are considered in the context of a forestry harvester machine such as Ponsse [29], John Deere [30], and Komatsu [31]. The example focuses on the control of the cylinders operating the crane of the machine. In this context, hydraulic cylinders are used to move parts of a crane to position a harvester head attached to the crane. In this example case, the crane is operated by a harvester operator, but the actual control of the crane is performed through a control system, which transfers the steering commands, given by the operator, into a movement of the crane. There are also safety functions considering the crane operation. For instance, the crane shall stop if the driver seat is not occupied, the cabin door is opened when the machine is operated, or the stability of the machine endangered.

Figure 2 illustrates the initial context of the running example. A hydraulic pump, typically driven by the diesel engine of a harvester, provides hydraulic pressure and flow. A control valve is used to direct the pressure to hydraulic cylinders that operate the crane. The cylinder affects the crane geometry producing movement. In Fig. 2 and subsequent illustrations of the example sections a solid line represents a hydraulic line or flow and a dashed line represents an electric signal used or produced by a control or a safety system.

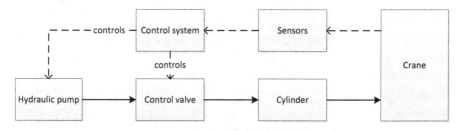

Fig. 2. Initial context of the running example considering control of hydraulic cylinders in harvester crane application.

The purpose of the example is to illustrate how the solutions described in the patterns affect a system in which they are applied. Please note that this running example does not stem from a real machine and it does not serve as a reference to build a safety system for a specific harvester crane or any application as such. The sole purpose of the running example is to illustrate the ideas of the solutions presented by the patterns. The circuits and illustrations given in the examples are simplified and omit various aspects, features, and functions of a complete safety system.

2 Separated Safety

Context

A control system for a machinery application or an industrial process needs to be designed and developed. According to performed hazard and risk analyses, the system to be controlled is capable of causing physical or financial harm to the environment or people working in its surroundings. The risks are mitigated with a functional safety system, which must be developed according to appropriate standards and needs to be possibly certified by authorities. The followed safety-related standards restrict the development process, tools and methods, and in addition require the usage of various techniques and measures not directly needed to develop a control system.

Problem

Designing a whole control system according to safety standards is a costly, bureaucratic, and slow process.

Forces

- Standards such as IEC 61508 [20] considering the development of functional safety systems require independence between safety-related and non-safety-related parts of the systems. Considering especially software elements, the justification of non-interference between the safety and the control system may be a difficult and burdensome task to accomplish.
- To ensure the safety of the system under development, the whole system could be developed according to a defined safety standard and using certified hardware intended for safety applications. However, the development of a whole control system according to safety standards would be difficult and increase the development costs substantially. Firstly, the development process according to IEC 61508 and similar standards is relatively burdensome and restricted compared to a typical control system development process. Secondly, hardware certified to be used as a part of a functional safety system is principally pricier than its non-certified counterpart.
- Certified components and processing units with limited instruction sets may not enable the development of all required control functionalities. For example, floating point arithmetic is not supported by all safety certified processing units, which makes it hard to use such units in control system development.

Solution

Divide and separate the system control functionality into two separate entities: a control system and a safety system. Requirements for the whole control system are first divided into safety-critical requirements and non-safety-critical requirements. Typically, the safety-critical requirements are related to the deviation and possibly hazardous situations whereas the non-safety-critical requirements are related to the normal operational conditions and the intended use of the system.

Safety-critical functionality is designed and implemented into the safety system according to the followed safety standard(s). The produced safety system shall fulfil the requirements given in the followed standards, but it also needs to achieve its intended purpose, that is, fulfil the requirements considering the application for which the safety system is designed. Non-safety-critical functionality is designed and implemented into the control system. This frees the development of the control system from the requirements of the safety system. Thus, all kinds of non-certified or safety approved devices, tools, methods, instruction sets, etc. are utilizable in control system development.

Figure 3 illustrates the approach. The *system under control* represents the (sub) process or machine under consideration. The *control system* controls the process. The *safety system* is separated from the control system(s). The safety system, as well as the control system, have their own hardware including, among others, processing units, actuators, and sensors. Both systems affect and measure the same process but they operate independently of each other.

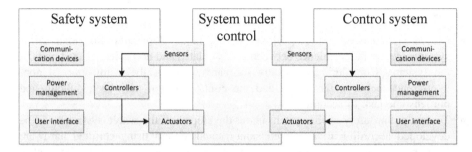

Fig. 3. Illustration of separated safety system within a process

The safety system and the control system(s) are separated from each other so that the correct functioning of the safety system is not dependent on the correct functioning of the control system. If necessary, the safety system may utilize certified hardware such as sensors, actuators, buses and safety PLCs. The control system may utilize the same components provided that it is not capable of disturbing the correct functioning of the safety system; otherwise, it must use different components. Because the control system is separated from the safety system, the requirements of safety standards do not apply to the development of it. Separation also potentially enhances the development processes of both systems. Because the systems are separated there are, or should be, no, or very few, dependencies between the systems. This supports the development of the systems in parallel and by different development teams, which is also beneficial from the diversity point of view.

Consequences

+ Safety of the whole system can be achieved with an appropriate safety system. Only the safety system side needs to be developed according to the functional safety system standards. As the safety is ensured with a separated system, the control system does not need a certification.

+ Control system development may utilize the development process, tools and techniques preferred by the vendor company – not the ones required by safety standards. For instance, full instruction set tools, computing units, and components can be applied in a development process of a control system.
+ The development costs of the control system can be reduced. This is due to the fact that the control system does not have to be developed according to the requirements considering safety systems.
+ Because the safety system and the control system are separated, the development of the systems can be outsourced separately or they can be developed independently from each other by different development teams. This can also have a positive effect on the schedule of the whole project.
– Two separate applications must be developed and they may require different instrumentation.
– The separated systems control the same process and process variables. For instance, a safety system, as well as a control system, could affect flow in the same pipeline. However, the preferences of the systems considering the target state of the process variable may be conflicting. For instance, a safety system might want to drive a process variable to a safe state whereas the respective control system is trying to keep the variable in the given set point value. This aspect needs to be taken into account in the design of the whole system.

Example

Consider a harvester machine utilizing a control system. The purpose of the control system is to operate the machine, automate its functionalities, and assist the operator of the harvester in a work task. The control system, for instance, operates hydraulics according to the operator input, controls energy source such as a diesel engine of the machine, collects and communicates operational data produced by the machine with fleet management and online service systems. The control system also reduces the risks introduced by the harvester by affecting the operation of it when a hazardous condition or event is detected. These safety functions halt harvester crane and harvester head operations such as crane movement and trunk processing when, for instance, an operator is not detected on the operator's seat, a cabin door is opened, or the machine stability is endangered in an operational state.

Application of the SEPARATED SAFETY pattern in a harvester context separates the safety functionalities from the control functionalities of the machine. A safety system is added to the machine which implements all the safety functions, especially the ones that need to be developed according to a standard such as EN 13849 or IEC 61508. When a safety system takes care of the safety functions, the rest of the control system does not have to consider the requirements given in the safety standard. This reduces the scope of the part of the control system for which the standard needs to be considered as illustrated in Fig. 4.

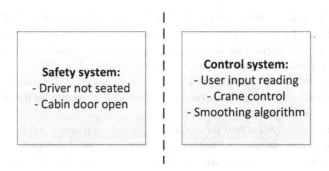

Fig. 4. Example of separation of functions between safety and control systems in a harvester application.

Known Uses

The solution is widely used in Finnish process industry and additionally known in the domain of mobile machinery.

Related Patterns

The PRODUCTIVE SAFETY describes how the responsibilities and complexity of the safety system can be decreased and how the activations of the safety system can be reduced to necessary situations only.

The HARDWIRED SAFETY pattern describes a way to avoid the need for safety related application software in safety system development. Elimination of application software development from the safety system development removes a significant amount of work, considering software development and related activities. However, the work is partly transferred to the design and development of the hardwired approach.

The SEPARATED OVERRIDE, CONTROL SIGNAL BLOCKING, and SAFETY LIMITER patterns provide solutions to override a control system with a safety system so that the safety system has the final word in the operation of the system.

3   Productive Safety

Context

A control system for a machine or an industrial process is being developed and the SEPARATED SAFETY pattern has been utilized so that the control functionality of the system is divided into two separate systems: a control system and a safety system. Some user requirements are related to safety aspects but they are not, or they do not need to be, directly assigned to the scope of the safety system. Quite often, these kinds of requirements can be due to customers willing to avoid financial consequences of production losses due to reduced production speed or costly activations of the safety system, such as shutting down a machine or plant.

Problem

A system under control should be kept in an operational region for as long as possible to avoid the activation of safety functionality while the functionality of a safety system should be kept minimal in comparison to control functionality.

Forces

- The purpose of the safety system is to drive and/or retain the system under control within the safe operating region. To achieve this purpose, the safety system needs to be able to drive the system into a SAFE STATE or similar state whenever required. However, financial impacts of, for example, shutting down a power plant or a paper machine are dramatic and not desired unless it is not absolutely necessary to achieve safety.
- To increase the availability and the robustness of the system, the customers and the users of the system may want the system to recover from disturbances. However, the recovery algorithms may require complex and advanced functionality and/or logic.
- Development of complex and advanced algorithms and functionalities in the context of the safety-critical systems is considerably burdensome and costly due to restrictions and the requirements of the safety-critical system development.

Solution

Implement corrective functions in a control system and use the simplest approach for the safety system functionality. The purpose of the corrective functions is to keep the system within the desired operation region and handle the disturbances, that is, "unwanted input signals" [32, p. 201]. From control system viewpoint disturbances may appear, for instance, in the form of changes in ambient temperature, load of an electric motor [32, p. 201], and feed composition [33, Sect. 2.9]. The corrective functions also implement protective operations such as interlockings to prevent undesired operations.

The corrective functions for disturbances are typically necessary for fulfilling the requirements of clients. The algorithms and techniques to implement corrective functions are potentially complex and advanced and thus they are problematic if implemented in a safety system according to the followed safety standards. These functions should be implemented in a control system. The safety system, on the other hand, can be designed to be as simple as possible. In many, though not all, cases, the system is in the safe state when the system is not powered. So, without trying to recover from disturbances, the safety system can often be designed to take relatively simple measures to drive the system into a safe state when critical safety limits are violated.

The scope of the control system is widened to include functions meant to keep the system in its operation region in which safety system never activates. In the control system, the corrective actions, including interlocking operations, can be as complex as required to achieve this goal.

Figure 5(a) represent situation before application of the productive safety. The dashed line represents a division of responsibility between the control system and the safety system. In Fig. 5(b) the responsibilities of the control system are widened, i.e., the safety system takes control later.

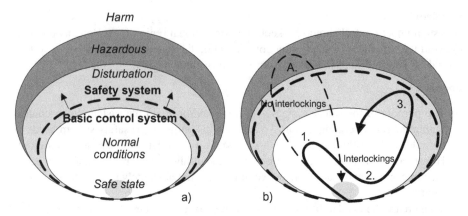

Fig. 5. System states of operation from a control system point of view.

In Fig. 5(b) a possible operation path of a process is illustrated (solid line arrow). The process is first in normal operation condition. Next, the state starts to shift towards a disturbed state. In point 1, the interlocking operations prevent the process from entering the disturbed state. Without interlockings, the state would have changed to hazardous where the safety system had taken control (point A) and returned the system into the safe state (dashed line arrow). After point 2, the process state leaves normal conditions and enters the disturbed state. However, the system state begins to move towards normal conditions from disturbed conditions at point 3 due to successful corrective functions with interlocking operations. The main idea of the corrective functions is to prevent the system from entering a hazardous state that would result in an intervention of a safety system and, for example, a complete shutdown of the system under control.

Consequences

+ The safety of the system can be achieved with a safety system that is designed to be as simple as possible which makes it easier to develop and certify.
+ The corrective functions, the purpose of which is to retain the system under control in a normal operational region, can be implemented without the need to follow safety standards. This eases the burden to develop the corrective functions as the functionality developed into the control system does not need to follow the development process of safety system parts.
+ As corrective functions are implemented to keep the system under control within the operational region, the amount of system shutdowns due to safety system operation is likely reduced.
− The complexity of the control system is increased as the control system needs to implement the corrective functions.

Example

Consider a forest harvester machine that needs to operate in a forest environment where the machine has to operate on uneven surfaces and lift and move heavy weight trunks. In such environments, it is possible that the stability of the machine can be lost due to the position of the machine and dynamic forces introduced by handling and moving of tree trunks. For the safety of the operator, the machine should retain stability and a safety function could be developed to identify and mitigate instability situation from occurring. Therefore, a safety function to halt the machine on an instability limit is implemented.

Applying the PRODUCTIVE SAFETY approach, the stability safety function is augmented with a control system function that tries to prevent an instability situation from occurring. In a control system, it easier to implement more complicated functionality. Therefore, the instability prevention algorithm in the control system can take multiple aspects into account to assess the dynamic forces, machine position, user inputs, etc., and calculate whether some operations of the machine should be restricted. For instance, if a heavy trunk is about to be lifted in an unfavourable position, the control system can reduce motion speed to maintain stability.

This way the control system can mitigate the need to activate the actual safety function. The safety function needs to exist, but it can be simpler as it does not have to restrict the machine operation in a sophisticated way because this is handled by the control system as illustrated in Fig. 6.

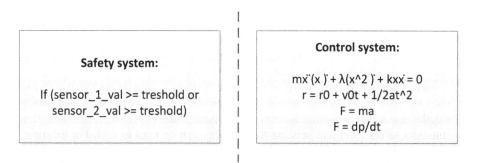

Fig. 6. Illustration of magnitude of complexity of algorithms in safety and control systems when PRODUCTIVE SAFETY is applied.

Known Uses

The approach is used in both process industry as well as mobile machinery systems.

Related Patterns

As the safety system simplicity is promoted, the usage of a sophisticated software-based safety system approach may become unnecessary for the application in hand. For such a case, the HARDWIRED SAFETY pattern describes a way to avoid the need for safety-related application software when implementing simple safety functions.

To implement the corrective or interlocking functionality, one could consider the OUTPUT INTERLOCKING pattern [24]. The purpose of the pattern is to take the interlocking logic out of control logic in order to keep the control logic simpler and promote its reusability.

4 Separated Override

Context

A control system for a machine or for an industrial process is being developed. The SEPARATED SAFETY pattern has been applied so that the control system functionality has been divided into two separate systems: a control system and a safety system. The separation between safety and control systems is followed strictly to, for instance, enable an easier certification process. The separated systems may in some places control the same functionalities or process variables.

Problem

A safety system needs to have the ability to drive the system under control or one of its process variables into a SAFE STATE regardless of the operations of a control system.

Forces

- A safety system must always be able to drive the system into a SAFE STATE, that is, a state where the system minimizes the risk of damaging itself or people around it, regardless of the state of a control system.
- For certain applications, such as mobile machinery applications, spatial and weight attributes are considerable and should be minimized. However, for other applications, such as process control systems, the liability of the additional hardware may not be a problem in terms of cost, space, and weight.
- A control actuator primarily driven by a control system could be potentially used to obtain a SAFE STATE. In such a case, the hardware architecture could be potentially simpler and utilize a smaller amount of hardware units. However, actuators with a sufficient safety level and suitable functionality can be hard to find. For example, hydraulic proportional control valves with SIL 3 certificate are not too widely available. This aspect is likely to become even more relevant when an actuator is used to control large quantities, such as high currents, high rates of flow, or high pressures.

Solution

Use separate actuators for safety and control systems. The purpose of a safety actuator is to drive a controlled process variable into a safe state as controlled by the safety system. A control system operates its own actuator for control purposes and a safety system operates a separate actuator for safety purposes.

The principle of the separated override architecture is presented in Fig. 7. A separate actuator for the safety system is added in the points in which the safety system needs to have control over the control system. The safety system must always be able to override the control system's operations. Ensure that the safety function cannot be circumvented or bypassed in any way by the control system. The safety system has the ability to drive the state of the controlled quantity to the safe state regardless of the control system state. Only the actuators controlled by the safety system have to comply with safety (standard) requirements whereas the actuators for the control system can be chosen freely.

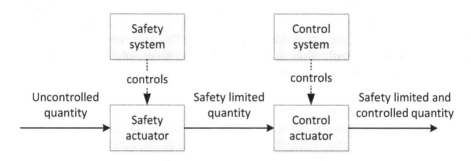

Fig. 7. Principle of separated override

Notice, that a safety function typically wants to either fully enable or disable the controlled variable. The actuator controlled by the safety system should then be placed in parallel or in series in terms of the control actuator respectively. In the latter case, one also needs to consider the order of the actuators, as the safety actuator may be positioned before or after the control actuator depending on the system. In either case, the safety actuator must be placed so that the normal control system cannot bypass it.

Consequences

+ (Complete) separation between safety and control systems can be achieved.
+ A safe state can be taken and retained by a safety system using its dedicated actuator even if the control system fails.
+ The selection of the safety system actuator is disengaged from the selection of the control actuator. Thus both actuators can be selected according to their needs. The control actuator does not need to be certified for use in the safety system context.
+ The simplest possible safety system approach can be chosen in terms of actuator type. In most cases, a binary on/off actuator is sufficient and the most cost efficient approach.
+ The approach promotes the freedom of selecting the data communication method between the controlling system and the controlled actuator. For example, the safety system may use analogue signalling and the control system can use a CAN-bus.
− Regardless of the benefits of choosing the actuators for the tasks, increased amount of hardware is needed in comparison with a case where the same actuator is used. This likely increases the cost and the spatial requirements.
− Additional hardware may increase the complexity of the hardware layout and design for example in terms of wiring and power supply arrangements.

– Each new hardware element added to a system also introduces a potential new failure point to the system.

Example

A possible application of the separated override principle can be considered in control of harvester crane cylinders. A safety system needs to be able to halt the crane movement, for instance, when a cabin door is opened while the harvester is in an operational state to prevent harm to the operator of the machine. A separate safety valve, controlled by the safety system, is added to the hydraulic line that operates a hydraulic cylinder of the crane as illustrated in Fig. 8. The purpose of the safety valve is to prevent any hydraulic flow in and out of the cylinder, effectively halting the cylinder and preventing its movement.

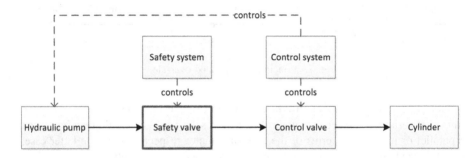

Fig. 8. Example of separated override in motor control application

Known Uses

The approach is used in process industry systems where large quantities and energies are present. The approach is suggested for a motor control applications [34, p. 11] and [35, p. 15]. The approach is also suggested to be used in hydraulic applications [36, p. 103].

Related Patterns

To reduce the total number of safety system actuators, one could consider SHARED SAFETY ACTUATOR approach, which proposes merging the actuation of multiple safety functions into a single or set of redundant safety actuators.

In case the safety system needs to activate and bring the system into a safe state, it should provide a CONTROL SYSTEM NOTIFICATION. The purpose of this is to let the control system know that its operation environment has been changed, and it may not be able to achieve its goal anymore. To further enhance the effect, CO-OPERATIVE SAFETY RELATED ACTUATION can be considered giving the safety system the ability to also drive the control system actuators to the safe state.

The CONTROL SIGNAL BLOCKING pattern describes an alternative solution to a similar problem. The pattern describes how a separated actuator of the safety system can be replaced with a relay (or similar switching device) to reduce the need for actuator hardware.

The SAFETY LIMITER describes an alternative solution to similar a problem. Safe operation can be achieved by circumventing the control signal calculated by the control system through a safety function that limits the value without a need for an additional relay or other hardware. Consequently, no additional hardware is required besides the control actuator, but potentially complex safety-related application software needs to be developed.

5   Control Signal Blocking

Context

A safety function for a control application is being designed. The SEPARATED SAFETY pattern has been utilized so that the control system functionality is divided into two separate systems: a control system and a safety system. The system has, in the context of the considered safety function, a well-defined SAFE STATE [8]. The safe state is always the same regardless of the state of the system, but tripping of the safety function can depend on various aspects. The safety system and the control system affect the same process variable(s). The system or system part, which the safety function considers, conforms to DE-ENERGIZED SAFE STATE. That is, the safety function must have a well-defined safe state that is independent of the system state.

Problem

A safety system needs to have the ability to drive the system under control or the process variable of interest into a SAFE STATE regardless of the operations of a control system.

Forces

- The SEPARATED OVERRIDE approach could be used to achieve the desired effect of the safety system becoming able to take the system into the SAFE STATE. However, the SEPARATED OVERRIDE approach requires additional hardware to affect a physical quantity or process variable of the system under control. That is, in this case, an additional safety actuator would be used to actuate the safety function. This may be problematic for numerous reasons. The actuator increases spatial requirements and adds weight to the system. The actuator increases the cost of the safety system as the actuator is likely to be a certified safety component.

Solution

Override a control signal produced by a control system with a suitable blocking device controlled by a safety system, which forces the controlled actuator and consequently the affected process variable and/or system into a safe state regarding the considered safety function. That is, when the safety function activates, the safety system effectively blocks the control signal produced by the control system and consequently forces the actuator, which is normally controlled by the control system, into a neutral state, which must represent a DE-ENERGIZED SAFE STATE. Now, regardless of the control system input, the actuator is in the safe state and the control system is overridden by the safety system.

In this approach, a dedicated safety actuator is replaced with a blocking element, that is, a relay or similar binary state device, which is used to block the control system signal. The safety system controls the blocking element. The principle of the approach is depicted in Fig. 9. The control system is responsible to providing the normal control signal to the actuator. Whenever the safety function trips, it de-energizes the actuator, which then enters the predefined safe state forced by a mechanical load.

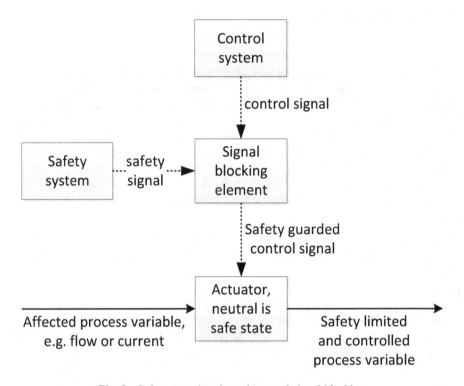

Fig. 9. Safety actuation through control signal blocking

A signal blocking element is typically more compact in terms of size and weight than a dedicated safety actuator such as a valve. Also, a signal blocking element is likely to be less expensive than its actuator counterpart.

However, the control actuator has to be mechanically loaded (e.g. spring loaded) to be able to enable the safe state when it receives a neutral control signal. In addition, the control actuator (or at least the mechanical loading system) has to be compatible with the dedicated safety integrity level of the safety function. This may increase the cost of the actuator significantly as complex actuators with high safety integrity properties are expensive. Notice that also the blocking element controlled by the safety system needs to have sufficient safety properties as it is part of the safety function.

The architecture is not suitable for all cases. One needs to consider whether or not the mechanical loading is sufficient to bring the actuator into the neutral (safe) state with a sufficient reliability. For example, if there is a risk of a blocking of the actuator, the applicability needs to be assessed. For instance, in some hydraulic systems/ environments control actuators may block open due to impurities. Also, in electronic circuits, the relays acting as actuators may be stuck open or weld closed. The architecture may not be applicable if there is a risk that the actuator type used in the control is not able to obtain the desired state to enable the safe state.

Ensure that the safety function cannot be circumvented or bypassed in any way by the control system. If such an architecture is used, it must be ensured that the safety system is able to drive all the actuators having an effect on the application of the considered safety function into the safe state.

Consequences

+ Safety is retained by the safety system regardless of the control system operation.
+ The separation between the safety system and the control systems remains. However, it is typically beneficial to at least provide CONTROL SYSTEM NOTIFICATION, which nevertheless implies only a weak connection between the systems.
+ As the safety system only needs to switch a control signal, there is no need for an additional safety actuator to control large energies, quantities etc. related to the process variable of interest. Thus reduced weight, size and (potentially) power consumption of the safety system can be achieved.
− The safety system can only block the control signal or pass it along as such. This induces some limits to the possibilities of the safety function. For instance, the safety system cannot manipulate the control value in any way except blocking it completely.
− The approach requires the application of the DE-ENERGIZED SAFE STATE PATTERN which leads to a safe state in the occurrence of system-wide power loss.
− The actuator operated by the control system needs to be suitable for the control task with sufficient safety properties, as it needs to take the safe state when receiving no control signal. Usually, this leads to a mechanically loaded and potentially expensive actuator element.
− There still needs to be a relay or similar switching device to detach the actuator from its control system.

Example

A possible application of the control signal blocking principle can be considered in control of harvester crane cylinders. A safety system needs to be able to halt the crane movement, for instance, when a cabin door is opened while the harvester is in an operational state to prevent harm to the operator of the machine. A safety relay is added between a control system output and the respective control valve operated by the control system as illustrated in Fig. 10. A safety system controls the state of the relay. In a normal operational state, the safety system keeps the relay in a such state that it passes the control signal to the control valve. In this case, the control system operates the control valve. When a safety function activates, the safety system changes the relay state to block the control signal and override it with a suitable signal. Typically, this signal is a ground or de-energized level signal, in which case control valve returns to a neural state. This prevents hydraulic flow in and out of the cylinder and effectively halts the cylinder and prevents its movement.

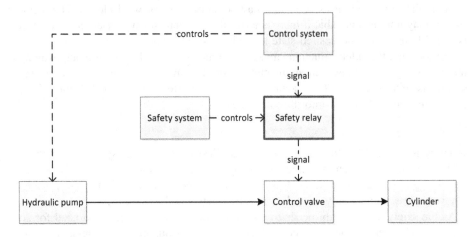

Fig. 10. Example of control signal blocking in a harvester hydraulics application

Known Uses
The principle is used in the machinery domain. It is also a recognized approach in [37, pp. 4–23], [36, p. 260], [38, p. 15 & 30].

Related Patterns
The SAFETY LIMITER pattern describes an alternative solution to the problem. Safe operation can be achieved by circumventing the control signal through a safety function that limits the value without a need for an additional relay or other hardware. Consequently, no additional hardware is required besides the control actuator, but potentially complex safety-related application software needs to be developed.

The SEPARATED OVERRIDE pattern describes an alternative solution to the problem. In this approach, the safety system is provided with a dedicated actuator. This gives the safety system more alternatives to actuate the safety function, but also requires an additional actuator.

The DE-ENERGIZED SAFE STATE pattern describes a generic design-related principle of constructing a system so that a safe state is obtained whenever power is lost.

When a safety system overrides a control system by blocking the control signal, a conflicting situation may appear. From the control system viewpoint, it should try even harder to achieve the desired operation. This leads to a situation where the control system tries to fight against the safety system and this could lead to the saturation of the control algorithm etc. Such side-effects can be mitigated by CONTROL SYSTEM NOTIFI-CATION, which suggests informing the control system when the safety system blocks or restricts its operation in any way.

6 Safety Limiter

Context
Safety function architecture is being designed. The PRODUCTIVE SAFETY pattern has been applied, so the safety system logic is minimized and the complex functionality is deployed on the control system. The amount of hardware needs to be minimized and thus no dedicated actuator or other supporting hardware for the safety system can be added. To retain safety in all situations, the safety system has to have full control over the process variable(s) affecting safety.

Problem
A safety system needs to have the ability to drive a system under control or a process variable of interest into a SAFE STATE regardless of the operations of a control system.

Forces

- A safety system must always be able to drive the system under control into a safe state, that is, a state where the system minimizes the risk of damaging itself or people around it, regardless of the state of a control system.
- In many cases, a safe state can be achieved relatively easily through de-energization, which takes the system into a DE-ENERGIZED SAFE STATE. However, in some cases, this is not sufficient or optimal approach and the safety function is context specific and may require arbitrary controls.
- Safety system logic could be, in principle, used to implement the whole control logic functionality related to a safety-related process variable control. However, as suggested in PRODUCTIVE SAFETY, it is not typically practical to do so as potentially complex logic should be included in the safety system and this is not desirable. However, in the control system one can more easily implement complex control algorithms and structures and on the other hand, in the safety system simple monitoring and reaction operations are more easily accessible.
- Providing a safety system with a dedicated way to control a process variable of interest would yield it the ability to achieve multiple and or time dependent safe states. However, this would, in practice, require a redundant actuator alongside the actuator operated by a control system. On the other hand, software has no drawback of hardware in terms of spatial requirements and can be duplicated for free in mass produced devices.

Solution
Let the safety system manipulate the control signal before directing the control signal to the actuator. Calculate the control signal in a control system and limit the value with a safety system. Provide the control value calculated by the control system to the safety system that checks the safety conditions and limits the control value to a safe range if necessary. The safety control system controls the actuator.

An illustration of the architecture is provided in Fig. 11. The control system cal-culates the control value for the actuator. The control system may use any kind of algorithm freely from the restrictions of safety regulations according to which the safety system has to be developed. The control system then passes the control value to the safety system. The purpose of the safety system is to limit the control value so that safety is retained. The safety system is developed to conform with safety regulations so it shouldn't contain any unnecessary functions. The safety system alone is connected to the actuator.

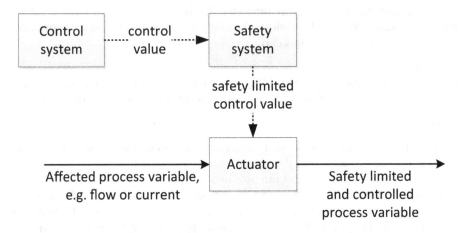

Fig. 11. Principle of software safety limiter in control system override

The logic elements (CPUs, PLCs, etc.) of the control and the safety systems can either be separated devices or a single device running both safety-critical and non-safety-critical functions. The latter approach requires additional measures to be taken to justify non-interference between the systems. The actuator needs to have sufficient capabilities to satisfy the safety standard requirements and it must also be suitable for the control task. Thus the actuator may prove to be expensive.

Data communication from the control system to the safety system is always a potential risk from the point of view of the safety system. However, the systems may communicate if certain conditions are met. Consequently, the software architecture of the safety control system needs special attention. These conditions are not too restrictive as, in general, communication through global data variable or similar data structure is not recommended. Communication should be established through a well-defined interface, for example, a class method or message bus message (with a strict structure).

Example

A possible application of the safety limiter principle can be considered in control of harvester crane cylinders. Consider a harvester safety function that only allows crane movement to a certain direction so that the operability is otherwise retained. In such a case, a safety system cannot completely disable crane control valves or block their hydraulic flow. One possible approach here is to deploy a safety system between a control system and a control valve so that safety system guards control signal produced by the control system as illustrated in Fig. 12.

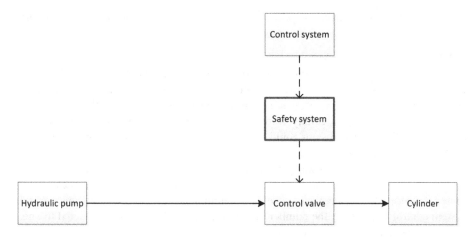

Fig. 12. Example of safety limiter approach in a harvester hydraulics application

Now, any control signal produced by the control system can be overridden by a safety system before it is passed to the control valve. Additional hardware elements are not needed, but the extra effort needs to be put to enable data communication between control and safety systems.

Consequences

+ A complex control algorithm can be used without a need to develop the algorithm according to safety standards as the safety system has the final word.
+ Advanced safety functions can be established through software-based safety functions. Certain types of safety functions are very hard to implement with hardware solutions such as restricting motion into complex-shaped space.
+ The solution is cost-effective especially when the system is mass produced as software is cheaper to multiply than hardware.
− The separation between safety and control systems is lost. However, if the notification approach is implemented rationally, strong (though not complete) independence can still be achieved.
− The safety system may increase the delay in control compared with a situation without an additional safety controller between the controller and the actuator. In many cases, however, the delay is manageable.
− Data communication from the control system to the safety system inflicts a potential risk and thus software architecture of the safety safety-critical system and the data communication, in general, requires special care due to data obtained from the system that does not conform to the applied safety standards.

Known Uses

The approach is applied in machinery applications. The idea is also utilized in airplane control applications. For instance, Boeing 777 employs flight envelope protection. In this approach, the input from the pilot is filtered by a flight envelope protection system [39]. A similar approach is also suggested in [40].

Related Patterns

As the safety system is inherently able to restrict or even block the control system control value, it is important to make the control system aware of the situation. Thus, use CONTROL SYSTEM NOTIFICATION to inform the control system about the state of the safety system. This is especially important when the control value is restricted or blocked, but the control system could also benefit from information when the restrictions are released.

The CONTROL SIGNAL BLOCKING pattern describes an alternative solution to a similar problem. The pattern describes how the safety system and the control system can use a shared actuator without the need to use data communication between safety and control system controls. However, the number of possible safety operations is restricted to one, i.e. only one safe state can be obtained.

The SEPARATED OVERRIDE pattern describes an alternative solution to a similar problem. The safety system is provided with a dedicated actuator. This gives the safety system more alternatives to actuate the safety function and provides complete separation between the control and safety systems. However, the approach requires an additional actuator.

7   Hardwired Safety

Context

Implementation for relatively simple safety functionality is being considered. For instance, the PRODUCTIVE SAFETY pattern has been applied so no advanced functionalities are implemented in the safety system.

Problem

Development of safety-related application software is costly and provides no real benefit in the context of the considered safety function.

Forces

- Development of safety-related software is costly as typically a standard needs to be followed which, for example, in the case of IEC 61508-3, leads to a burdensome development process for safety system software. Thus software development becomes time consuming. Software needs to be run on suitable (and oftentimes certified) processing units which are also expensive in comparison with their non-certified counterparts.
- The simpler the system the more understandable it is and thus faults are less likely to be introduced. Safety systems should be simple and understandable.
- Software provides freedom to implement different kinds of functionalities in safety systems. However, this comes at the cost of the development process. In addition, commercially-off-the-shelf (COTS) safety hardware products for various environments and purposes are available.

Solution

Use a hardware-based safety system instead of application software to implement the safety functionality. That is, remove the need for safety-related application software (and controller) by implementing the required logic with hardware means. For instance, establish a direct link between sensors and actuators to implement the functionality or implement the functionality using electronics. Also, simple hardware based logic components can be used if logic is required.

Hardwired safety systems can be used to implement simple and generic safety functions such as over and under temperature, pressure and speed related to a process variable. Advanced and custom safety functions are, however, easier to be implemented with custom software-based safety applications.

A hardwired functional safety system typically consists of a sensor, an actuator, and potentially logic elements. The sensors measure the system state and inform/control the actuators to apply the safe state when predefined conditions apply. The devices need to be compatible in terms of communication. That is, the sensor must provide a suitable output signal and the actuator needs to be able to use the signal generated by the sensor. Any communication method from an analogy signal to a message bus (as far as compatible with safety regulations) is applicable. Notice that the elements used in the safety function can contain software, if the element manufacturer provides certification or correspondence with appropriate functional safety standards such as IEC 61508 or EN ISO 13849-1.

The following guidelines can be used to identify safety functions, which could be implemented with hardwired solutions.

- The safety function requires no complex logic or calculations. In principle, any logic can be implemented with simple hardware devices (such as logic gates), but in practice merely simple logic (AND, OR, NAND, etc., or their small scale combinations) functions are sensible as hardware implementations.
- There should be a well-defined trigger for the safety function. In this context, a trigger means an event, state, process variable value etc. in the system that triggers the safety function active (e.g. liquid level rises above a maximum value). Simple logics can be used to connect several trigger conditions (e.g. liquid level high and exhaust valve closed). However, more advanced conditions are problematic, e.g. mean values.
- The safety function should be able to actuate the safety function in relatively simple manners. That is, positioning multiple outputs to arbitrary states is problematic whereas controlling a single binary output is (typically) a considerably easier task.

Example

A possible application of the separated override principle can be considered in control of harvester crane cylinders. The movement of a crane has to be halted, for instance, when a cabin door is opened or the operator is not detected on a seat while the harvester is in an operational state to prevent harm to the operator of the machine. In such a simple case, the safety function does not necessarily need to utilize application software. In this example, a safety system consists of two switches and an AND gate as illustrated in Fig. 13. The switches illustrate sensors, which detect if the cabin door is closed and whether the operator's seat is occupied. The output of the AND gate is used to control a separate safety valve as suggested in SEPARATED OVERRIDE.

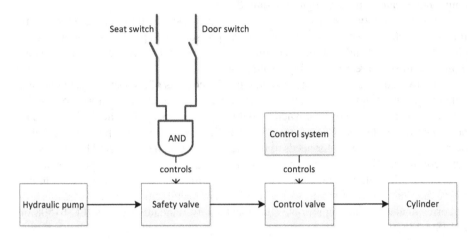

Fig. 13. Example of hardwired safety approach in a harvester hydraulics application

In a normal operational state, the cabin door is closed and the operator's seat occupied. In this case the, switches are closed and they energize the AND gate inputs that consequently open the safety valve, which allows the flow of hydraulic fluid in and out of the cylinder. If either or both of the switches are open, the AND gate output goes low and the safety valve closes causing a SAFE STATE [8].

Consequences

+ No need to develop safety-related application software. This is a major benefit as the development process of even simple safety-related application software is typically a burdensome process.
+ As there is no application software to be run, there is also no need for a dedicated safety-related controller. This potentially reduces the number of devices of the safety system.
+ Intelligibility of the system is increased. This is partly due to inherently encouraged simplicity and partly due to lack of software, which - from a high abstraction level viewpoint - represents a black box in the safety system.
− The advanced features of the safety system may be hard to implement with pure hardware solutions unless suitable ready-made components are available.
− Expansion and further development of hardwired solutions are harder than software based solutions.

Known Uses
The approach is known, applied, and encouraged to be used in several companies including engineering offices and component manufacturers.

Related Patterns
DE-ENERGIZED SAFE STATE is typically a beneficial principle to be applied alongside the approach. This ensures that if the energy source is lost from the (safety) system, a safe state is obtained.

8 Control System Notification

Context
The SEPARATED SAFETY pattern has been applied, so safety and control systems are separated. The safety system is capable to control/affect one or more process variables that are also controlled or used by the control system. For instance, the safety system can affect the state of steam flow in a pipeline that is used by the control system to regulate the temperature of a container. To ensure safety, the safety system is able to override the control system regardless of the state of it (e.g. SEPARATED OVERRIDE, CONTROL SIGNAL BLOCKING, or SAFETY LIMITER pattern have been applied). The context is illustrated in Fig. 14.

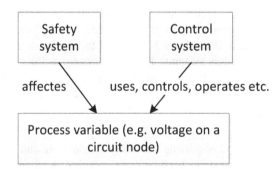

Fig. 14. Context of the CONTROL SYSTEM NOTIFICATION pattern

Problem
The operation of a control system is disturbed when a safety system overrides or restricts the operation of the control system, which may cause the unexpected behaviour of the control system.

Forces

- A safety system needs full control over the process variable regardless of possible side effects on a control system. However, the control system cannot operate normally if the safety system has restricted its operating environment. For example, a control system that uses an electric current to regulate an electric motor speed cannot operate correctly when a safety system has cut off the current. This may lead to a situation where the safety and control systems are fighting against each other.

- A control system could be given required hardware to sense the state of a safety system. However, this would very likely increase the cost and complexity of the control system.

Solution

Make a control system aware of the state changes of a safety system so that the control system can react accordingly. Notify the control system about any operation or event that affects the operation of the control system. Such events include, for instance, a restriction of a variable. A restriction may appear, for example, in form of a limited speed or a load force control of a variable to fully enabled or disabled.

Implement the notification system so that the safety system is kept as independent of the control system as possible to prevent a blocking of the safety system due to the failures of the control system. Three approaches to achieve such an information transfer mechanism can be identified:

- Analogue signalling: The safety system provides an analogue signal for the control system. This approach is simple and releases developers from considerations of the additional requirements of the IEC 61508-3 [20] for digital message busses. However, analogue signalling requires a dedicated cable between the communicating nodes and is more prone to interference from the environment.
- Message bus: The safety system and the control system communicate through a message bus. Safe communication is established through the bus. Additional requirements as given in IEC 61508-3 [20] need to be considered.
- Integrated control and safety systems: The safety system and the control system are executed in the same integrated device. The device and the underlying operating system provide a communication scheme between the entities. However, in such a mixed criticality system there has to be separation between the systems in spatial and temporal domains [20].

Regardless of the method of passing the safety system state and event information to the control system, both systems become more complex. A communication method between the systems needs to be established, which may increase hardware requirements, unless the communication method already exists. In any way, the amount of logic in the safety and control systems will increase. To enable communication and successful reaction the safety system has to produce the state and event information for the control system and the control system has to receive and use the information in a meaningful way. This adds the requirements to the both systems and increases complexity.

Consequences

+ The control system can react and adapt to the state changes and actions of the safety system as it is informed about the safety system state changes.

+ The system safety is increased overall by decreasing the likelihood of unexpected behaviour related to inconsistencies between safety and control systems.
− Full separation between the safety system and the control systems is lost. There needs to be a way to communicate between the safety and control systems. However, depending on the communication method the separation can still be rather strong.
− Increases complexity of both safety and control systems, a notification must be produced and transferred by the safety system and received, interpreted and reacted on by the control system.

Example
Consider a hydraulics cylinder control approach utilized in a harvester application as illustrated in Fig. 15. The cylinder under consideration is attached to a crane that is capable of causing hazardous movement. A SEPARATED SAFETY approach supplement with a SEPARATED OVERRIDE capability has been applied to implement a safety function mitigating the risk of hazardous movement. The safety system has been provided with the ability to notify the control system considering the state and status changes of the safety system. The safety system enables a safe state through the safety valve, but it also notifies the control system regarding the event. As the control system is aware of the situation, it does not need to try to compensate a deviation from user input as the crane cannot be moved regardless of the state of the control valve.

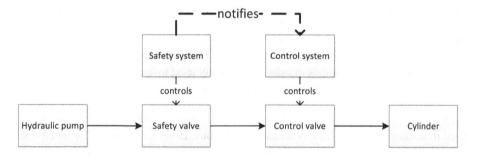

Fig. 15. Example of a control system notification approach in a harvester hydraulics application

Known Uses
The approach is common in the context of machinery system design. Also, for instance, the functionality and system structure illustrated in [35, p. 245] supports the principle.

Related Patterns
The CO-OPERATIVE SAFETY RELATED ACTUATION pattern describes an application for the notifications from the safety system to the control system. Consistency between the safety system and control system can be increased by forcing the control systems actuators to actuate the SAFE STATE [8].

9 Co-operative Safety Related Actuation

Context
An actuator of a control system affects a process variable related to a safety function operation. The CONTROL SYSTEM NOTIFICATION pattern has been applied to enable safety system notifications from the safety system to the control system.

Problem
How to increase the consistency between the operation of a safety system and a control system during situations where the safety system overrides the control system partly or completely?

Forces
- A conflicting state between safety and control systems may cause an undesired operation of the control system and increase a risk of malfunctioning of a safety function.
- A consistent state of a safety and control systems regarding the process variable affected by both systems increases the reliability of a successful actuation of the safety function. This is because in a case of failure of either actuator the other may still be able to actuate and result in the correct safety function outcome.

Solution
Let a safety system drive a control system into a safe state whenever a safe state needs to be obtained (according to the safety system). As the safety system already can notify the control system about the state of the safety system, it is relatively simple to go further and use this asset to increase consistency between the systems.

The actuators of the control system are primarily used to control the process/system to produce the desired output, but they can also affect the state of the system similarly to the actuators of the safety system, that is, change the state of the process variables such as fluid flow or electric current. Thus, the actuators of the control system can be used to actuate similar operations as safety functions. However, it should be noted that control actuators can only support the safety system, but cannot take its responsibilities. In such a case, the control system would act as a safety system.

Two primary approaches to implement the co-operative safety related actuation can be described. Firstly, the CONTROL SIGNAL BLOCKING approach can be taken to force the control actuator in a consistent safe state with the safety system. Another approach is to provide the control system with information that effectively forces the control system in a safe state regarding the actuator(s) of interest. This approach is depicted in Fig. 16. In practice, the safety system first drives its own actuator to the safe state and then commands the control system to operate similarly. The OUTPUT INTERLOCKING [24] pattern may help to implement the described functionality in the control system logic.

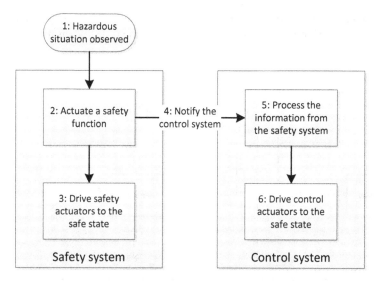

Fig. 16. Co-operative safety related actuation through control system notification using an OUTPUT INTERLOCKING approach.

Consequences

+ Increased consistency between the states of the safety and control systems which decrease the possibility of malfunctions due to state inconsistencies (when giving the control back to the control system).
+ The reliability of the desired outcome of safety function actuation is increased due to redundancy in actuators. When the actuators of the safety and control systems are in a consistent state, the reliability of a successful outcome of a safety function is increased.
+ The consistency between the states of the control and safety systems decreases the state space where the system can be when a safety function is active (after transitions).
− Although the overall reliability would increase, the control system side provides only additional "peace of mind" reliability which cannot be counted into safety system attribute as such.
− The complexity of the control system algorithm is increased as it needs to take the safety system input algorithmically into account.
− In some cases, the approach could mask safety system actuator faults. However, system diagnostics should identify such situations.

Example

Consider a hydraulics cylinder control approach utilized in a harvester application as illustrated in Fig. 17. The cylinder under consideration is attached to a crane that is capable of causing hazardous movement. A control system operates the hydraulic system by controlling a hydraulic pump and a control valve. A safety system primarily operates a safety valve that is used to achieve a SAFE STATE [8] when required.

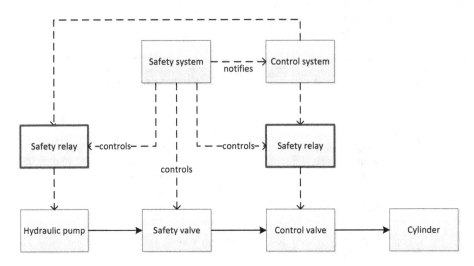

Fig. 17. Example of a co-operative safety related actuation approach in a harvester hydraulics application

The co-operative safety related actuation principle is also used in the setup. The safety system has the ability to notify the control system of state changes, for instance, regarding the activation and release of safety functions. The control system can adjust its operation if the safety function activates. In addition, the safety system can override the control signal to the control valve and the pump (CONTROL SIGNAL BLOCKING). This way, the safety system can force the safe state for the control actuators to complement the state of the safety valve.

Related Patterns
The OUTPUT INTERLOCKING pattern [24] suggests the usage of interlocking elements alongside each control output used to control a physical device. These interlocking elements provide a way to implement the driving of the control system into a suitable state. That is, when an interlock element of the control system receives a request to obtain a safe state, the element forces the control output to a predefined safe state.

The CONTROL SIGNAL BLOCKING describes a way to implement the co-operative actuation. This way the safety system does not have to rely on the operation of the control system logic.

10 Shared Safety Actuator

Context
A system under control consists of subsystems that use an input produced by a single source as illustrated in Fig. 18 (typically the source is an energy source). A similar safety function is related to all the subsystems (e.g. an emergency stop). The safety function operates in the same direction and has the same safe state in terms of the shared input between the subsystems. That is, each subsystem takes a safe state, e.g., when the input is disconnected from the subsystem. The SEPARATED OVERRIDE pattern has been applied, that is, the safety system has a dedicated actuator to control the operation of the system.

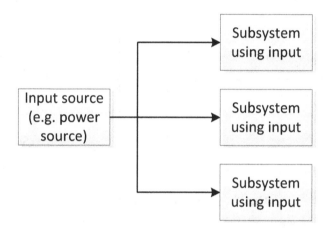

Fig. 18. The context of the shared safety actuator

Problem
Providing each subsystem with a dedicated safety actuator when the same input variable is used by multiple subsystems increases the number of needed safety actuators in the system.

Forces

- The independent operability of the subsystems in terms of the shared input could promote productivity, flexibility, and availability of the system by letting each independent subsystem continue operation in case one of the subsystems needs to obtain a safe state. However, dedicated safety actuators for each subsystem increases hardware cost, weight, space requirements and complexity of the safety system

- Suitable safety actuators are considerably more expensive or there are space and/or weight requirements considering the actuator and thus the number of the actuators should be kept low.

Solution

Use a shared safety actuator for all the subsystems. The safety actuator is positioned so that it can control the safety function considering all the subsystems (in the context of the shared input). The principle of the solution is depicted in Fig. 19. In the figure, a safety actuator is added between the input source and the subsystems which use the input and which are safety-critical. The safety actuator controls the input. Whenever the safety function (related to the input) is triggered in any of the subsystems, the safety actuator is used to obtaining a safe state. The safe state propagates to all subsystems regardless of their state.

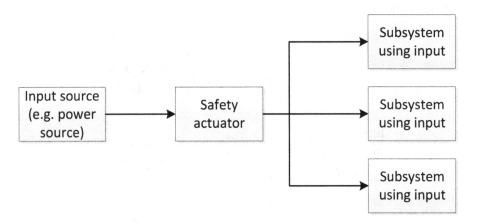

Fig. 19. Shared safety actuator principle

The solution requires thorough consideration before application. There are many aspects that might result in problems. Subsystem decoupling is one, but also the topology, structure, and functions for exceptional operation may cause undesired side-effects when the approach is used. In this solution, only the main approach is presented. The actual application of the solution depends on the details of the target system. For instance, in a hydraulic lifting system, one should consider potential energy stored in a lifted object and prevent object movement and drifting.

The input source is typically a power/energy source of some kind such as hydraulic (hydraulic motor), electric (power source) or pneumatic (air compressor) energy source. However, the input source can be any controlled variable of the system. The input source itself can also act as a "safety actuator". That is, the whole source of the considered variable can be turned on or off controlled by the safety system. This, as well, requires a thorough analysis of the effects to prevent undesired functionality.

Consequences

+ The number of safety actuation hardware is decreased as one set of safety actuators is needed instead of N (sets of) safety system actuators.

+ Due to a lower amount of safety system actuation hardware, space, weight, and (potentially power consumption) requirements for a safety system are decreased.
+ The approach likely decreases the overall cost of the safety actuator hardware.
− Potentially decreased productivity, flexibility, and availability of the system because the subsystems (sharing the input) lose independence considering safety function(s) related to the shared input.
− The potential safety functions are (practically) restricted to on-off type because it is hard to arrange the distribution of the shared input between the subsystems. In practice, this would need additional hardware which hinders the original objective of the approach.
− The subsystem design may obtain new requirements to meet the requirements for a correct operation of the safety system. That is, one needs to ensure that, for example, the pressurized fluid does not enter from one subsystem in another in an uncontrolled manner.
− The shared safety actuator requires a dedicated control element (e.g., a software component that is responsible for the actuator control).
− The approach is prone to unpredictable side-effects, due to, for example, insufficient decoupling between the subsystem in terms of the shared input.
− Requires detailed and throughout analysis to ensure correct operation in various operational cases.
− The safety system has to be developed and the safety actuator needs to be chosen according to the highest safety criticality/integrity level of the subsystems.

Example

Consider a hydraulics cylinder control approach utilized in a harvester application as illustrated in Fig. 20. The hydraulics operates a harvester crane, that utilizes three hydraulic cylinders in total to operate the separate crane parts. All three cylinders are controlled by a control system with dedicated control valves. A safety system has been deployed to implement stopping function of the crane when, for instance, a cabin door of the harvester is opened. The safety system controls a single safety valve that is shared among all the cylinder lines. When the safety valve is taken into a safe state, all the cylinders also go to the respective safe state, that is, stop any movement.

Notice that the illustration is heavily simplified. For instance, the decoupling between the cylinders is not shown. In a real application, one should consider how to establish decoupling between the cylinders so that movement or load in one does not result in movement or load in another.

Known Uses

The approach is used in the domain of the machinery applications. The BGIA Report (Sect. 8.2.27) [37] illustrates a similar solution. However, the approach given in the report focuses on redundancy and employs safety related actuators also in the subsystems to avoid a single point of failure problem. The decoupling aspect is not considered. Nevertheless, it is mentioned that the shared safety actuator is sufficient to enable the considered safety stop function.

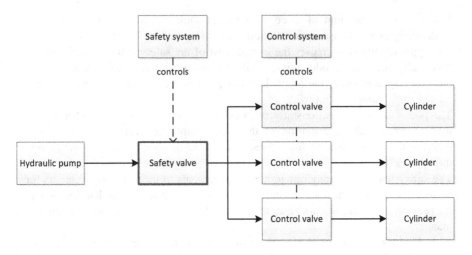

Fig. 20. Example of a shared safety actuator approach in a harvester hydraulics application

Related Patterns
The safety system should notify the control systems of the related subsystems as illustrated in the CONTROL SYSTEM NOTIFICATION.

Acknowledgments. The patterns presented in this article have originally been published in [41] and [24], and a grant to reuse the content has been kindly provided by VikingPLoP 2012 and 2013 organizers. The publications were written in co-operation with Timo Vepsäläinen and Seppo Kuikka.

The authors would like to thank the people who have helped us with these patterns. The authors would like to thank VikingPLoP 2012 members: Veli-Pekka Eloranta, Ville Reijonen, Dirk Schnelle-Walka, and Joonas Salo and especially our shepherd Farah Lakhani for their valuable feedback in the VikingPLoP 2012.

In addition, with no less importance, the authors would like to thank the workshop group members in the VikingPLoP 2013: Samuel Lehtinen, Christopher Preschern, Johannes Koskinen, Pekka Alho, Marko Leppänen, Stefan Radomski, Ville Reijonen, and Veli-Pekka Eloranta and especially our shepherd Dirk Schnelle-Walka for their valuable feedback and input to improve the patterns and the paper.

References

1. Gamma, E., Helm, R., Johnson, R., Vlissides, J.: Design Patterns: Elements of Reusable Object-Oriented Software. Addison-Wesley, Boston (1995)
2. Freeman, E., Freeman, E., Sierra, K., Bates, B.: Head First Design Patterns. O'Reilly, Newton (2004)
3. Buschmann, F., Meunier, R., Rohnert, H., Sommerland, P., Stal, M.: Pattern-Oriented Software Architecture: A System of Patterns, vol. 1. Wiley, Hoboken (1996)
4. Schmidt, D., Stal, M., Rohnert, H., Buschmann, F.: Pattern-Oriented Software Architecture: Patterns for Concurrent and Networked Objects. Wiley, New York (2000)

5. Hohpe, G., Woolf, B.: Enterprise Integration Patterns: Designing, Building, and Deploying Messaging Solutions. Addison-Wesley Professional, Boston (2003)
6. Fowler, M.: Patterns of Enterprise Application Architecture. Addison-Wesley, Boston (2002)
7. Erl, T.: SOA Design Patterns. Prentice Hall, Upper Saddle River (2009)
8. Eloranta, V.-P., Koskinen, J., Leppänen, M., Reijonen, V.: Designing Distributed Control Systems: A Pattern Language Approach. Wiley, Sussex (2014)
9. Hanmer, R.S.: Patterns for Fault Tolerant Software. Wiley, Chichester (2007)
10. Douglass, B.P.: Doing Hard Time: Developing Real-Time Systems with UML, Objects, Frameworks, and Patterns. Addison-Wesley, Boston (1999)
11. Armoush, A.: Design patterns for safety-critical embedded systems (2010). http://aib. informatik.rwth-aachen.de/2010/2010-13.pdf
12. Alho, P., Rauhamäki, J.: Patterns for light-weight fault tolerance and decoupled design in distributed control systems. In: Noble, J., et al. (eds.) TPLOP IV. LNCS, vol. 10600, pp. 1–21. Springer, Heidelberg (2019)
13. Preschern, C., Kajtazovic, N., Kreiner, C.: Building a safety architecture pattern system. In: Proceedings of the 18th European Conference on Pattern Languages of Program, EuroPLoP 2013 (2015)
14. Koskinen, J., Vuori, M., Katara, M.: Safety process patterns: demystifying safety standards. In: 2012 IEEE International Conference on Software Science, Technology and Engineering, pp. 63–71. IEEE Computer Society (2012)
15. Douglass, B.P.: Real-Time Design Patterns: Robust Scalable Architecture for Real-Time Systems. Addison-Wesley, Boston (2003)
16. Gomaa, H.: Real-Time Software Design for Embedded Systems. Cambridge University Press, Cambridge (2016)
17. Zalewski, J.: Real-time software architectures and design patterns: fundamental concepts and their consequences. Ann. Rev. Control 25, 133–146 (2001)
18. Pont, M.J.: Patterns for Time-Triggered Embedded Systems: Building Reliable Applications with the 8051 Family of Microcontrollers. Addison-Wesley, New York (2001)
19. Sanz, R., Zalewski, J.: Pattern-based control systems engineering - using design patterns to document, transfer, and exploit design knowledge. IEEE Control Syst. Mag. 23, 43–60 (2003)
20. Electrotechnical Commission: IEC 61508:2010 - Functional safety of electrical/electronic/ programmable electronic safety-related systems (2010)
21. International Organization for Standardization: EN ISO 13849-1 - Safety of machinery, safety-related parts of control systems, part 1: general principles for design (2006)
22. Rauhamäki, J., Vepsäläinen, T.: Functional Safety System Designer's Handbook - Design Patterns for Safety Development. Forum for Intelligent Machines. Internal report (2016)
23. Buschmann, F., Henney, K., Schmidt, D.C.: Pattern-Oriented Software Architecture: A Pattern Language for Distributed Computing, vol. 4. Wiley, Chichester (2007)
24. Rauhamäki, J., Kuikka, S.: Patterns for control system safety. In: Proceedings of the 18th European Conference on Pattern Languages of Program, EuroPLoP 2013 (2015)
25. Liebherr LTM 1030-2.1 technical datasheet. https://www.liebherr.com/external/products/ products-assets/261930/liebherr-ltm-1030-2-1-200-00-us04-2016.pdf
26. Manitou Man'go 12. https://www.manitou.com/en/p/VO2gPCwAAGQy0auV#p
27. Gasparini. http://www.gasparini.it/en/press-brakes
28. Caterpillar 302.7D CR Mini Hydraulic Excavator. http://www.cat.com/en_US/products/new/ equipment/excavators/mini-excavators/18254186.html

29. Ponsse: Scorpion, product brochure. http://www.ponsse.com/fi/content/download/9107/ 203130/file/PONSSE_Scorpion_ENG.pdf
30. John Deere: 1470G Wheeled harvester. https://www.deere.com/en_US/products/equipment/ harvesters/wheeled_harvesters/1470g_ft4/1470g_ft4.page
31. Komatsu: Komatsu 911 harvester. http://www.komatsuforest.com/default.aspx?id= 115891&productId=115641&rootID=1475
32. Dorf, R.C., Bishop, R.H.: Modern Control Systems. Pearson Education, Upper Saddle River (2005)
33. Smith, C.L.: Distillation Control: An Engineering Perspective. Wiley, Hoboken (2012)
34. Rockwell Automation: Bul. 440R—Guardmaster® Safety Relays. Publication 440R-SG001C-EN-P (2012). http://www.movetec.fi/images/pdf/440r-sg001_-en-p.pdf
35. Pizzato: Introduction to Safety. http://www.pizzato.com/PizzatoWeb/UserFiles/File/pdf/ document/introduction_safety.pdf
36. Hauke, M., et al.: Functional Safety of Machine Controls: Application of EN ISO 13849. DGUV, Berlin (2009)
37. Bittner, C., et al.: The Safety Compendium. Pilz (2013). https://www.pilz.com/imperia/md/ content/editors_mm/safety_compendium_en_2014_01.pdf
38. Apfeld, R., Zilligen, H., Köhler, B.: Safe Drive Controls with Frequency Converters (IFA Report 7/2013e). DGUV, Berlin (2014)
39. Bartley, G.F.: Boeing B-777: fly-by- wire flight controls. In: Spitzer, C.R. (ed.) The Avionics Handbook. CRC Press, Boca Raton (2001)
40. Falkena, W., Borst, C., Chu, Q.P., Mulder, J.A.: Investigation of practical flight envelope protection systems for small aircraft. J. Guid. Control Dyn. **34**, 976–988 (2011)
41. Rauhamäki, J., Vepsäläinen, T., Kuikka, S.: Functional safety system patterns. In: Eloranta, V.-P., Koskinen, J., Leppänen, M. (eds.) Proceedings of VikingPloP 2012 Conference, pp. 48–68. Tampere University of Technology (2012)

Internet of Things Patterns for Communication and Management

Lukas Reinfurt[1,2](✉), Uwe Breitenbücher[1], Michael Falkenthal[1],
Frank Leymann[1], and Andreas Riegg[2]

[1] Institute of Architecture of Application Systems, University of Stuttgart,
Stuttgart, Germany
{lukas.reinfurt, uwe.breitenbuecher,
michael.falkenthal,
frank.leymann}@iaas.uni-stuttgart.de
[2] Daimler AG, Stuttgart, Germany
{lukas.reinfurt, andreas.riegg}@daimler.com

Abstract. The Internet of Things is gaining a foothold in many different areas and industries. Though offerings vary in their scope and implementation, they often have to deal with similar problems: Constrained devices and networks, a vast amount of different vendors and technologies, security and privacy issues, etc. Over time, similar solutions for these problems appear, but the amount of available information makes it hard to identify the underlying principles. We investigated a large number of Internet of Things solutions and extracted the core principles into patterns. The eight patterns presented in this paper are: DEVICE GATEWAY enables devices that do not support a networks technology to connect to this network. DEVICE SHADOW allows other components to interact with offline devices. RULES ENGINE enables non-programmers to create rules that trigger actions. DEVICE WAKEUP TRIGGER informs sleeping devices that they should wake up. REMOTE LOCK AND WIPE allows lost or stolen devices to be secured. DELTA UPDATE only sends data that has changed since the last communication. REMOTE DEVICE MANAGEMENT enables remote device management with a client-server architecture. VISIBLE LIGHT COMMUNICATION uses existing lights to send messages to other devices.

Keywords: Internet of Things · Patterns ·
Embedded and cyber-physical systems · Device management

1 Introduction

In the last years, the *Internet of Things* (IoT) has gathered more and more attention in very different areas. It is driven by several developments, such as decreasing sensor and device sizes, energy consumption, or cost of chips and sensors. Additionally, widespread broadband connectivity and new communication technologies are also pushing the IoT forward. A future where many things will be connected to the internet seems increasingly palpable. This, in turn, would allow us to collect and analyze data about practically all aspects of our lives. The gathered knowledge could then be used for widespread improvements and automation.

© Springer Nature Switzerland AG 2019
J. Noble et al. (Eds.): TPLOP IV, LNCS 10600, pp. 139–182, 2019.
https://doi.org/10.1007/978-3-030-14291-9_5

There are a few core components that are combined to realize IoT systems, as shown in Fig. 1. Central to the IoT are the things, which usually resemble some kind of *device*. These devices are often limited in their capabilities due to cost, size, energy, or technological constraints. The typical device contains a combination of *sensors* and/or *actuators*, a *processing component*, some means of *communication*, and an *energy supply*. Sensors are used to translate changes in the environment to electrical signals, whereas actuators are used to act on the environment by translating electrical signals into some kind of physical action [1]. They are controlled by the processing component, which can range from a simple circuit to complex chips. A device can also communicate with other components through wired or wireless communication technologies. These other components could be, for example, other devices or a backend server that runs in a data center or in the Cloud. A *backend server* is usually used to aggregate and process data from many devices. It uses this data to gain new insights and knowledge as well as to send commands to the actuators connected to the devices. It is also used to manage all the connected devices, e.g., for registering new devices, updating software and firmware, or managing security credentials. It might also communicate with *other components*, such as web services for analytics or data storage provided by other companies.

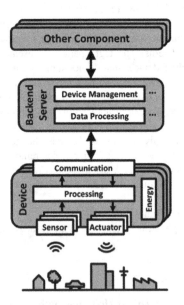

Fig. 1. Components overview

As the IoT is not particular to any specific industry or domain, many different movements or solutions have developed over time that in some way incorporate the IoT. These include *Smart Homes, Smart Offices* [2, 3], *Smart Grids* [4], or the *Smart City* concept [5, 6], as well as initiatives like *Industrie 4.0* in Germany [7], or the *Industrial Internet* [8]. They all do essentially the same on a different scale: They integrate a manifold of independent, distributed, and, sometimes, also physically accessible sensors in public environments to achieve two things: (i) to enable analyzing the gathered data and (ii) to use the processed analysis results to automate control of domain specific actuators. All these solutions share some significant similarities but have been developed mainly in closed off silos in the past. Several standardization efforts have been initiated that try to break up these silos on different levels. They include network connectivity standards [9–12], protocols [13–15], device management [16–18] or device communication frameworks [19–21]. It remains to be seen if all of these efforts can lead to a more unified IoT.

Getting to grips with all these developments is a challenge for companies. Because of the fragmented nature of the IoT space, it is not enough for them to look at different providers, solutions, and technologies in one IoT sector. Instead, they have to look in multiple separate sectors to find the most appropriate solution. Most corporations will come in contact with the IoT on one or multiple levels. A company might realize that it has to produce IoT-enabled products in the future to stay competitive. It might be able to save costs by introducing *Smart Factory* or *Smart Office* capabilities. It might find entirely new business opportunities that are connected to the IoT. When trying to build a good IoT solution, IT architects and developers at these companies are faced with the problems of:

- how to conceive application architectures to be robust for IoT challenges, i.e., how to receive and process data from a huge amount of sensors at the same time,
- how to assure security in terms of communication of devices as well as physical access to these devices,
- how to deal with energy and processing limitations of devices, and
- how to integrate multiple proprietary protocols supported by heterogeneous devices, sensors, and actuators into an IoT platform.

However, the prerequisite to tackling these issues is to understand the core design principles for developing IoT solutions. It is, therefore, valuable to extract and author a collection of proven design principles from production ready IoT solutions, which are already established in many IoT-platforms and related technologies.

Patterns have been used before to describe proven best practices that have stood the test of time in a specific domain. Examples include patterns for architecture [22], Cloud Computing [23], software design [24], or messaging systems [25]. Their abstraction of very similar and often reoccurring solutions into a structured form can be helpful to dissect and understand complex fields. They are also useful for comparing different solutions and solution providers for suitability for a specific task. Last but not least they can be used as a guideline for new implementations.

In this paper, which is an extended version of our former work that we have presented at the *21st European Conference on Pattern Languages of Programs (EuroPLoP)*, we describe eight patterns for the IoT, as seen in Table 1. The new contributions of this extended version to the original paper [26] are the three patterns, marked in Table 1 as new: DELTA UPDATE, REMOTE DEVICE MANAGEMENT, and VISIBLE LIGHT COMMUNICATION. As these patterns are also interlinked with the five original patterns, some minor adjustments have been made to the original patterns to reference the new patterns. We also added a pattern map showing the relations between the patterns in this paper, as well as an overview of the evolving IoT Pattern Language.

The patterns are aimed at IT architects and developers. We have abstracted them from a systematic information collection process focusing on IoT-platforms and related technologies. We believe that these patterns help IT architects and developers working on IoT application with selecting, designing, and building better solutions. Although these patterns are presented as IoT patterns, some of them may also be applicable in other areas. For example, a RULES ENGINE may also be used in an IT system that does not involve things connected over the internet. However, these patterns are listed here as IoT patterns as they often play a vital role in IoT system.

Table 1. Overview of the presented patterns.

	DEVICE GATEWAY (p.11)	Some devices cannot directly connect to a network because they do not support the required communication technologies. These devices can be connected through a gateway.
	DEVICE SHADOW (p.15)	Other components can interact with currently offline devices by communicating with a persistently stored virtual representation of the device that is synchronized once the device reconnects.
	RULES ENGINE (p.18)	Users can define simple rules without needing to program. These rules tell the system with what action it should react to incoming events.
	DEVICE WAKEUP TRIGGER (p.22)	A device that is not currently connected to the backend server can be informed to do so by sending a message to a low-power communication channel where the device listens for such messages.
	REMOTE LOCK AND WIPE (p.26)	When a device is lost or stolen, its functionality can be remotely locked or data on it can be wiped, either fully or partially, to protect it from possible attacks.
	DELTA UPDATE (new) (p.29)	Only the values that have changed since the last communication are sent in a message to reduce the required traffic.
	REMOTE DEVICE MANAGEMENT (new) (p.32)	A central device management server allows remote management by sending management commands to management clients located on the devices who translate and execute these commands locally.
	VISIBLE LIGHT COMMUNICATION (new) (p.32)	Visible light is modulated to send messages, which can be received by photodiodes or cameras. Normal use of the lights is still possible.

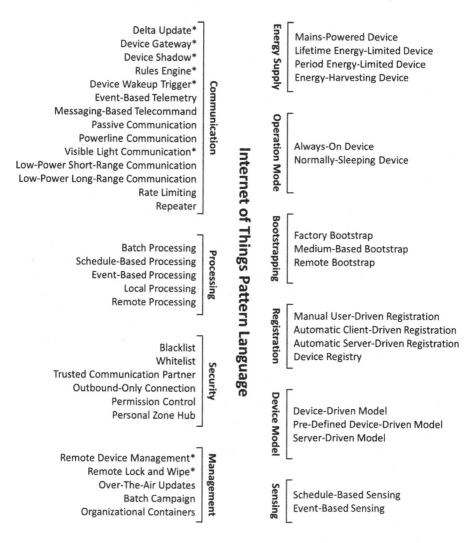

Fig. 2. The presented patterns and other well-founded pattern ideas as part of an evolving IoT pattern language.

These patterns do not stand alone but are part of an evolving pattern language, which we want to expand in the future with more patterns in several categories. Figure 2 shows the patterns presented in this paper in the context of a larger pattern language. Several potential categories and additional well-founded pattern ideas are also shown. All these pattern ideas are based on examples (several each) that we collected during the information collection process.

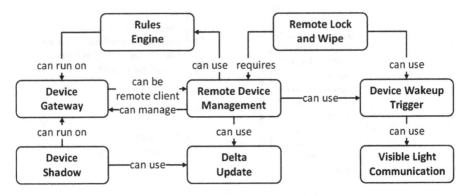

Fig. 3. Relations between the patterns presented in this work.

The patterns presented here are interconnected with each other. Figure 3 shows a pattern map, where each connection from one pattern to another pattern is labeled. Most of these connections, e.g., *can use* or *can run on*, describe how one pattern can be optionally enhanced or combined with another pattern. However, some connections, like *requires*, describe that one pattern is a mandatory prerequisite to be able to apply another pattern. These connections can therefore provide a guideline for a sensible reading and application order of the patterns. The connections are described in more detail in the patterns themselves.

The remainder of this paper is structured as follows: For a better comprehension, the original contribution of our previous work [26] is repeated in Sects. 2, 3, 4, 5.1, 5.2, 5.3, 5.4, 5.5, and 6. Section 2 elaborates on how the patterns presented in this paper have been identified. Section 3 briefly describes the pattern format used for these patterns. Section 4 introduces definitions that are helpful in the scope of the IoT and that are frequently used in the pattern descriptions. Sections 5.1, 5.2, 5.3, 5.4 and 5.5 present the five IoT patterns that we identified for the original paper [26]. Sections 5.6, 5.7 and 5.8 contain the new patterns. Section 6 presents related work in the field of patterns and the IoT. Section 7 summarizes the paper and gives an outlook on planned future research.

2   Pattern Identification Process

The patterns presented in this paper have been identified by collecting and reviewing information from existing products and technologies following the pattern authoring process defined by Fehling et al. [27]. They divide the pattern writing process into three iterative phases: *Pattern Identification*, *Authoring*, and *Application*. They further divide each phase into several steps [27]. The patterns presented here are the result of the first two phases. The pattern language is currently applied in the SePiA.Pro[1] project. In the first step of the first phase, *Domain Definition*, we started by defining our understanding of the IoT domain by identifying common knowledge in this area. Some results of this

---

[1] http://projekt-sepiapro.de/en/ (last accessed on 13.06.2018).

step are the IoT overview presented in Fig. 1 and the terminology and definitions in Sect. 4. In the next step, *Coverage Consideration*, we decided that we do not want to be limited to a specific sector or user group when looking for IoT patterns. Thus, commercial and open-source solutions for enterprises, developers, and end users alike were included. The exact sources for each pattern are detailed in the respective pattern's example section and include:

- **Product pages** that describe the functionality of IoT solutions
- **User manuals** that explain how to use IoT solutions
- **Technical documentation** of IoT solutions intended for developers
- **Standard documents** of technologies used in IoT solutions
- **Whitepapers** of companies that provide IoT solutions
- **Research Papers** that investigate technologies used in IoT solutions.

During the *Information Format Design* step, we decided to use Citavi[2] to collect and manage all information. Citavi's quoting features can be used to extract information out of all kinds of documents and store them in a database. These quotes can then be tagged to assign them to a category, creating groups by similarity. These features where used in step four, *Information Collection*. A random selection of possible sources was created based on searches on Google and Google Scholar for IoT related keywords. These sources were scanned briefly. If the content of a source seemed relevant, it was added to the Citavi database and all relevant sections where marked as quotes and tagged, using the same tags for similar quotes. In the final step of the first phase, *Information Review*, the resulting collection of tagged quotes was reorganized. Some tags with quotes describing very similar concepts were combined, some tags with quotes describing disparate concepts were split up. Each tag then represents a rough pattern indicator or idea. Several tags belonging to a similar area were organized under a larger parent category. This resulted in the hierarchy shown in Fig. 2.

During the second phase, *Pattern Authoring*, each tag containing at least three different examples [28] was authored into a pattern. In the first step, Pattern Language Design, the pattern format described in Sect. 3 was created based on other existing formats (see Sect. 3). In the next step, *Primitive Design*, additional graphical features commonly used in our patterns were defined. For example, each pattern's problem and solution section are put into a gray box to make them easy to find at a glance. Or, to ensure a unified look of the pattern sketches, graphical primitives for commonly used objects (such as *Device* or *User*) were created.

In the *Composition Language Definition* step, design rules for the pattern sketches were created to further ensure a consistent look. This includes defining common colors, line thicknesses, line types, etc. Then, in step four, *Pattern Writing*, the essence and core principles contained in the considered sources were abstracted to form a high level, provider independent description of the particular solution. Using these descriptions, patterns were authored following the advice of [29–32]. Finally, in step five, *Pattern Language Revision*, the links between the resulting patterns and pattern candidates (future patterns that have not yet been fully formulated) were checked for

---

[2] https://www.citavi.com/en (last accessed on 13.06.2018).

completeness. As this is an iterative process, phases and steps were revisited when new information was found, feedback of workshops was implemented, or ideas for other improvements appeared.

3 Pattern Format

This section describes the pattern format that is used to describe the patterns presented in this paper. It is based on pattern formats, approaches, and guidelines described in several publications about pattern writing or publications that contain patterns [23, 29–33]. While some elements are required in every pattern description, others are optional and are only used when necessary.

The **Name** is used to identify the pattern. Other names by which the pattern might be known in the industry are listed under **Aliases**. Additionally, the **Icon** adds a graphical representation of the pattern that is intended to be used in architecture diagrams or sketches [23]. The **Problem** section captures the core problem that is resolved by the pattern in an abstract manner, i.e., independent from a concrete domain or technology since the general problem might exist in many different use cases. Thus, more technical patterns [34] are out of the scope of this work. The **Context** then further describes the circumstances in which the problem typically occurs, which might impose constraints on the solution. Next, the **Forces** state the considerations that must be taken into account when choosing a solution to a problem. These can often be contradictory.

The **Solution** states the core steps to solve the problem and is often closed with a sketch depicting the architecture of the solution. Then, the **Result** section elaborates the solution in greater detail and describes the situation we find ourselves in after applying the pattern. **Variants** of the pattern are listed if they do not differ enough to need their own separate pattern description. Connections between patterns, such as patterns that are often applied together or patterns that exclude each other can be listed in the **Related Patterns** section. A final **Example** section lists concrete examples that illustrate the application of the pattern and could also contain links to concrete solution artifacts as conceptually introduced in [35] and validated for different domains in [36].

4 Terminology and Definitions

In this section, we define the basic terminology used to describe the IoT Patterns following Bormann et al. [37], who presented a terminology for constrained-node networks. The terminology defines different (i) device types, (ii) device energy supply types, and (iii) device operation modes. The following is a short summary to provide a clear understanding of the presented patterns.

4.1 Device Types

Devices in the IoT can be categorized into groups according to their computational and communication capabilities.

Unconstrained Devices have no significant constraints regarding their computational and communication capabilities. They are able to run arbitrary software and can use communication technology that is not specifically designed for low energy consumption, limited storage, or limited performance.

Semi-Constrained Devices are constrained in their computational power and/or storage space in such a way that they cannot use a common full protocol stack to communicate over the internet. However, they can use protocol stacks that are specifically designed for *Semi-Constrained Devices*, such as the Constrained Application Protocol (CoAP)[3], IPv6 over Low-power Wireless Personal Area Networks (6LoWPAN)[4], or Open Platform Communications Unified Architecture (OPC UA) Binary[5]. This enables them to act as fully integrated peers in a network without the help of a gateway or similar components. These nodes often also have a limited energy supply.

Constrained Devices are severely constrained in their computation, storage, and communication capabilities, often caused or accompanied by strong limitations of their energy supply. Therefore, they do not have the resources to support direct internet communication. Consequently, they use communication technology specifically designed for *Constrained Devices*, such as Bluetooth Low Energy[6], ZigBee[7], or Z-Wave[8].

4.2   Device Energy Supply Types

The energy supplies available for devices in the IoT can be divided into four groups.

Mains-Powered devices have no direct limitation to available energy, i.e., they are plugged into a wall socket. Unless there is an outage, they can use all the power they need.

Period Energy-Limited devices have a power source that has to be replaced or recharged in regular intervals, such as easily replaceable or rechargeable batteries or fuel in some kind of generator.

Lifetime Energy-Limited devices contain a non-replaceable and non-rechargeable power source, such as a battery that is directly soldered onto the circuit board. Once this power source is depleted it cannot be easily replaced.

Energy Harvesting devices convert ambient energy into electrical energy. Ambient energy can be in form of radiant energy (solar, infrared, radio-frequency), thermal energy, mechanical energy, or biomechanical energy. The energy available to the device depends on the ambient energy available at the location of the device and might vary significantly over time. Energy harvesting can supply a device with perpetual power in some cases, but the available amount of energy is usually very small. Often,

---

[3] https://tools.ietf.org/html/rfc7252 (last accessed on 13.06.2018).

[4] https://tools.ietf.org/html/rfc4944 (last accessed on 13.06.2018).

[5] https://opcfoundation.org/ (last accessed on 13.06.2018).

[6] https://www.bluetooth.com/bluetooth-technology/radio-versions (last accessed 13.06.2018).

[7] http://www.zigbee.org/ (last accessed on 13.06.2018).

[8] http://www.z-wave.com/ (last accessed on 13.06.2018).

these devices will be mostly sleeping while they collect enough energy for short bursts of activity.

4.3   Device Operation Modes

Devices can operate in different modes depending on their communication frequency and their need to save energy.

Always-On devices have no reason to change operation modes to save power. They can stay connected and operational all the time.

Low-Power devices usually need to operate on small amounts of power but are still required to communicate frequently. They will sleep for short periods of time between communicating, but will generally stay connected to the network. This requires optimized hardware and communication solutions.

Normally-Off devices will be asleep most of the time and reconnect to the network at specific intervals to communicate (duty cycling).

5   Internet of Things Patterns

In this section, we present eight IoT Patterns that were identified following the procedure described in Sect. 2. The format follows the definition presented in Sect. 3.

5.1   Device Gateway

Aliases: Gateway, Field Gateway, Intermediate Gateway, Physical Hub, Protocol Converter.

Context: A number of devices have to be connected to a network. These might include *Constrained Devices* or *Semi-Constrained Devices* that are limited in their processing power and do not support the communication methods of the network. These might also include *Unconstrained Devices* from legacy systems that cannot connect to the network due to outdated technology. A backend server reachable over this network is intended to process data from these devices.

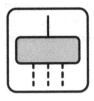

Problem: You want to connect many different devices to an already existing network, but some of them might not support the networks communication technology or protocol.

Forces:

- **Connectivity:** Devices have to be connected to a network because you want to access their data and functionality regularly. Doing this manually is not an option.

- **Upgradability:** Changing or building up a network so that it supports the communication technology required by the device is often not possible. You might not control the network, or the purpose of the network cannot be realized with the device's technology, e.g., you need a long-range network but the device only supports short-range communication.
- **Effort:** Adding communication capabilities that are supported by the network to all device types would mean a high investment in time and resources, or might not be possible at all because of technological limitations.
- **Diversity:** Other devices with different communication technology might also have to be connected to the same network and will face the same problem.
- **Device Numbers:** Your network can only support a certain amount of simultaneous connections. The number of devices you want to connect exceeds this limit. Extending the network is not an option.

Solution: Connect devices to an intermediary DEVICE GATEWAY that translates the communication technology supported by the device to communication technology of the network and vice-versa.

Result: A DEVICE GATEWAY is usually a dedicated hardware appliance that can translate between a number of heterogeneous communication technologies. In many cases, it will be located at the edge of the network, close to the devices that it connects to the backend. It is possible to integrate a DEVICE GATEWAY into the backend, but this is often not practical. It is often used to translate low-power short-range communication to IP communication, so it has to be located close to these devices, whereas the backend is usually located far away in a data center (Fig. 4).

For communication translation, it has to support at least two, but more commonly multiple communication technologies. On the interface towards the backend it usually supports IP communication over Ethernet, Wi-Fi, or mobile networks. On the interfaces towards the devices, it usually supports some kind of low energy communication technology. Depending on its application, it might also contain additional interfaces supporting other protocols. A translation layer converts messages received from either the backend or the devices to messages that can be sent to the respective opponent interface and vice versa. To be able to route the messages to their intended receivers the messages have to container some kind of identifier.

Benefits:

- **Connectivity:** Devices that do not directly support the networks communication technology can be connected to the network.
- **Separation of Concerns:** Device implementations can focus on only one arbitrary protocol or technology, which makes them simpler. On the other hand, the DEVICE GATEWAY can be optimized for protocol translation.
- **Effort:** One DEVICE GATEWAY can support multiple different communication technologies. The devices do not have to be modified.

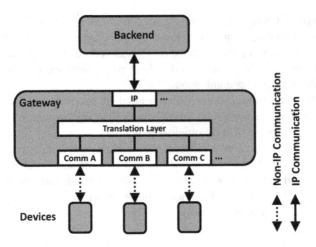

Fig. 4. Exemplary sketch of the DEVICE GATEWAY pattern used to transform to and from IP communication.

- **Cost:** Many devices can be connected to a network via one DEVICE GATEWAY, without needing to support multiple communication technologies over the whole network, which saves costs.
- **Reusability:** It might be possible to reuse existing hardware as a DEVICE GATEWAY, for example, smartphones or routers, which might further decrease the effort and cost needed.
- **Technological Limitations:** Devices can use very limited communication technology in the form of a specifically reduced software stack. Therefore, they can exploit their limited power elsewhere, while still being able to connect to a network that requires more sophisticated technology through a DEVICE GATEWAY.
- **Additional Functionality:** A DEVICE GATEWAY might have enough resources to be able to implement additional functionality, such as management or monitoring capabilities, data aggregation or filtering, or enhanced security mechanisms.
- **Resilience:** A DEVICE GATEWAY with additional local functionality, like a RULES ENGINE and a backup battery, can add a layer of resilience and keep local processes running regardless of power or network outages and backend server failures.

Drawbacks:

- **Connectivity:** The DEVICE GATEWAY might become a single point of failure for the network connectivity of the connected devices. Adding redundant DEVICE GATEWAYS with a failover mechanism could alleviate this problem, but at an increased cost.
- **Security:** As a single point of attack, the DEVICE GATEWAY also poses a security risk. If compromised, an attacker could gain access to all attached devices or the backend server.

- **Complexity:** Another layer of components is introduced that has to be managed and maintained. This becomes even more difficult if multiple kinds of gateways are used.
- **Cost:** The DEVICE GATEWAY usually has to support multiple communication technologies and, thus, needs more processing power, which makes it expensive. In addition, if devices are distributed, possibly multiple DEVICE GATEWAYS are required to connect all of them. Costs might be reduced by using a modular DEVICE GATEWAY design, where only the required technologies can be added with extension boards.
- **Compatibility:** Some technologies might be incompatible on a conceptual level. A DEVICE GATEWAY might only be able to create a partial translation between these technologies, or it might not be able to translate between certain technologies at all.

Variants: Common variants of a pure DEVICE GATEWAY usually include some kind of local processing power. Some examples are listed below. They are not mutually exclusive and can be combined.

- **Aggregating Device Gateway:** Besides translating communication technologies this gateway also aggregates the messages it receives from the devices in some meaningful way. For example, it might average the temperature readings of several devices and send it on once a minute. This is usually done to reduce the number of individual messages that have to be sent to the backend.
- **Local Processing Device Gateway:** In addition to translating communication technologies, this gateway also contains some local processing functionality, which could mirror or replace functionality located in the backend. For example, it could contain a local RULES ENGINE, which decides some actions directly on the gateway. This is usually done to minimize communication with the backend and therefore reduce latency or to insulate from connection loss between gateway and backend.

Related Patterns:

- MESSAGE GATEWAY: The MESSAGE GATEWAY pattern is similar to the DEVICE GATEWAY, but describes how one or more gateways can be used to combine several different messaging technologies in a single machine [38].
- ADAPTER: The DEVICE GATEWAY can be seen as a physical version of the ADAPTER pattern that describes how two incompatible interfaces can work together by converting one interface to the other [24].
- RULES ENGINE: A DEVICE GATEWAY might contain a RULES ENGINE to trigger actions locally. This can prevent unnecessary round trips to a remote server and might decrease latency.
- REMOTE DEVICE MANAGEMENT: A DEVICE GATEWAY might act as a management client for *Constrained Devices* connected to it when using the *Remote Client* variant of REMOTE DEVICE MANAGEMENT.

Examples: Central hubs are a common occurrence in the product portfolios of home automation companies. Here, they often act as an indispensable central point for integrating and managing the actual home automation devices. Examples are the Samsung SmartThings Hub [39] which supports ZigBee, Z-Wave, and IP, or the Wink

Hub [40] that additionally supports Bluetooth Low Energy and Lutron Clear Connect[9]. The SmartThings Hub v2 also introduced local processing capabilities, which is also supported by other DEVICE GATEWAYS like the THNGHUB [41]. Various companies offer development kits and appliances to implement DEVICE GATEWAYS for industrial use, such as Intel, Dell, or Nexcom [42–44]. The Eclipse Kura project is an Open Source framework for building the software side of DEVICE GATEWAYS [45]. Zachariah et al. [46] proposed to use smartphones with Bluetooth Low Energy as universal gateways for other devices. In a way, smartphones are already used as DEVICE GATEWAYS for many wearable devices, like fitness trackers or smartwatches, which completely rely on the smartphone to communicate the data they collected to the backend. Many IoT platform documentations mention physical hubs or field gateways as a way to connect devices to their platforms that cannot connect to the internet on their own, even though they do not offer any products or solutions in this space [47–51]. Thus, these follow the idea of DEVICE GATEWAYS.

5.2 Device Shadow

Aliases: Thing Shadow, Virtual Device.

Context: Devices, such as *Constrained Devices*, *Semi-Constrained Devices*, and *Unconstrained Devices*, might operate in *Normally-Off*, *Low-Power*, or *Always-On* modes. Either because of their operation modes or because of external circumstances, these devices might be offline at various times.

Problem: Some devices will be only intermittently online in order to save energy or because of network outages. Other components want to interact with them but do not know when they will be reachable.

Forces:

- **Availability:** Sending commands to or reading state from offline devices is not possible.
- **Timeliness:** Waiting for currently offline device to come online again to send or receive data in a synchronous fashion can lead to long idle times and should be avoided.
- **Consistency:** Often a slightly out-of-date state is better than no state.

---

[9] http://www.lutron.com/en-US/Residential-Commercial-Solutions/Pages/Residential-Solutions/IntegrationConnectivity.aspx (last accessed on 13.06.2018).

Solution: Store a persistent virtual representation of each device on some backend server. Include the latest received state from the device, as well as commands not yet sent to the device. Do all communication from and to the device through this virtual version. Synchronize the virtual representation with the actual device state when the device is online.

Result: By storing persistent virtual representations of the devices on the backend server and communicating only through those, device communication can be decoupled. This allows reading device state as well as sending device commands even if the device is offline (Fig. 5). Essential to this is a persistent storage on the backend that can store virtual device representations reliably for many devices and that can handle read and write access from multiple sources. If commands are saved, they should be queued, unless only the newest command is regarded as relevant. When a device reconnects to the backend, which can happen according to a schedule or based on certain events, it can retrieve and process the stored command and update the last known state. To let other components know that a device is online, a flag can be stored with the device shadow. When a device connects or gracefully disconnects it enables or disables this flag itself. Otherwise, the flag is set to false after a certain time of inactivity or by another mechanism, for example by the last will and testament of the Message Queue Telemetry Transport (MQTT)[10] protocol.

Conceivably, DEVICE SHADOW functionality could also be implemented on DEVICE GATEWAYS to allow localized decoupling between devices connected to one DEVICE GATEWAY. This would bring the benefits of a DEVICE SHADOW to these devices, even if the Gateway might be disconnected from the rest of the network from time to time. A problem here could be that a DEVICE GATEWAY might not be able to provide the reliable persistent storage that is needed.

Benefits:

- **Unified Handling:** The communication with devices can be handled as if they are *Always-On*, even if they really are not. Therefore, time autonomy between backend and devices is established.
- **Additional Functionality:** If all communication goes through a DEVICE SHADOW, additional functionality can be implemented, such as batch messaging, filtering, or caching.
- **Security:** By only communicating with a single, well-known target, security can be increased, because devices can categorically deny communication attempts from any other source.

---

[10] http://mqtt.org/ (last accessed on 13.06.2018).

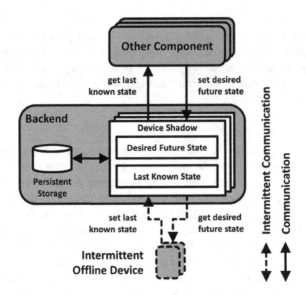

Fig. 5. Sketch of the DEVICE SHADOW pattern.

Drawbacks:

- **Eventual Consistency:** The virtual device representation is only eventually consistent with its actual state.
- **Synchronization Issues:** State updates could be lost if a new state update is written to the device shadow that is based on a state that is older than the current last known state. One way to avoid such issues is versioning the states and using OPTIMISTIC OFFLINE LOCK [52]. Other issues include transactional synchronization and issues depending on the semantics of the synchronized data.
- **Obsolescence:** By the time an offline device reconnects and receives stored commands, these commands might have become obsolete. In the same way, sensor values or other data send by the device to the Device Shadow may be too old to be useful by the time the device synchronizes. To avoid stale commands and data, the MESSAGE EXPIRATION pattern [25] can be used.
- **Quality of Service**: If all communication is forced through the backend server, latency and decreased availability for communication that could be done locally can be a problem.

Related Patterns:

- **Remote Proxy:** Gamma et al. describe remote proxy as one application of the PROXY pattern. Here, the remote proxy locally represents an object in another address space to hide the fact that the object is remote [24]. DEVICE SHADOW can be seen as a device specific version of a remote proxy.

Examples: AWS IoT stores a persistent virtual version of each connected device that includes the last reported state and the desired future state of the device. This allows applications to read and write device state irrespective of the actual availability of the device [53, 54]. Azure IoT Suite stores device models in a device registry that is an eventually consistent view of device data [55]. Kii IoT Platform's Thing Interaction Framework saves the latest state of registered things on the backend server. Applications that request a device's state get the state stored on the server [56].

5.3   Rules Engine

Aliases: Action Engine, Trigger Conditions.

Context: A wide range of differing messages from devices and other components are received at the backend server. These might include measurements from sensors, errors, a heartbeat, registration information, etc. These messages can arrive regularly or irregularly. There are different kinds of actions that have to be executed depending on the type of the received message, its content, the time it is received, or other factors.

Problem: Throughout its operation, a system receives a wide range of messages from devices and other components. You want to react in different ways to these messages.

Forces:

- **Flexibility:** The actions to trigger might change over time, new actions might be added, old ones removed, or you might want to temporarily test or disable an action. Hard-coding them into some software component would be possible, but is not flexible enough.
- **Data Sources:** In some cases, additional data apart from the device message might be needed to decide if a particular action should be taken.
- **Diversity:** The type of action to be triggered can vary significantly depending on the circumstances. In some cases, you might want to add an entry into a log file or send an email. In other cases, you might want to route a message to another service for further processing or store it in some kind of database.

Solution: Pass all messages received from devices through a RULES ENGINE. Allow non-programmers to define and manage rules using a graphical user interface. Provide an API for programmers. Use these rules to evaluate the content of incoming messages or metadata about the message against a set of comparators. Allow external data sources to be included in these comparisons. Let users associate a set of actions with these rules. Apply each rule on each message and trigger the associated actions if a rule matches.

Result: A Rules Engine contains a set of rules and actions that should be executed if a particular rule is met. Usually, these rules and associated actions are user definable through a graphical user interface on the backend server, which allows non-programmers to implement and manage these rules. But an API may provide developers with more flexible options. Another possibility is to provide a domain specific language (DSL) for creating the rules. During operation, each incoming message is compared against these rules. If a rule matches, the associated action is triggered. Rules Engines are often located on a central backend server but can also be located on a Device Gateway.

The rules usually allow comparing incoming data to static values, historical data, data from other sources, or a combination thereof. Different comparators allow a user to check if incoming data is, e.g., equal to, unequal to, larger than, or smaller than a certain value, or if it contains a certain value. Regular expressions or SQL statements might be allowed for comparisons that are more complex. Rule matching for a particular message could be stopped after the first match, or it could be continued until all rules are evaluated. It could also be possible to let a rule trigger only once and never again, or only once in a specific time window.

Actions can vary in their scope and complexity. Simple actions might trigger some functionality that is built into the platform that is used, such as sending an alert to a user. They might also act as a router that passes data on to services on the same backend server or to external services of other companies for further processing. One rule could only trigger one action, but it could also be possible to associate multiple actions to one rule that then could be executed in serial or in parallel (Fig. 6).

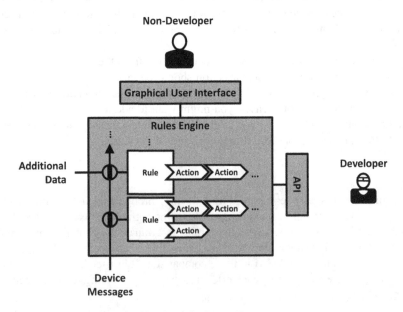

Fig. 6. Sketch of the Rules Engine pattern.

Benefits:

- **Flexibility:** Rules can be flexibly added, changed, temporarily disabled, or removed, because they are not hard-coded into software.
- **Ease of Use:** A graphical user interface allows non-programmers to manage rules.
- **Configurability:** The RULES ENGINE usually offers a wide range of options for how to evaluate the rules and trigger the actions, but users without extensive programming knowledge can configure simple rules.
- **Automation:** A RULES ENGINE allows creating automatic responses for certain situations.
- **Analytics:** A RULES ENGINE might track certain values to enable monitoring and analytics on the messages it receives and the rules and actions that are or are not triggered.

Drawbacks:

- **Suitability:** Depending on the functionality offered by the inbuilt rules and actions, a RULES ENGINE might not be suitable for certain complex transformation or routing tasks. A possible way to mitigate this drawback is to support user defined rules and actions via some scripting language.
- **Configurability:** While simple rules are easy to configure, complex rules might require more insight or special training.
- **Security:** A compromised or misconfigured RULES ENGINE can be a security risk.
- **Single Point of Failure:** If all messaged are passed through a RULES ENGINE it becomes a single point of failure.
- **Effort:** Creating and maintaining good rules might be a lot of work. Creating a marketplace for rules could be one solution to decrease effort and duplication and increase efficiency.

Related Patterns:

- PRODUCTION RULE SYSTEM: As described by Fowler [57], a PRODUCTION RULE SYSTEM organizes logic into a set of rules, where each rule has a condition and an action. While the PRODUCTION RULE SYSTEM is just a formalism to represent and organize logic into rules and conditions, the RULES ENGINE is the component that controls the execution of these rules.
- CONTENT BASED ROUTER: A RULES ENGINE can be seen as an extended CONTENT BASED ROUTER as described by Hohpe and Woolf [25]. A CONTENT BASED ROUTER examines only the message content and then routes the message to exactly one system. A RULES ENGINE can route to multiple systems based on the message content, other data, or a combination thereof.
- REMOTE DEVICE MANAGEMENT: A RULES ENGINE can be used on the management server to automate certain management tasks.

Examples: The AWS IoT Platform includes a RULES ENGINE that can transform and deliver inbound messages to other devices or Cloud services. Its rules can be applied to multiple data sources at once and multiple actions can be triggered in parallel. The rules can be created in an SQL-like syntax [53]. IBM IoT Real-Time Insights has an action engine that lets users define automated responses to detected conditions. Inbuilt actions include sending an email, triggering an IFTTT[11] recipe, or executing a Node-RED[12] workflow. Arbitrary other web services can be included with webhooks [58]. Many other IoT Platforms also include a Rules Engine [56, 59–63]. There are also standalone services like Waylay, IFTTT, and Zapier or apps like Stringify that offer RULES ENGINE functionality without a complete IoT platform [64–67]. Some RULES ENGINES, like EVRYTHNG's Reactor, can be located on DEVICE GATEWAYS to enable low latency message processing close to the devices [41].

5.4   Device Wakeup Trigger

Aliases: Update Trigger, Device Triggering.

Context: You have a *Constrained Device* or *Semi-Constrained Device* that is *Lifetime Energy-Limited* or *Period Energy-Limited* and operates in a *Low-Power or Normally-Off* mode. You have a backend server where the device is registered, i.e., the server knows its identity and other metadata. From time to time, you have a situation where you want to contact the sleeping device immediately. For example, this could be the case if a critical security fix has to be applied, if you need current sensor values or send commands for one-off time critical situations, or if the device has been lost or stolen and you want to use REMOTE LOCK AND WIPE immediately.

Problem: Some devices might go into a sleep mode to conserve energy and only wake up from time to time to reconnect to the network. During sleep, they are not reachable on their regular communication channels. In some instances, other components may have to contact a sleeping device immediately.

Forces:

- **Irregularity:** You need to establish a connection at non-regular times.
- **Predictability:** You do not know the point in time when you need to connect to the device in advance.
- **Timeliness:** The device might reconnect on its own, but you cannot wait that long.
- **Power Consumption:** The device has to maintain low power consumption in terms of entering *Low-Power* or *Normally-Off* operation modes to save energy.

Solution: Implement a mechanism that allows the server to send a trigger message to the device via a low energy communication channel. Have the device listening for these triggering messages and immediately establish communication with the server when it receives such a message.

---

[11] https://ifttt.com/ (last accessed on 13.06.2018).

[12] http://nodered.org/ (last accessed on 13.06.2018).

Result: A triggerable device can be in a *Low-Power* or *Normally-Off*[13] operation mode, where most of its functionality is dormant. However, it is still listening on a specific communication channel for triggering messages using a low energy communication module. When a server wants to wake up a device, it has to know the device and this channel in advance. Therefore, a prerequisite for the DEVICE WAKEUP TRIGGER is that the device has previously registered some kind of identifier and its listening channel with the backend server. This can either be done manually when the server or the device is provisioned, or it could be done automatically by the device when it communicates with the server.

If the server wants to initiate communication with a triggerable device, it looks up the device in its registry and uses the stored information to send a trigger message to the channel that the device is listening on. The trigger message can contain a payload, e.g., to trigger some specific action on the device after the wake-up. Depending on the content and the existence of a payload, the triggered device might react in two ways: (i) If a payload was sent, it can process it and send a response to the server without establishing a long lasting connection (piggybacked response). (ii) If no payload was sent or the payload indicates that further communication is needed, the device can establish a long lasting connection to the server and wait for further instructions. The maximum time to wait for further instructions can be configured by a timeout, either directly on the device or in the payload of the wake-up message (Fig. 7).

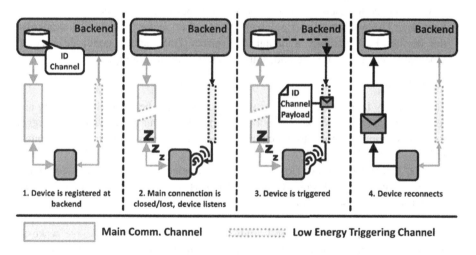

1. Device is registered at backend
2. Main connection is closed/lost, device listens
3. Device is triggered
4. Device reconnects

Main Comm. Channel   Low Energy Triggering Channel

Fig. 7. Sketch of the DEVICE WAKEUP TRIGGER pattern.

---

[13] The device can be NORMALLY-OFF when a passive trigger mechanism, such as passive RFID is used [68].

Benefits:

- **Efficiency:** If no constant connection has to be kept alive, it allows the device to operate in a *Low-Power* or *Normally-Off* mode where the only active component is a low energy communication module listening for trigger messages.
- **Responsiveness:** Even though the device can be in a *Low-Power* or *Normally-Off* operation mode most of the time, it can be triggered to reconnect at any time if needed.

Drawbacks:

- **Efficiency:** At least the communication module has to be active to listen for triggering messages. To maximize efficiency, a very low power communication module should be used to listen for trigger messages. There are also passive RFID-based modules that eliminate this drawback but at a loss of range compared to active modules [68].
- **Cost:** There might be costs associated with sending a trigger message, for example, when using SMS to trigger devices.
- **Infrastructure:** New infrastructure might be needed on the server side for a low energy communication channel, which is only used for device triggering.
- **Effort:** The device needs a second communication circuit which increases cost and complexity.
- **Responsiveness:** Although it is possible to wake up the device when needed, the wakeup procedure itself takes some time that should be accounted for.
- **Security:** The wakeup triggering channel is another vector for potential attacks on the device. For example, a denial of service (DoS) attack could be used to repeatedly wake up a device and, thus, quickly drain its battery.

Related Patterns:

- CORRELATION IDENTIFIER: A CORRELATION IDENTIFIER can be used when sending and replying to a DEVICE WAKEUP TRIGGER so that the server from which the trigger message originated knows to which trigger message the answer it received belongs [25].
- VISIBLE LIGHT COMMUNICATION: One way to implement a low-energy communication channel for a DEVICE WAKEUP TRIGGER is a circuit with a photodiode and VISIBLE LIGHT COMMUNICATION.

Examples: There have been several studies proposing active and passive wake-up receivers [68]. In general, active receivers provide remote wakeup capabilities at higher ranges while using some energy, while passive receivers use no energy but sacrifice range. One example is RFID, which is passive and low range. It's range can be extended by adding a power source to the receiver and, thus, turning it into active RFID [68, 69]. Device Triggering was introduced in release 11 of the 3rd Generation Partnership Project (3GPP) as a way to allow server initiated communication with UMTS or LTE devices when their IP address is not known. SMS is used as triggering mechanism, but a direct response to the payload is not supported [70]. 3GPP2 also supports Device Triggering using SMS, broadcast SMS, or IP transport [71].

OneM2 M uses these mechanics to trigger devices to wake them up, to force them to establish a connection to the server, or when their IP address is not known [72]. Starsinic et al. [73] argue that LTE devices always have an IP address and using SMS as triggering mechanism makes applications using a DEVICE WAKEUP TRIGGER more platform dependent, because they always need to support SMS. Additionally, the lack of direct response to a trigger message requires devices to always establish a connection, which may be inefficient in cases where a simple reply to the trigger messages would have been sufficient. They propose an IP-based triggering method that is LTE backwards compatible and utilizes UDP packages. It supports direct responses to triggering messages, for example by using CoAP confirmable data packages. Open Mobile Alliance Lightweight Machine to Machine (OMA LWM2 M) supports an update trigger mechanism where the server can wake up devices via SMS. An LWM2 M client can disconnect if it does not receive a message after a certain time but stays reachable via SMS. The LWM2 M server queues operations for the client while it is offline. The server can send an update trigger message via SMS to the client. After the client received the SMS it reconnects and receives the queued operations [17]. The CPE WAN Management Protocol, also known as TR-069, includes a mechanism called asynchronous auto-configuration server-initiated notifications. It allows a configuration server to instruct a device to establish a connection with the server when a new configuration is available [18]. Examples of products are the PawTrax pet trackers. They stay in a sleep mode to save energy until activated by SMS. As a piggyback response, they send the current location of the pet, but they can also be switched to periodically send the location to an app or web platform [74].

5.5   Remote Lock and Wipe

Aliases: Remote Factory Reset, Remote Locking, Remote Wiping.

Context: A device is connected to a backend server and is in danger of being lost or stolen. This might be the case because it is installed at an easily accessible public location, or a remote and unmonitored location. The device might have functionality that must not be accessed by a thief. It might also contain classified data that has to be kept protected. The data might or might not be encrypted. The device might be retrievable when it is lost or stolen, but it might also vanish forever.

Problem: Some devices might be lost or stolen. You want to prevent attackers from misusing the functionality of the device, or from gaining access to the data on the device or to the network through the device.

Forces:

- **Long-term Data Security:** If the device is irretrievably stolen, an attacker might have ample time to break encryptions if data on the device is encrypted.

- **Fine-grained Control:** Depending on the situation, the type of device and the content on the device, different actions might be necessary in the case of loss or theft.
- **Reversibility:** A lost or stolen device might eventually be returned, so any actions taken should be reversible if possible.
- **Remote Control:** Since the device is no longer physically available, the activation of additional security mechanisms has to work remotely.

Solution: Make the device a managed device that can receive and execute management operations from the backend server. Allow authorized users to use the backend server to trigger functionality on the device that can delete files, folders, applications or memory areas, revoke or remove permissions, keys, and certificates, or enable additional security feature. Execute triggered functions as soon as the device receives them and provide acknowledgment to the backend.

Result: To be able to offer REMOTE LOCK AND WIPE functionality, a device has to be a managed device that is connected to a management backend, which is a component on the backend server that can remotely execute management functionality on the device. This can be achieved by applying REMOTE DEVICE MANAGEMENT. Once an authorized user successfully authenticated to the backend, he or she can choose between different lock or wipe options depending on the circumstances (Fig. 8). Which exact options are provided depends on the particular device. The device should provide a list of lockable or deletable data and functionality to the backend server.

In some circumstances, it might be enough to disable only some functionality but leave on location tracking to facilitate the retrieval of a lost or stolen device. The user might also only erase certain sensitive data to prevent data theft. In more severe cases, he or she might reset the device to its factory state, which would leave it operational but without any data on it. He or she might also completely disable the device to make it unusable.

Wiping data can be done by utilizing existing functionality to delete files and folders, or by directly deleting certain memory areas. Data can also be encrypted with a key stored on the device, which is used by applications to access this data. When this key is deleted, access to this data is effectively revoked. Functionality can be locked by revoking permissions, keys, or certificates that are required for execution, or by enabling security checks that were previously not enabled. Functionality could also be completely removed by deleting the associated code from the device. Once the requested operations are executed, the device should send back an acknowledgment to the backend server if possible.

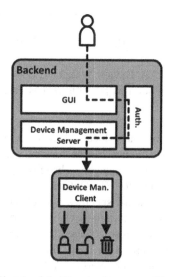

Fig. 8. Sketch of the REMOTE LOCK AND WIPE pattern.

Benefits:

- **Long-Term Data Security:** Wiping sensitive data from the device prevents an attacker from stealing the data, even when he has enough time to circumvent some kind of encryption.
- **Fine-grained Control:** Partially or fully locking or wiping and full factory reset allow reactions appropriate to the situation and the sensitivity of the data on the device, or its functionality.
- **Reversibility:** Locked device functionality can be unlocked if the device is retrieved.
- **Remote Action:** To execute lock and wipe functionality the device does not have to be under physical control. It only has to be connected to the backend so that the lock and wipe functionality can be triggered.

Drawbacks:

- **Reversibility:** Wiped data and a factory reset cannot be reversed. A backup mechanism could be used to be able to restore at least some data.
- **Connectivity:** The device has to be connected to receive the REMOTE LOCK AND WIPE commands. A DEVICE WAKEUP TRIGGER could be used to get the device to connect to the backend server.
- **Security:** If attackers gain access to the REMOTE LOCK AND WIPE functionality they could lock devices for ransom or wipe or disable them to cause damage. Proper authentication and authorization mechanisms, as well as end-to-end encryption, should be used at all times.

Related Patterns:

- **REMOTE DEVICE MANAGEMENT**: REMOTE LOCK AND WIPE is a specific use case of REMOTE DEVICE MANAGEMENT.
- **DEVICE WAKEUP TRIGGER**: A DEVICE WAKEUP TRIGGER could be used to get the device locked or wiped as soon as possible if it is currently not connected to the backend server.

Examples: Functionality to remotely locate, lock or wipe a phone is common on modern smartphones. Android phones can be located, set to ring, locked, or erased remotely with the Android Device Manager website or app [75]. Apple offers similar functionality through the iCloud [76, 77]. Options for other kinds of devices do also exist. The OMA LWM2 M standard specifies a Lock and Wipe object. It supports functionality for partially or fully locking a device, for partially or fully wiping data on a device, and for doing a factory reset. These operations can be performed with or without user confirmation or notification [17]. The Kii IoT Platform allows users to lock and unlock devices over their web interface. When locked, the device is not able to access its data resources in the Cloud, while the owner and admin users still have access to these resources [78]. TR-069 and the IBM IoT Foundation Platform both support remote factory reset functionality [18, 79].

5.6 Delta Update

Aliases: Delta State, Delta Records.

Context: You have devices with which you communicate using messages. The network they use to communicate has limited bandwidth. You want to add new devices to the network but you do not want to overwhelm the network. You cannot extend or change the network.

Problem: You want to reduce the size of messages containing sensor data without losing any information.

Forces:

- **Message Size:** You want to reduce the size of messages to fit more messages in existing connections but you do not want to lose any information.
- **Compression:** Compression alone does not give the desired results or using compression is impossible because you use severely *Constrained Devices*.
- **Structure:** Messages can have structured or unstructured content but in your case they have a common structure with multiple identifiable fields.
- **Repetition:** The messages may contain values that have been sent before without a change.

Solution: Store the last message sent. Calculate the delta from the current data to this message. Also, calculate a hash of the current full data set. Send only the delta and the hash to the receiver. Let the receiver merge the delta with its current state and check, if it matches the received hash.

Result: DELTA UPDATES reduce message size without losing information as they contain only the data that has changed since the last communication, but not more. As such, they need messages to have a common structure, which has multiple identifiable fields whose values do not change at once. Examples are devices that periodically send multiple sensor values. Other examples are backend servers that send configuration messages to devices to adjust their settings. If such messages are sent with values that have not changed, DELTA UPDATES reduce their size by omitting these unchanged values.

To send a DELTA UPDATE, the sender first has to calculate the delta, as shown in Fig. 9, step 1 and 4. The sender does this based on the data it wants to be sent, for example, a set of sensor values or configuration parameters. The delta is the difference between the latest full data set and the last data set that the sender communicated. Thus, the sender has to store two or more full data sets: The current data set and the last communicated data set for each communication partner. The exact algorithm for calculating the delta depends on the format of the data set. The resulting delta is empty if there were no changes to the data since the last communication. The delta is equal to the current data set if every value changed since the last update. If a value disappeared since the last update, the DELTA UPDATE has to include this change. One solution is to mark such a value with a reserved word to let the receiver know it has to delete this value.

Besides the delta, the sender calculates the hash value of its current full data set. It sends this value together with the delta to the intended receiver, as shown in step 2 and 5. The receiver merges the delta into its latest version of the dataset, as shown in step 3 and 6. The exact algorithm for merging the delta depends on the format of the data set. To make sure the data is consistent the receiver calculates the hash value of the resulting merged data set. If this hash value is equal to the hash value in the DELTA UPDATE the update was successful. Otherwise, the receiver asks the sender for a full update to synchronize their states.

The communication frequency for DELTA UPDATES varies depending on the use case. One way is to send DELTA UPDATES periodically at fixed intervals, regardless of changes. If there have been no changes since the last update, an empty Delta State message is comparable to a heartbeat and is thus no unnecessary overhead. Another way is to send DELTA UPDATES event-based. In this case, the sender emits a DELTA UPDATE when an event occurs, for example, if a sensor value has changed. A third way is to send a DELTA UPDATE once a parameter reaches a threshold. This limits communication to those situations where a relevant change has happened.

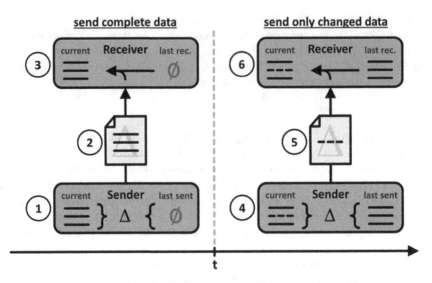

Fig. 9. Sketch of the DELTA UPDATE pattern.

Benefits:

- **Message Size:** Messages are smaller as they no longer contain any unnecessary data.
- **Information:** Messages do not loose information. They still contain the data that has changed since the last communication and only omit data which has not changed.
- **Bandwidth:** The decreased message size lowers the bandwidth required on involved components, such as devices, DEVICE GATEWAYS, etc.
- **Energy Consumption:** Communication is the biggest energy consumer on *Constrained Devices*. DELTA UPDATES are smaller than full updates and thus devices need less time to send them. This, in turn, allows devices to switch off communication modules for longer periods, which lowers their energy consumption.

Drawbacks:

- **Suitability:** DELTA UPDATES may not be suited for data that does not contain an identifiable structure which allows an algorithm to create and merge in deltas.
- **Data Consistency:** If messages containing DELTA UPDATE get lost, and the receiver merges a later message, the updates from the lost message are not present in the dataset. This leaves the receiver in an inconsistent state. To prevent this, use hash values to check for data consistency or reliable messaging technologies for transportation.
- **Increased Storage:** The sender has to store the last sent data set for each of its communication partners. Depending on the number of communication partners, this increases the storage space required by orders of magnitude. *Constrained Devices* with severe storage limitations may not have the required storage space.

- **Incompatibility:** Sending DELTA UPDATES leads to problems with communication patterns where receivers are not directly addressable. For example, a PubSub network distributes one message to multiple receivers. If a hash check fails and the receiver requests a full update, the network distributes the update to every receiver. If one hash check fails with each update this leads to more messages than before. Therefore, if multiple receivers are involved, they need a way to communicate with senders directly in case of data inconsistencies.

Examples: Libelium [80] mentions DELTA UPDATE in its Waspmote programmer guide. They describe sending only changed data as one way to lower the power consumption of the communication module. The OMA LWM2 M standard [81] describes a client registration update operation. When executed, this operation sends the parameters that have changed since the last update. The Kaa IoT platform [82] uses delta messages to send configuration updates to endpoints. They make sure the data is consistent by comparing hashes between endpoint and server.

5.7   Remote Device Management

Aliases: Device Management.

Context: You have a large number of devices, which need to be managed throughout their lifecycle. From time to time, you have to update the firmware or software installed on the device, or adjust configuration values. The locations of the devices are remote, or hard- or dangerous-to-reach.

Problem: You want to manage a large number of devices remotely.

Forces:

- **Location:** You have devices located in remote or dangerous areas. The placement of the devices makes management on location difficult.
- **Scalability:** You have to manage a large number of devices. Manual work does not scale for these numbers.
- **Outsourcing:** Device management is not part of your core business. You want the ability to have a third party to do the device management for you.
- **Security:** Managing devices includes handling sensitive information such as passwords. You want this information to stay secure.

Solution: Set up a management server on the backend. Add management clients to the device which you want to manage. Send management command from the server to the client and have the client execute these commands locally on the device.

Result: REMOTE DEVICE MANAGEMENT enables a remote party to execute management procedures on devices. If desired, even a third party is able to manage the devices. Otherwise, the device user, operator, owner, vendor, or a combination of them handles management. For example, router modems provided by internet service providers to customers include functionality, which enables the provider to set up the router remotely. However, users are able to override these settings with a local web interface or remote management interfaces accessible via the web or mobile apps.

Available management operations vary from device to device. The ability to create, read, update, and delete configuration values remotely enables managers to initially configure devices and adjust them to changing surroundings. Functionality for downloading and updating firmware and software on the device keeps versions up-to-date and allows quick reaction to security vulnerabilities. Besides, it allows the introduction of new features after you have installed the device. Other functionalities, such as remote rebooting and factory resets, are helpful for troubleshooting.

REMOTE DEVICE MANAGEMENT provides this remote management functionality with a client-server architecture. It involves three key components as shown in Fig. 10: One or several management server, management clients, and a connection between them. The management servers are used to send management commands to the management clients. They handle authentication and authorization to ensure that only users or applications with proper authorization are able to trigger management commands. Other components are able to trigger management commands if a management server offers an external application programming interface (API). Users access the server through a graphical user interface, which allows them access to the management operations. The management server has the ability to store multiple device configurations and to give an overview of manageable devices. Users select existing configurations or create new ones, change them if needed, and apply them to one or more devices.

The messages containing the management commands are sent using a device management protocol. It is a bi-directional protocol where the server sends a command and receives a response when the device has processed the command. These commands are not timed out because the server cannot predict the time that a device needs to process a command. It has to be secure since management messages involve confidential data. End-to-end encryption is one solution that offers this security. Usually, there are many different devices connected to one management server and these devices may support different management protocols. Thus, the management server also has to be able to support different management protocols. This can be done with a plugin architecture, where a common internal representation of the management commands is translated into the required management protocols.

A device management model defines the parameters and functions, which are manageable and executable by the management server. It comprises a set of generic features common to devices, such as changing configuration values, updating the firmware, or doing a factory reset. Besides, vendors are able to extend and customize it for vendor-specific functionality.

The management client is a piece of software, which runs directly on a device and receives management messages from the server. The client translates the generic message format into the specific actions, which are necessary to execute the management operations on the device. It executes these operations on the device and sends a response to the server. A device managed by such a client is a *Managed Device*.

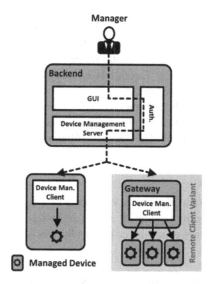

Fig. 10. Sketch of the REMOTE DEVICE MANAGEMENT pattern.

Benefits:

- **Remote Management:** Managers do not have to physically go to a device to change its configuration.
- **Decoupling:** The employed management protocol and model can hide differences between devices. This decouples the device management commands on the server from their implementation on the devices.
- **Regular Updates:** REMOTE DEVICE MANAGEMENT enables managers to apply regular updates to firmware and software on devices. This reduces the risk of devices with outdated and insecure software on them.
- **Bulk Management:** Managers do not have to manage devices individually. REMOTE DEVICE MANAGEMENT enables bulk management of devices, where the server applies changes to a large number of devices.
- **Automation:** Managers do not have to trigger management operations manually. A RULES ENGINE allows automatic management by triggering management operations, for example, when a device connects for the first time.

Drawbacks:

- **Security:** The management server, the clients, and the communication between them create new attack vectors. One solution to limit exposure is to use outbound-only communication for devices where they start communication and do not accept connection requests.
- **Scalability:** Sending bulk management operations to a large number of devices without limitations overwhelms networks with limited bandwidth. Bulk campaigns prevent this as they divide large bulk operations into smaller parts and issue these commands in stages. Besides, if the server sends pending notifications to a device that reconnects after a longer period of time, the number of notifications may overwhelm the device. One solution is to queue these notifications and have the device retrieve them one by one when it is ready.
- **Connectivity:** *Constrained Devices* cannot keep up connections because of power constraints. A DEVICE WAKEUP TRIGGER is one solution to tell devices when they need to connect to the server.
- **Compatibility:** Multiple device management standards exist and vendors create custom implementations. Managing a heterogeneous group of devices requires a device management solution that handles different standards. However, this is complex to implement.

Related Patterns:

- **REMOTE LOCK AND WIPE:** REMOTE LOCK AND WIPE uses REMOTE DEVICE MANAGEMENT to implement security features. It allows authorized managers to remotely lock or wipe a device when it is no longer physically reachable due to loss or theft.

Variants:

- **Remote Client:** Severely *Constrained Devices* do not have the capabilities to run a resource-intensive management client. In such a case, other more capable devices in their vicinity host the client for them. For example, a DEVICE GATEWAY running a management client manages the *Constrained Devices* connected to it.

Examples: Multiple IoT platforms include remote device management functionality. IBM's Watson IoT platform includes a device management service. It communicates via a device management protocol based on Message Queuing Telemetry Transport (MQTT) with management agents located on the devices. The available management operations include location updates, firmware updates, as well as reboot and factory reset functionality [83]. Oracle mentions lifecycle management in its IoT Cloud Service documentation [84].

Multiple specifications and standards for device management exist. The Broadband Forum created the Customer Premise Equipment (CPE) Wide Area Network (WAN) Management Protocol, known as TR-069, for remote management of end-user devices. It includes an auto-configuration server, which automatically and dynamically provisions and configures devices based on criteria. These criteria include device specific requirements or general criteria, such as vendor, model, or software version.

Besides, the protocol has software and firmware management, monitoring, and diagnostics functionality [18].

The Open Mobile Alliance (OMA) defines the Device Management (DM) protocol for remote management of mobile devices. It includes functionality for provisioning, configuration, software upgrades, and fault management. A DM server controls these functions on the DM clients. It has the ability to trigger sessions, but the clients start the sessions themselves. The protocol defines a common core parameter set, but vendors who need specific functionality are able to extend the protocol [16].

OMA Lightweight Machine to Machine (LWM2M) is a protocol optimized for remote management of *Constrained Devices*. An LWM2M server communicates with LWM2M clients to reach management goals. These goals include device bootstrapping, registration, and management [81].

Nokia Motive Connected Device Platform is one solution that combines TR-069, OMA DM, and OMA LWM2M and other protocols into a single device management system. The platform automatically detects and configures devices. It is able to manage devices attached through gateways. Besides, its functionality includes remote firmware and software updates, diagnostics, fault management, and REMOTE LOCK AND WIPE [85, 86].

5.8   Visible Light Communication

Aliases: LiFi, Free-space Optical, Optical Wireless.

Context: Today, wireless communication uses the radio spectrum, which is a part of the electromagnetic spectrum, because of its beneficial properties. Humans cannot perceive this spectrum and its waves are not harmful to the environment. Depending on their frequency, they travel long distances and through objects. Organizations that manage the radio spectrum further divide it into frequency bands for specific purposes, for example, broadcasting, air, and marine communication, or radar. This leaves a limited amount of frequencies for wireless communication technologies such as WiFi or Bluetooth. As more and more devices communicate wirelessly, these limited radio bands become increasingly crowded. This is problematic in areas with dense connectivity, such as office or apartment buildings, or high traffic public areas.

Problem: You need to use wireless communication in a crowded area, but the limited radio spectrum and the interference from many other devices lead to performance problems, which you want to avoid.

Forces:

- **Wireless:** You have to use wireless communication because devices are mobile or because using cables is not an option.

- **Limited Spectrum:** The radio spectrum used for wireless communication is limited and increasingly crowded.
- **Safety:** Wireless communication technology has to be safe to use near humans and other lifeforms. Besides, the technology has to minimize adverse effects on machinery that is sensible to electromagnetic effects.
- **Security:** Wireless communication has to be secure to avoid attackers from eavesdropping or tampering with messages.
- **Speed:** You need communication speed comparable to wireless communication technologies such as Bluetooth or WiFi.
- **Cost:** You want to keep costs for wireless communication low.
- **Infrastructure:** Building up a new wireless communication network requires investment into infrastructure.
- **Communication Distance:** Communication technologies have different distances at which they are usable. Finding a suitable technology often requires trade-offs in other areas.

Solution: Use visible light for short distance wireless communication. Modulate messages into the light by turning the light on and off. Do it fast to not impede normal light usage and to be invisible to the human eye.

Result: Visible Light Communication (VLC) uses light in the visible spectrum between 380 to 720 nm wavelength to transport messages. A sender encodes a message into a sequence of binary states, similar to Morse code. It sends out the sequence by turning a light source on and off in rapid succession, thereby modulating the sequence into the light. A receiver near the light decodes the sequence and reads the message (Fig. 11).

Senders for Visible Light Communication make use of existing infrastructure. A large amount of today's wireless communication happens in densely populated and frequented areas, in particular in buildings. In these areas, light fixtures are densely deployed and suitably positioned for data transmission. Lights using Light Emitting Diodes (LED) are now increasingly used as light sources because of their beneficial properties. LEDs are cheap and reliable and support the rapid modulation which encoding messages into the light requires. Using other components, such as lasers, is an option, but is not a concern of this pattern.

Multiple options exist for the form factor of the sender. One option is to integrate the sender into the fixture, but this requires large infrastructure investments. Another option is to have the sender as a separate part and connect it to the fixture, which allows retrofitting of Visible Light Communication capabilities. A third option is to integrate the sender directly into LED lights.

The sender encodes messages into the lighting with intensity modulation. The modulation is not visible to the human eye since its frequency exceeds the flicker fusion threshold. Lights are dimmable by changing the relative periods of light and darkness. It is even workable to communicate data while the human eye perceives the light as off. Thus, VISIBLE LIGHT COMMUNICATION does not impede normal light functionality.

The receiver consists of a photodiode and a circuit for decoding the messages. Another option is to use a camera, for example, on a smartphone. Photodiodes support high-speed data reception while their framerate limits cameras to lower speeds. Cameras are able to extract data from multiple senders at once, which makes them great for positioning. They support positioning in three dimensions, including orientation, with high accuracy. Both photodiodes and cameras work with indirect light reflected from a surface, but direct line of sight to the sender is helpful. LED lights with integrated photodiodes act as both sender and receiver and thus enable bi-directional communication.

Hybrid systems exist which combine VISIBLE LIGHT COMMUNICATION with other wireless communication technologies, such as WiFi or Bluetooth. In these scenarios, the traditional wireless communication technologies act as backup when light communication is not working because of obfuscation. On the flip side, VISIBLE LIGHT COMMUNICATION frees up the wireless spectrum.

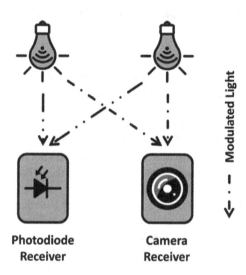

Fig. 11. Sketch of the VISIBLE LIGHT COMMUNICATION pattern.

Benefits:

- **Datarate:** The datarate benefits from the speed of light and is, thus, higher than in other wireless communication technologies that use radio waves.
- **Cost:** VISIBLE LIGHT COMMUNICATION uses low-cost off-the-shelf LEDs. Besides, it reuses existing lighting infrastructure, further reducing infrastructure cost. Energy cost is lower because the light has a dual functionality as it now additionally transports data.

- **Power:** Lights have a direct connection to power lines and, thus, do not need extra power sources. Besides, this allows you to combine them with Powerline Communication, where data is communicated over electrical wires [87].
- **Directional Propagation:** Directional propagation of light allows high spatial reuse and larger total network capacity.
- **Interference:** The visible light spectrum does not interfere with the radio spectrum. Opaque materials are one way to control and limit self-interference.
- **Safety:** Unlike other wireless communication technology, VISIBLE LIGHT COMMUNICATION does not cause electromagnetic interference. This makes it safe in areas where such interference is harmful and where authorities have banned other technologies, such as airplanes or hospitals. Besides, visible light does not pose a health risk.
- **Security:** Eavesdropping needs line-of-sight to the light source or a surface it illuminates. By confining the VISIBLE LIGHT COMMUNICATION to one room, security is controllable. Besides, security problems are identifiable as the communication channel is visible to the eye.
- **Localization:** Receivers are able to locate themselves using VISIBLE LIGHT COMMUNICATION. They use the strength of the received signal to calculate the distance to the transmitter.

Drawbacks:

- **Distance:** Long distance VISIBLE LIGHT COMMUNICATION becomes increasingly complicated to implement. Focused light needs to hit the receiver, which long distance solutions achieve with lasers and mechanical stabilization systems. This increases the cost and complexity of such solutions.
- **Infrastructure:** For VISIBLE LIGHT COMMUNICATION to play out its advantages, a suitable light infrastructure has to exist. In areas that do not need lighting, this is not given. You also need the components that modulate the lights if they do not already exist.
- **Line of Sight:** Direct line of sight is not needed, but beneficial. In situations where direct line of sight is not given at times, performance suffers. If no line of sight to a surface illuminated by a transmitter exists, communication does not work.
- **Security:** Using visible light as communication medium may pose new security risks. It may also be possible to launch attacks to disrupt communication, for example by using additional lights to overwhelm the receivers, similar to denial of service (DoS) attacks.

Related Patterns:

- **DEVICE WAKEUP TRIGGER:** VISIBLE LIGHT COMMUNICATION is one option to implement a DEVICE WAKEUP TRIGGER. In this case, a device uses a photodiode and a simple detection circuit to catch trigger messages sent using the lights in its environment.

Examples: Bell patented the idea of using optical signals for communication in 1880 [88]. Research in this general field, called Free Space Optical (FSO) communication, has steadily advanced the technology. FSO is now used in multiple forms and applications, including infrared remote controls and communication with spacecrafts and satellites [89]. In recent years, the availability and increased usage of low-cost LEDs have made a particular form of FSO, VISIBLE LIGHT COMMUNICATION, a practical option.

Realizing VLC using modified off-the-shelf LED bulbs is workable [90]. Photodiodes and cameras work as receivers and both are addressable with the same signal. Besides, photodiodes enable always-on VLC receivers that are suitable as a low-energy channel to receive DEVICE WAKEUP TRIGGER. The power available to *Energy Harvesting* devices is insufficient for using LEDs as uplink for VLC. An alternative is to use retro-reflective materials to reflect light from the transmitter and other light sources to form an uplink. An LCD-shutter modulates messages into the reflected light [91]. OpenVLC [92] is a project that offers an open-source VLC research platform based on off-the-shelf components.

Disney researches LED to LED communication between toys. Pointing a magic wand with a VLC enabled LED at a dress activates the lights in the dress. A smartphone add-on placed in the headphone jack or other VLC enabled lights control the lights of a toy police car [93].

Light-Fidelity (LiFi) [94] extends VLC by adding common wireless networking features. These include bi-directional multiuser communication and seamless handover between cells. PureLiFi [95] offers commercial solutions, such as the LiFi-XC system. It consists of access points that modulate existing light fixtures and stations which plug into laptops via USB.

Qualcomm Lumicast [96] is a commercial technology, which uses VLC for indoor mobile device positioning where GPS is not available. They offer a software framework that allows developers to access the location information in their apps. Position accuracy is higher than with methods that use WiFi or Bluetooth. Besides, the framework offers orientation determination and three-dimensional positioning. It allows using auxiliary positioning methods as a backup. Other companies offer VLC services based on Lumicast, such as Acuity's BiteLight [97].

The Institute of Electrical and Electronics Engineers (IEEE) has created the 802.15.7 standard for VLC [98]. It describes a physical and media access control layer for short-range optical wireless communication. IEEE designed the standard for audio and video services, mobility, and compatibility with existing light infrastructure. During design, they considered impairments due to noise and eye safety.

6 Related Work

The concept of patterns, as introduced by Alexander et al. [22] is of course nothing new. Over the years, many publications either included new patterns for a specific field or talked about the pattern creation process in general. A selection of the latter was already mentioned in Sect. 3 and includes [23, 29–33]. Additional publications include [27, 99, 100]. Further, research about efficient pattern application via pattern refinement and concrete solutions organized in solution repositories emerges [34, 36].

Some patterns for topics in IoT or related areas exist. Eloranta et al. [101] describe patterns for building distributed control systems for moving machinery used for foresting, mining, construction etc. These patterns focus on aspects of reliability and fault-tolerance within these large machines but are not concerned with communication between small, *Constrained Devices* [101]. Qanbari et al. [102] present four patterns for edge application provisioning, deployment, orchestration, and monitoring. In addition to their narrow focus on edge applications, these patterns use existing technologies like Docker and Git, which are not suited for all *Constrained Devices*.

Publications in other contexts exist that contain patterns that are applicable in the IoT domain. The *Messaging Patterns* by Hohpe and Woolf [25] contain several patterns that can be used to describe communication aspects in the IoT. For example, the COMMAND MESSAGE and EVENT MESSAGE patterns fit neatly with the two types of messages that are exchanged in the IoT, namely messages that are sent to devices that contain a command, e.g., to activate some kind of actuator, and messages that are sent from devices to the backend for further processing by other components, e.g., sensor values. Other patterns that are applicable include EVENT-DRIVEN CONSUMER, PUBLISH-SUBSCRIBE CHANNEL, or GUARANTEED DELIVERY. However, these patterns only cover some aspects of IoT communication.

The *Cloud Computing Patterns* by Fehling et al. [23] also contain some patterns that are applicable in the IoT domain. For example, a variant of the WATCHDOG pattern can be found on DEVICE GATEWAYS where it resets the system when it detects a problem with a critical component [103]. The EXACTLY-ONCE DELIVERY and AT-LEAST-ONCE DELIVERY patterns apply to device communication, for example when the MQTT protocol is used. The different workload patterns could be used to describe workloads generated by device messages and the LOOSE COUPLING pattern discusses principles to decouple devices from other components that consume their data or trigger some actuator functionality of the device, respectively. Again, these patterns only cover some aspects that are relevant for IoT.

7 Summary and Outlook

The vision of the IoT has existed for a few years now. While not fully realized yet, recent developments have added numerous solutions, technologies, and standardization efforts to various areas of this field. However, their ever-increasing number and heterogeneity make it hard to grasp the underlying principles. To help to understand this complex field, we presented IoT patterns, which summarize recurring solutions to various problems in the IoT space. In our original work [26], we presented five patterns: DEVICE GATEWAY, which enables devices which do not support the technology of a network to communicate with this network, DEVICE SHADOW, which allows other components to interact with offline devices, RULES ENGINE, which enables non-programmers to design rules which trigger actions, DEVICE WAKEUP TRIGGER, which notifies sleeping devices when they should wake up, and REMOTE LOCK AND WIPE, which allows lost or stolen devices to be secured.

In this extended version of our original work [26], we added three new patterns: DELTA UPDATE, which only sends data which has changed since the last communication, REMOTE DEVICE MANAGEMENT, which allows remote device management using a client-server architecture, and VISIBLE LIGHT COMMUNICATION, which modulates visible light to send messages to devices. These patterns already show relations between them and the new patterns added in this extended version also added new relations. They also hint at other patterns that have not yet been published. We are working on expanding this pattern catalog into a full pattern language by adding new patterns and investigating relations between these patterns. In the future, this pattern language will guide developers towards useful pattern combinations, give companies a tool to evaluate different IoT providers and solutions, and help other interested readers to understand the different aspects of the IoT.

Acknowledgements. We would like to thank our shepherd Marko Leppänen for the discussions and comments that helped to improve this paper. This work was partially funded by the BMWi projects NEMAR (03ET4018B), SmartOrchestra (01MD16001F) and SePiA.Pro (01MD16013F).

References

1. Anjanappa, M., Datta, K., Song, T.: Introduction to sensors and actuators. In: Bishop, R.H. (ed.) The Mechatronics Handbook, pp. 327–340. CRC Press, Boca Raton (2002)
2. Röcker, C.: Services and applications for smart office environments - a survey of state-of-the-art usage scenarios. Int. J. Soc. Behav. Educ. Econ. Bus. Ind. Eng. **4**, 51–67 (2010)
3. Le Gal, C., Martin, J., Lux, A., Crowley, J.L.: SmartOffice: design of an intelligent environment. IEEE Intell. Syst. **16**, 60–66 (2001)
4. Kopp, O., Falkenthal, M., Hartmann, N., Leymann, F., Schwarz, H., Thomsen, J.: Towards a cloud-based platform architecture for a decentralized market agent. In: Cunningham, D., Hofstedt, P., Meer, K., Schmitt, I. (eds.) INFORMATIK 2015, P-246, pp. 69–80. Gesellschaft für Informatik e.V. (GI), Bonn (2015)
5. Nam, T., Pardo, T.A.: Conceptualizing smart city with dimensions of technology, people, and institutions. In: Proceedings of the 12th Annual International Digital Government Research Conference: Digital Government Innovation in Challenging Times, pp. 282–291. ACM, New York (2011)
6. Su, K., Li, J., Fu, H.: Smart city and the applications. In: 2011 International Conference on Electronics, Communications and Control (ICECC), pp. 1028–1031. IEEE, Piscataway (2011)
7. Kagemann, H., Wahlster, W., Helbig, J.: Recommendations for implementing the strategic initiative INDUSTRIE 4.0 (2013). http://www.acatech.de/fileadmin/user_upload/ Baumstruktur_nach_Website/Acatech/root/de/Material_fuer_Sonderseiten/Industrie_4.0/ Final_report__Industrie_4.0_accessible.pdf. Accessed 13 June 2018
8. Industrial Internet Consortium: Overview (2015). http://www.iiconsortium.org/pdf/IIC-Overview-11-24-15.pdf. Accessed 13 June 2018
9. ZigBee Alliance: Control your World. http://www.zigbee.org/. Accessed 13 June 2018
10. Z-Wave Alliance: The Internet of Things is powered by Z-Wave. http://z-wavealliance.org/. Accessed 13 June 2018
11. Bluetooth: Bluetooth Technology Website. https://www.bluetooth.com/what-is-bluetooth-technology/how-it-works. Accessed 13 June 2018
12. Thread Group. http://www.threadgroup.org/. Accessed 13 June 2018
13. IETF: The Constrained Application Protocol (CoAP) (2014). https://tools.ietf.org/html/ rfc7252. Accessed 13 June 2018

14. OASIS: MQTT Version 3.1.1. OASIS (2014). http://docs.oasis-open.org/mqtt/mqtt/v3.1.1/os/mqtt-v3.1.1-os.pdf. Accessed 13 June 2018
15. OPC Foundation: Unified Architecture - OPC Foundation. https://opcfoundation.org/about/opc-technologies/opc-ua/. Accessed 13 June 2018
16. Open Mobile Alliance: OMA Device Management Protocol. Open Mobile Alliance (2015). http://www.openmobilealliance.org/release/DM/V2_0-20150122-C/OMA-TS-DM_Protoc ol-V2_0-20150122-C.pdf. Accessed 13 June 2018
17. Open Mobile Alliance: Lightweight M2 M - Lock and Wipe Object (LwM2 M Object - LockWipe) (2015). http://technical.openmobilealliance.org/Technical/Release_Program/docs/LWM2M_LOCKWIPE/V1_0-20150217-C/OMA-TS-LWM2M_LockWipe-V1_0-20150217-C.pd. Accessed 13 June 2018
18. Bernstein, J., Spets, T.: DSL Forum TR-069. CPE WAN Management Protocol (2004). https://www.broadband-forum.org/technical/download/TR-069.pdf. Accessed 13 June 2018
19. AllSeen Alliance: AllSeen Alliance. https://allseenalliance.org/. Accessed 13 June 2018
20. Open Interconnect Consortium: Open Interconnect Consortium. http://openinterconnect.org/. Accessed 13 June 2018
21. Object Management Group: Data Distribution Service (DDS) (2015). http://www.omg.org/spec/DDS/1.4/PDF/. Accessed 13 June 2018
22. Alexander, C., Ishikawa, S., Silverstein, M.: A Pattern Language: Towns, Buildings. Construction. Oxford University Press, New York (1977)
23. Fehling, C., Leymann, F., Retter, R., Schupeck, W., Arbitter, P.: Cloud Computing Patterns. Fundamentals to Design, Build, and Manage Cloud Applications. Springer, Wien (2014). https://doi.org/10.1007/978-3-7091-1568-8. Accessed 13 June 2018
24. Gamma, E., Helm, R., Johnson, R., Vlissides, J.: Design Patterns: Elements of Reusable Object-Oriented Software. Addison-Wesley, Reading (1995)
25. Hohpe, G., Woolf, B.: Enterprise Integration Patterns. Designing Building, and Deploying Messaging Solutions. Addison-Wesley, Boston (2004)
26. Reinfurt, L., Breitenbücher, U., Falkenthal, M., Leymann, F., Riegg, A.: Internet of things patterns. In: Proceedings of the 21st European Conference on Pattern Languages of Programs (EuroPLoP). ACM (2016)
27. Fehling, C., Barzen, J., Breitenbücher, U., Leymann, F.: A process for pattern identification, authoring, and application. In: Proceedings of the 19th European Conference on Pattern Languages of Programs (EuroPLoP). ACM, New York (2015)
28. Coplien, J.O.: Software Patterns. SIGS, New York (1996)
29. Meszaros, G., Doble, J.: Metapatterns: a pattern language for pattern writing. In: Third Pattern Languages of Programming Conference. Addison-Wesley, Boston (1996)
30. Wellhausen, T., Fießer, A.: How to write a pattern? A rough guide for first-time pattern authors. In: Proceedings of the 16th European Conference on Pattern Languages of Programs. ACM, New York (2012)
31. Harrison, N.B.: Advanced pattern writing. Patterns for experienced pattern authors. In: Pattern Languages of Program Design 5, vol. 5, pp. 433–452. Addison-Wesley, Upper Saddler River (2006)
32. Harrison, N.B.: The language of shepherding. a pattern language for shepherds and sheep. In: Pattern Languages of Program Design 5, vol. 5, pp. 507–530. Addison-Wesley, Upper Saddler River (2006)
33. Fehling, C., Barzen, J., Falkenthal, M., Leymann, F.: PatternPedia - collaborative pattern identification and authoring. In: PURPLSOC (In Pursuit of Pattern Languages for Societal Change): The Workshop 2014, pp. 252–284. epubli GmbH, Berlin (2015)

34. Falkenthal, M., et al.: Leveraging pattern application via pattern refinement. In: Proceedings of the International Conference on Pursuit of Pattern Languages for Societal Change (PURPLSOC) (2016)
35. Falkenthal, M., Barzen, J., Breitenbücher, U., Fehling, C., Leymann, F.: From pattern languages to solution implementations. In: Proceedings of the Sixth International Conferences on Pervasive Patterns and Applications (PATTERNS 2014), pp. 12–21. IARIA, Wilmington (2014)
36. Falkenthal, M., Barzen, J., Breitenbücher, U., Fehling, C., Leymann, F.: Efficient pattern application: validating the concept of solution implementations in different domains. Int. J. Adv. Softw. **7**, 710–726 (2014)
37. Bormann, C., Ersue, M., Keranen, A.: Terminology for Constrained-Node Networks (2014). http://www.rfc-editor.org/rfc/pdfrfc/rfc7228.txt.pdf. Accessed 13 June 2018
38. Eloranta, V.-P., Koskinen, J., Leppänen, M., Reijonen, V.: Patterns for the Companion Website. http://media.wiley.com/product_ancillary/55/11186941/DOWNLOAD/website_patterns.pdf. Accessed 13 June 2018
39. SmartThings: Architecture. http://docs.smartthings.com/en/latest/architecture/index.html. Accessed 13 June 2018
40. Wink: Wink Hub. http://www.wink.com/products/wink-hub/. Accessed 13 June 2018
41. EVRYTHNG: THINGHUB Local Cloud Gateway. https://evrythng.com/wp-content/uploads/THNGHUB-data-sheet.pdf. Accessed 13 June 2018
42. Intel: Intel IoT Gateways. https://www-ssl.intel.com/content/www/us/en/embedded/solutions/iot-gateway/overview.html. Accessed 13 June 2018
43. Dell: Dell IoT solutions. http://www.dell.com/learn/us/en/04/oem/oem-internet-of-things. Accessed 13 June 2018
44. Nexcom: IoT Gateway. http://www.nexcom.com/Products/industrial-computing-solutions/iot-solutions/iot-gateway. Accessed 13 June 2018
45. Eclipse Foundation: Kura - Open Source Framework for IoT. http://www.eclipse.org/kura/. Accessed 13 June 2018
46. Zachariah, T., Klugman, N., Campbell, B., Adkins, J., Jackson, N., Dutta, P.: The internet of things has a gateway problem. In: Proceedings of the 16th International Workshop on Mobile Computing Systems and Applications - HotMobile 2015, pp. 27–32. ACM, New York (2015)
47. Amazon Web Services: AWS IoT FAQs. https://aws.amazon.com/iot/faqs/. Accessed 13 June 2018
48. Microsoft: Azure and IoT. https://azure.microsoft.com/en-us/documentation/articles/iot-hub-what-is-azure-iot/. Accessed 13 June 2018
49. Microsoft: Azure IoT Hub guidance. https://azure.microsoft.com/en-us/documentation/articles/iot-hub-guidance/. Accessed 13 June 2018
50. Comarch Technologies: Comarch IoT Platform. In the pursuit of becoming smart (2015). http://technologies.comarch.com/wp-content/uploads/2015/10/CT_IoT-white-paper_22092015_WEB.pdf. Accessed 13 June 2018
51. Bosch Software Innovations: The Bosch IoT Suite. Technology for a Connected World (2015). https://www.bosch-si.com/media/en/bosch_si/iot_platform/bosch-iot-suite_product-brochure.pdf. Accessed 13 June 2018
52. Fowler, M., Rice, D., Foemmel, M., Hieatt, E., Mee, R., Stafford, R.: Patterns of Enterprise Application Architecture. Addison-Wesley, Boston (2002)
53. Amazon Web Services: How the AWS IoT Platform Works. https://aws.amazon.com/iot/how-it-works. Accessed 13 June 2018
54. Amazon Web Services: Device Shadows Documents. http://docs.aws.amazon.com/iot/latest/developerguide/thing-shadow-document.html. Accessed 13 June 2018

55. Microsoft: Overview of device management with IoT Hub. https://docs.microsoft.com/en-us/azure/iot-hub/iot-hub-device-management-overview. Accessed 13 June 2018

56. Kii: State Registration and Retrieval. http://documentation.kii.com/en/starts/thingifsdk/model/states/. Accessed 13 June 2018

57. Fowler, M.: Domain-Specific Languages. Addison-Wesley, Upper Saddle River (2011)

58. IBM: Getting started with IoT Real-Time Insights. http://www.ng.bluemix.net/docs/services/iotrtinsights/index.html. Accessed 13 June 2018

59. myDevices: myDevices Connected Device Platform for the Internet of Things. https://www.mydevices.com/platform. Accessed 13 June 2018

60. Wind River: Wind River Helix Device Cloud (2015). http://www.windriver.com/products/product-overviews/wr-device-cloud_overview.pdf. Accessed 13 June 2018

61. Comarch Technologies: Digital Lifestyle & IoT Solutions (2015). http://www.comarch.com/files-com/file_91/Comarch-Digital-Lifestyle-and-IoT-Solution-283522.pdf. Accessed 13 June 2018

62. Ayla Networks: Ayla Architecture. Focusing on the 'Things' and Their Manufacturers (2015). https://www.aylanetworks.com/wp-content/uploads/2015/06/Ayla_Architecture_White_Paper_preview.pdf. Accessed 13 June 2018

63. EVRYTHNG: Evrythng Platform Overview. https://evrythng.com/wp-content/uploads/EVRYTHNG-IoT-Platform-Overview.pdf. Accessed 13 June 2018

64. waylay.io: Waylay.io Documentation. https://docs.waylay.io/usage/tasks-and-templates/. Accessed 13 June 2018

65. IFTTT: IFTTT. https://ifttt.com/. Accessed 13 June 2018

66. Zapier: Connect Your Apps and Automate Workflows. https://zapier.com/. Accessed 13 June 2018

67. Stringify: Home – Stringify. https://www.stringify.com/. Accessed 13 June 2018

68. Ba, H., Parvin, J., Soto, L., Demirkol, I., Heinzelman, W.: Passive RFID-based Wake-Up Radios for Wireless Sensor Networks. In: Smith, J. (ed.) Wirelessly Powered Sensor Networks and Computational RFID, pp. 113–129. Springer, Heidelberg (2013). https://doi.org/10.1007/978-1-4419-6166-2_6. Accessed 13 June 2018

69. Ruzzelli, A.G., Jurdak, R., O'Hare, G.M.P.: On the RFID wake-up impulse for multi-hop sensor networks. In: The 1st ACM Workshop on Convergence of RFID and Wireless Sensor Networks and their Applications (SenseID) at the 5th ACM International Conference on Embedded Networked Sensor Systems (ACM SenSys 2007) (2007)

70. ETSI: 3GPP TS 23.682. Architecture enhancements to facilitate communications with packet data networks and applications (2015). http://www.etsi.org/deliver/etsi_ts/123600_123699/123682/12.04.00_60/ts_123682v120400p.pdf. Accessed 13 June 2018

71. 3GPP2: Network Enhancements for Machine to Machine (M2M) (2014). http://www.3gpp2.org/public_html/specs/X.S0068-0_v1.0_M2M_Enhancements_20140718.pdf. Accessed 13 June 2018

72. oneM2 M: Functional Architecture (2015). http://www.onem2m.org/images/files/deliverables/TS-0001-Functional_Architecture-V1_6_1.pdf. Accessed 13 June 2018

73. Starsinic, M., et al.: An IP-based triggering method for LTE MTC devices. In: 2015 Wireless Telecommunications Symposium (WTS). IEEE (2015)

74. PawTrax: Welcome to PawTrax. http://www.pawtrax.co.uk/. Accessed 13 June 2018

75. Google: Remotely ring, lock, or erase a lost device - Accounts Help. https://support.google.com/accounts/answer/6160500. Accessed 13 June 2018

76. Apple: iCloud: Use Lost Mode. https://support.apple.com/kb/PH2700. Accessed 13 June 2018

77. Apple: iCloud: Erase your device. https://support.apple.com/kb/PH2701. Accessed 13 June 2018

78. Kii: Disable/Enable Things. http://documentation.kii.com/en/guides/thingifsdk/thingsdk/ thing-client/things-status/. Accessed 13 June 2018
79. IBM: Device Management Operations - Device Actions. https://console.bluemix.net/docs/ services/IoT/devices/device_mgmt/requests.html#requests. Accessed 13 June 2018
80. Libelium: Waspmote Programming Guide (2015)
81. Open Mobile Alliance: Lightweight Machine to Machine Technical Specification (2015). http://technical.openmobilealliance.org/Technical/Release_Program/docs/ LightweightM2M/V1_0-20151030-C/OMA-TS-LightweightM2M-V1_0-20151030-C.pd. Accessed 13 June 2018
82. CyberVision: Configuration - Kaa - Kaa documentation. http://docs.kaaproject.org/display/ KAA/Configuration. Accessed 13 June 2018
83. IBM: About Watson IoT Platform. https://console.bluemix.net/docs/services/IoT/ iotplatform_overview.html#about_iotplatform. Accessed 13 June 2018
84. Oracle: Using Oracle Internet of Things Cloud Service. http://docs.oracle.com/cloud/latest/ iot/IOTGS/IOTGS.pdf. Accessed 13 June 2018
85. Nokia: Nokia Motive connected device platform (2016). http://resources.alcatel-lucent. com/asset/196246. Accessed 13 June 2018
86. Nokia: Motive Connected Device Platform. Release 6.0 (2016). http://resources.alcatel-lucent.com/asset/196247. Accessed 13 June 2018
87. Komine, T., Nakagawa, M.: Integrated system of white LED visible-light communication and power-line communication. IEEE Trans. Consumer Electron. **49**, 71–79 (2003)
88. Bell, A.G.: Apparatus for Signaling and Communicating, called Photophone (1880)
89. Sevincer, A., Bhattarai, A., Bilgi, M., Yuksel, M., Pala, N.: LIGHTNETs: smart LIGHTing and mobile optical wireless NETworks – a survey. IEEE Commun. Surv. Tutorials **15**, 1620–1641 (2013)
90. Schmid, S., Richner, T., Mangold, S., Gross, T.R.: EnLighting: An Indoor Visible Light Communication System Based on Networked Light Bulbs. https://s3-us-west-1.amazonaws. com/disneyresearch/wp-content/uploads/20160615205959/EnLighting-An-Indoor-Visible-Light-Communication-System-based-on-Networked-Light-Bulbs-Paper.pdf. Accessed 13 June 2018
91. Li, J., Lie, A., Shen, G., Li, L., Sun, C., Zhao, F.: Retro-VLC: enabling battery-free duplex visible light communication for mobile and IoT applications. In: Manweiler, J., Choudhury, R.R. (eds.) Proceedings of the 16th International Workshop on Mobile Computing Systems and Applications (HotMobile 2015), pp. 21–26. ACM, New York (2015)
92. Wang, Q., de Donne, D., Giustiniano, D.: Demonstration abstract: research platform for visible light communication and sensing systems. In: Proceedings of the 15th ACM/IEEE International Conference on Information Processing in Sensor Networks (IPSN). IEEE (2016)
93. Schmid, S., et al.: (In)visible Light Communication: Combining Illumination and Communication. https://s3-us-west-1.amazonaws.com/disneyresearch/wp-content/uploads/ 20140915070828/Pub_InvisibleLightCommunication_Siggraph14_paper.pdf. Accessed 13 June 2018
94. Haas, H., Yin, L., Wang, Y., Chen, C.: What is LiFi? J. Lightwave Technol. **34**, 1533–1544 (2016)
95. pureLiFi: LiFi-XC. https://purelifi.com/lifi-products/. Accessed 13 June 2018
96. Jovicic, A.: Qualcomm Lumicast: A high accuracy indoor positioning system based on visible light communication (2016). https://www.qualcomm.com/media/documents/files/ lumicast-whitepaper.pdf. Accessed 13 June 2018

97. Acuity: Illuminating the In-Store Experience. Indoor Positioning Services Using LED Lighting Benefit Shoppers and Retailers (2016). http://www.acuitybrands.com/-/media/Files/Acuity/Solutions/Services/Indoor%20Positioning%20White%20Papers/indoor%20positioning%20white%20paperrevised%2011110315%20pdf.pdf. Accessed 13 June 2018

98. IEEE: Part 15.7: Standard for Short-Range Wireless Optical Communication using Visible Light (2011)

99. Reiners, R., Falkenthal, M., Jugel, D., Zimmermann, A.: Requirements for a collaborative formulation process of evolutionary patterns. In: Proceedings of the 18th European Conference on Pattern Languages of Programs (EuroPlop). ACM, New York (2013)

100. Falkenthal, M., et al.: Pattern research in the digital humanities: how data mining techniques support the identification of costume patterns. In: Proceedings of the 10th Symposium and Summer School on Service-Oriented Computing (SummerSOC 2016). Springer, Heidelberg (2016)

101. Eloranta, V.-P., Koskinen, J., Leppänen, M., Reijonen, V.: Designing Distributed Control Systems A Pattern Language Approach. Wiley, Hoboken (2014)

102. Qanbari, S., et al.: IoT design patterns: computational constructs to design, build and engineer edge applications. In: Proceedings of the First International Conference on Internet-of-Things Design and Implementation (IoTDI), pp. 277–282. IEEE (2016)

103. Eclipse Foundation: Kura Documentation – Introduction. http://eclipse.github.io/kura/intro/intro.html. Accessed 13 June 2018

A Pattern Language for Knowledge Handover When People Transition

Kei Ito[1], Joseph W. Yoder[2], Hironori Washizaki[1,3(✉)],
and Yoshiaki Fukazawa[1,3]

[1] Department of Computer Science and Engineering, Waseda University,
3-4-1 Ohkubo, Shinjuku-ku, Tokyo 169-8555, Japan
`k-win@toki.waseda.jp`, {`washizaki, fukazawa`}`@waseda.jp`
[2] The Refactory, Inc., 7 Florida Drive, Urbana, IL 61801, USA
`joe@refactory.com`
[3] Global Software Engineering Laboratory, Waseda University,
27 Waseda-cho, Shinjuku-ku, Tokyo 162-0042, Japan

Abstract. Handover of knowledge and responsibilities can cause problems when people transfer to other parts of a company or retire. Handover issues became apparent in Japan when many people from the Baby Boomer Generation retired simultaneously in 2007. In particular, this was a resounding issue in the software industry. Most business people are familiar with the concept of a handover. Although effective handovers are crucial for seamless business operations during personnel changes, the preferable elements for a handover are ambiguous. In this paper, we outline a "Pattern Language for Knowledge Handover when People Transition". The pattern language consists of handover patterns. Actual handover patterns were pattern mined from our experience as well as from industrial interviews. We originally started with handover anti-patterns which identify actual problems for a handover. This led us to pattern mine the handover patterns that provide strategies to mitigate these problems. The examples are from software industry, but these patterns are applicable to other domains.

Keywords: Project and people management · Design patterns

1 Introduction

Personnel changes, including transitions of responsibilities and knowledge, are integral to prosperous businesses. A key factor in seamless personnel changes is successfully transferring responsibilities as people depart or transition to other areas within a company. A handover is a necessary activity to preserve superior knowledge and skills within an organization. In fact, a handover is a critical stage in the software life cycle [1].

Despite its importance, handover problems are not well studied [2] and many undesirable handovers occur in business [3]. One study mentioned that insufficient knowledge of the successor is the main problem in a handover [2], while another found that the information sharing process contains complex problems [4].

© Springer Nature Switzerland AG 2019
J. Noble et al. (Eds.): TPLOP IV, LNCS 10600, pp. 183–209, 2019.
https://doi.org/10.1007/978-3-030-14291-9_6

Although knowledge management systems and toolkits such as [20] can support handovers, efficient and practical utilization of such systems is unclear. Some practices and lessons learned from successful and failed handover projects are available [21, 22]. Because these are not described in the form of a pattern language, why, when, how, and under which contexts to adopt such systems and toolkits remain hazy. Moreover, these do not comprehensively cover all combinations of roles (such as predecessors, successors and third parties) and the timing of knowledge handover (such as preparation, during handover and after handover).

Some companies, especially software outsourcing companies, have their own internal processes to deal with knowledge transfers and personnel changes. Organizational knowledge transfer processes together with the concept of knowledge and business continuity are discussed in [23]. However, clarifying and documenting such processes in the form of a pattern language is beneficial to identify commonly recurring problems in knowledge handovers and their corresponding solutions.

Pattern languages provide desirable solutions based upon best practices. They help guide a solution for a given context and problem domain. This paper outlines a pattern language to solve handover issues. Our patterns are written as a mixture of the Alexandrian Pattern and the Fearless Change Pattern forms [5, 6, 7]. Stories are used to write the context, problems, solutions, and forces. We use a consistent story format where each pattern begins with a quote followed by a brief description of the pattern. We then use a scenario to write the context, problem, forces, and solution. This storytelling format, which can be easily understood, is similar to the presentation in the Fearless Change patterns. To describe concrete stories, we assume a fictitious company called Waseda Co., Ltd. It should be noted that we list related patterns, alternatives, and consequences after the last set of "***".

Previously, we identified handover problems using anti-patterns. We presented three handover anti-patterns at Asian PLoP 2016 (*Unsupported to review*, *Background is omitted*, and *Necessary knowledge is omitted*) [3], which were confirmed by questionnaires sent to businesses. Analysis of these anti-patterns revealed their origins. A contributing factor of an undesirable handover is the predecessor's failure to communicate clearly with his or her successor. This led us to outline 25 potential handover patterns. We believe that these patterns address the abovementioned problem. More problems and corresponding patterns may exist, but this is a future work. We presented our analysis and described three of these handover patterns at PLoP 2016 (*Spread of knowledge*, *Handover space*, and *Firewall for the handover*) [24]. We also investigated the effects of these 25 handover patterns using questionnaires targeting businesspersons working for systems departments. Because the handover anti-patterns and handover patterns are related, herein we organize their relationships and outline a "Pattern Language for Handovers".

Although our example focuses on the software domain, these patterns are intended for anyone involved in the handover process. The scenarios herein assume a systems department, but even those without a systems' background should find this paper useful since a handover is a common business concept. The patterns are illustrated using a concrete scenario where someone transfers within a company, but these patterns should be applicable to other contexts such as retirement and job changes. This study assumes that there is adequate time for a handover (e.g., the predecessor will not transfer or leave the job for at least a few weeks or months). It should be noted these patterns do not directly address handover issues when someone is fired or leaves immediately.

The rest of the paper is organized as follows. Section 2 defines our concept of a handover using an activity diagram, which expresses the actors and each actor's activity. Section 3 introduces concrete scenes where the pattern occurs for a fictitious company. Section 4 introduces problems with handovers as anti-patterns (three handover anti-patterns). In addition, the section outlines our pattern language for knowledge handovers, explains how the language resolves the anti-patterns, and describes three handover patterns in detail. Section 5 introduces a case study. In Sect. 6, we describe the workshops, which included pattern mining and focus groups that were held to refine our pattern language. Finally, Sect. 7 concludes this paper and outlines future work.

2 Concept of a Handover

A handover is a process to transfer responsibilities and knowledge from the predecessor to the successor [2, 8]. This paper considers a knowledge handover at the personnel level such as worker's retirement[1]. Because handovers occur in most organizations, they are a persistent problem. They range from straightforward and simple to extremely complex. In general, a handover has three phases (preparation, the actual handover, and after the handover) and up to three actors (predecessor, successor, and preferably a third party assisting with the handover). Normally, all the actors are employees of the organization. The best scenario occurs when sufficient time is allocated for an incremental handover with a lot of mentoring. In this case, it is possible to extend the handover over a longer period and the process may only involve the predecessor and the successor.

Often a handover is conducted in a short amount of time. This paper examines shorter handover situations where a third party plays an important role. The third party, which may be more than one person, is an interested party responsible for the handover such as the project manager. In every phase, each actor must perform specific tasks.

Handover activities can be decomposed into nine areas. Figure 1 overviews the handover activities. These activities can be executed in parallel.

- Predecessor's preparation activity
- Successor's preparation activity
- Third party's preparation activity
- Predecessor's activity during the handover
- Successor's activity during the handover
- Third party's activity during the handover
- Predecessor's activity after the handover
- Successor's activity after the handover
- Third party's activity after the handover

---

[1] Some of patterns presented in this paper may be useful for other levels such as an organizational level and department level. Our future work is to investigate such applicability.

In the preparation phase, the predecessor chooses the knowledge to be shared while the successor begins preparations for the new post. Note that selected knowledge consists of both explicit and tacit knowledge[2]. The predecessor formalizes explicit knowledge into the proper form to be communicated or documented. The successor prepares for the new post (e.g., by studying or receiving formal training to understand the knowledge to be communicated by the predecessor).

Tacit knowledge contains formless elements like experiences and ideas (e.g., the predecessor shares the knowledge while the successor performs the tasks). Some explicit knowledge can be difficult to formalize because it is complex and time consuming to characterize. Such explicit knowledge is best shared via a mentoring process. Regardless, it is critical that the predecessor selects an effective form of communication for the handover process.

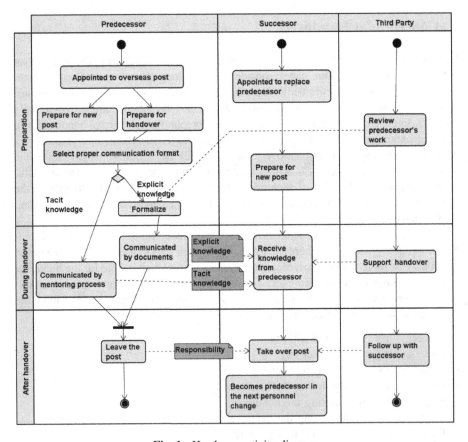

Fig. 1. Handover activity diagram

<hr />

[2] In this paper, we regard "tacit knowledge" as the concept defined in Ikujiro Nonaka's model of organizational knowledge creation [18]. Tacit knowledge can be transformed into explicit knowledge and communicated with others. This definition differs from the original concept of "tacit knowledge" proposed by Michael Polanyi in Personal Knowledge [19].

Ideally the third party reviews any formalized knowledge documented by the predecessor. During the handover period, the predecessor exchanges knowledge with the successor. The third party assists by supporting the predecessor during the handover. Upon completion of the handover process, the successor assumes the predecessor's responsibilities. Since the successor might be unfamiliar some aspects of the job, the third party follows up regularly with the successor to answer questions as they arise.

3   Scene

For consistency, we use a concrete scenario to explain the context, forces, problems, and consequences, to describe our patterns. A concrete scenario helps conceptualize the pattern language for handovers. The following example scenario is used to help illustrate the patterns throughout this paper.

3.1   Example Scenario

Hiro works at Waseda Co., Ltd., which is one of the largest companies in Japan. Its business focuses on systems auditing and consulting. Hiro is part of the internal systems department. He is responsible for the development, operation, and maintenance of internal systems. He has been in charge of the financial system since its inception, but is being transferred overseas. Kei, a mid-level employee, has been appointed as Hiro's successor. Before leaving, Hiro must handover knowledge of the financial system to Kei.

The financial system, which was developed in Java about ten years ago, is one of Waseda's biggest internal systems. The system outputs the settlement of accounts for external auditors and the government for tax purposes. The system must be revised and updated when the tax law or other requirements change.

3.2   Characters

In this scenario, a handover consists of the activities of three actors (predecessor, successor, and third party). However, there are four people involved because the third party role is shared by two people.

Hiro (the predecessor), a veteran worker in charge of the financial system, is being transferred overseas. Although Hiro will remain with the organization, he is moving to a different department in another location. After the handover, he will no longer be directly involved with the financial system, but he can answer questions for his successor. Kei is a mid-level employee in a different department. She has been at Waseda for a couple of years and has been appointed as Hiro's replacement. Joe is a veteran worker and a colleague of Hiro. He also works for the internal systems department but is in charge of a different system. Yoshiaki is the person responsible for the internal systems department as he is the project manager of the financial system and Hiro's boss.

4   A Pattern Language for Knowledge Handover

In this section, we introduce a concrete pattern language for a knowledge handover during a personnel transition. The pattern language consists of 25 handover patterns. These patterns were identified using a two-step process (Fig. 2). First, we analyzed the three previously discussed anti-patterns. Then handover issues were mined by talking with businesses that have experienced handover problems.

We originally held a handover workshop to collect data about handover experiences. Participants recollected failures and shared their experiences, which helped us identify three handover anti-patterns. These anti-patterns were subsequently used to identify concrete handover problems. We noted the root causes of these problems and outlined them as problems and solutions.

To validate the extracted handover patterns, we created questionnaires and targeted businesses. We interviewed ten industrial engineers and managers from five companies. In the questionnaires, we explained each pattern's success story and asked the respondents to indicate whether they have had similar experiences. The questionnaire focused on the three patterns presented in this paper (*Spread of knowledge, Handover space*, and *Firewall for the handover*). Our questionnaire confirmed that these patterns can be effective for successful handovers. (See Sect. 5).

Additionally, we conducted two workshops on pattern mining and classification at Waseda University and at PLoP 2016. In these workshops, we overviewed our handover patterns and handover concepts. Then we organized groups and let attendees brainstorm to identify and categorize new possible patterns as well as note relationships between the patterns.

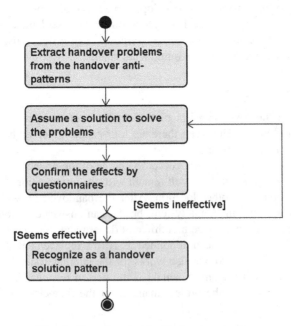

Fig. 2. Procedure to identify handover pattern

4.1   Handover Anti-patterns

Anti-patterns can provide insight and the necessary knowledge to prevent or recover from an undesired situation. Examples of anti-patterns include *death march, god class,* and *vendor lock-in* [9, 10]. In this section, we introduce three anti-patterns: *Unsupported to review, Background knowledge is omitted,* and *Necessary knowledge is omitted.* These anti-patterns are caused by defective knowledge (inaccurate or insufficient knowledge) being transmitted to the successor (Fig. 3).

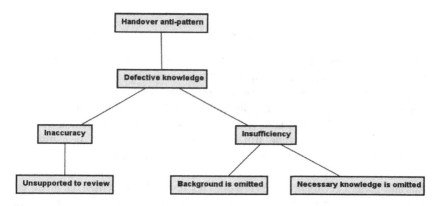

Fig. 3. Map of handover anti-patterns

Inaccuracy is related with *Unsupported to review.* The review is an opportunity to correct errors in documents. Consequently, *Unsupported to review* may transfer erroneous knowledge. However, failure to convey important knowledge to the success is responsible for *Background is omitted* and *Necessary knowledge is omitted.* A detailed background and some knowledge can be difficult to document or is unclear if included. Consequently, necessary knowledge is often lost by the predecessor's omissions. These anti-patterns arise from defects in the handover elements (Fig. 4).

As confirmed in Sect. 2, a handover is the process where the predecessor communicates his or her knowledge to the successor through documents or a mentoring process. The causes of the handover anti-patterns can be roughly divided into five issues: documents, predecessor's communication, successor's understanding, time, and the organizational structure (e.g., human resources and systems problems).

Document issues may lead to *Unsupported to review, Background is omitted,* and *Necessary knowledge is omitted.* The predecessor's communication issue may cause *Background is omitted* and *Unsupported to review,* whereas gaps in the successor's understanding may be due to *Background is omitted.* Time issues may cause *Unsupported to review* and *Necessary knowledge is omitted.* Finally, organizational issues may result in *Background is omitted* and *Necessary knowledge is omitted.* The rest of this section outlines the handover anti-patterns as they relate to our example scenario. Appendix A includes class diagrams that describe anti-patterns situations and subsequent problems.

Unsupported to Review (i.e., Un-updated Documents Under Review)

A review conference to identify defects is an opportunity to correct deficiencies in a document. However, documents are not always revised after a review.

Consider the following scenario. Hiro has been in charge of the financial system since its inception, but was recently appointed to an oversea post. Kei has been named his successor. Upon learning of his transfer, Hiro creates a To-Do list.

His colleague Joe reviews the list. Joe points out that one of the planned repairs is not on the list. Although important, Hiro forgets to revise the list because he is busy preparing for his new post while still performing his daily tasks. As a result, Kei receives defective knowledge because the list lacks an important task.

***

This anti-pattern occurs because Hiro does not revise the list. Often the predecessor cannot determine whether a document is updated because a method to verify the document status does not exist. Thus, defective documents can be shared during a handover.

***

Intention for responsible handover enables the predecessor to recognize the importance of the handover. Therefore, the predecessor will maintain the documents. Sometimes the predecessor misunderstands the status of the documents. *Update history* will help the predecessor determine whether the documents are updated.

Using *Quick correspondence for the review*, the predecessor can avoid forgetting to revise the documents. Additionally, *Timing of appointment* helps Hiro find time to make the necessary revision. If unsupported to review occurs, *Supporting development of the successor* might help the successor obtain the proper knowledge.

Background Is Omitted

All systems have background knowledge such as design concepts, requests from customers, and restrictions regarding budgets. Although background knowledge indirectly affects the system, it tends to be lost because it is typically not recorded in the handover documents.

Consider the following scenario. Kei has been Hiro's successor for one year. Kei determines that the system needs to be repaired. Kei reviews the program and finds a method (i.e., a program API) to calculate some values, which are not used. Additionally, the method is not described in the documents that Hiro handed over because it is a mistake. The method should have been deleted, but Kei is unaware of this fact. Consequently, an unnecessary method remains in the program.

***

Once background knowledge is lost, it is very difficult to rediscover. However, a third party might know the background since he or she worked with the predecessor. Sometimes the background is written in unexpected documents.

***

By *Neighboring excavation*, Kei might find the missing information. *Witness for the knowledge* also helps the successor. *Spread of knowledge* must be implemented by the predecessor to generate the *Witness*. If the background is lost, third parties can use *Reunion for old members* to ask the predecessor about the fact. *Secure an emergency contact* also helps the successor in the investigation of the background knowledge.

However, the successor's capacity shortage is also one of the causes. *Successor as capable as the predecessor, Mercenary, Questions checking the successor's understanding,* and *Mentor for the successor* might avoid this anti-pattern.

Necessary Knowledge Is Omitted

The predecessor chooses the necessary knowledge to be shared, and records it in the documents. However, necessary knowledge may be omitted from the documents.

Consider the following scenario. As part of the documents for the handover Kei, Hiro creates a manual about regular inspections. However, Hiro forgets to write the procedure to shut down the abnormality sensing function. Kei received the manual without a description of the necessary procedure. During her first regular inspection, she shutdowns the system without the necessary procedure, and the system malfunctions.

***

The absence of a method to verify omitted knowledge objectively is the main cause of this anti-pattern. Although the predecessor verifies whether the handover documents contain all necessary knowledge, a self-check tends to be a subjective ad-hoc review, making it difficult for the predecessor to determine if knowledge is omitted.

***

To improve the self-check, the predecessor should use *Check by other similar documents. Review of the handover documents* also helps to avoid the *Necessary knowledge is omitted.* By using *Apprentice* and *Immediate questions on the unclear spot,* the omitted knowledge might become apparent.

Additionally, *Professional writer for documentation* would prevent the necessary knowledge from being omitted. The predecessor might find the lack of the document or knowledge by concentrating on the handover. Therefore, using *Handover space* and *Firewall for the handover* are effective to avoid the anti-pattern.

4.2   Handover Patterns

In this subsection, we overview of the handover patterns, which are divided into the nine areas outlined in Table 1. Each pattern belongs to a specific area and effectively mitigates the anti-patterns.

The handover patterns can address potential issues (Fig. 4). That is, employing the patterns can mitigate handover failures as the handover patterns provide solutions to assist with an efficient handover, provide countermeasures to prevent the loss of superior skills and knowledge, avoid troubles caused by personnel changes, and reinforce know-how that can be used during handover. We found 25 handover patterns using the procedure described in Fig. 2.

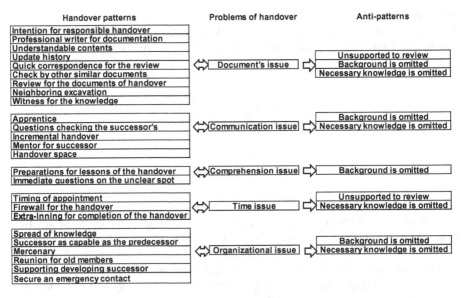

Fig. 4. Relation between anti-patterns and handover patterns

Figure 5 shows the sequences of the patterns listed in Table 1. The sequence is both a summary of the language and an index of the patterns [11]. In Fig. 5, we show the connection between each pattern and the outline of this language. These patterns are distributed over the nine areas described in Sect. 2. We categorized the patterns into the area that they are most relevant, although they could possibly be placed in other areas. (See Table 1).

Table 1. List of handover patterns

	Preparation for handover	During handover	After handover
Predecess or	*Intention for responsible handover* Handover is not a temporary thing. The predecessor must consider the handover as a project	*Apprentice* Have the successor imitate the predecessor's action	*Extra-inning for completion of the handover* Contact the successor to communicate information not conveyed during the handover
	Spread of knowledge Share knowledge with third parties	*Questions checking the successor's understanding* Check the successor's knowledge by asking questions	
	Professional writer for documentation Ask a good writer to create handover documents	*Handover space* Move to a different room while communicating with the successor	
	Understandable contents Make a list to arrange it what is written in the document	*Incremental handover* Handover little by little, and enhance the handover content while working with successor	
	Update history Confirm the revision status by the update history	*Mentor for successor* Support the successor during the handover	
	Quick correspondence for the review Deal with the review immediately		
	Check by other similar documents Utilize other similar documents as a framework when verifying knowledge is not omitted		
	Review for the documents of handover Have third parties verify documents objectively.		
Third party	*Timing of appointment* Allow sufficient time for the handover	*Firewall for the handover* Protect the successor from sudden work to support the handover	*Reunion for old members* Gather with the predecessor to maintain a relationship

(*continued*)

Table 1. (*continued*)

	Preparation for handover	During handover	After handover
	Successor as capable as the predecessor Appoint successor just as capable as the predecessor		*Supporting developing successor* Support the successor as they learn the post
	Mercenary Appoint an external person if a proper person does not exist in the department		
Successor	*Preparations for lessons of the handover* Study the duties of the predecessor before the handover and make an effort to understand the responsibilities.	*Immediate questions on the unclear spot* Immediately ask questions for clarity	*Neighboring excavation* If there were no data in the handed over document, survey other data
			Witness for the knowledge Ask the person who seems to have neighboring knowledge
			Secure an emergency contact Exchange contact information with the predecsssor to keep in touch

Handover patterns are related to each other and share a purpose. In Fig. 5, patterns with the same purpose are surrounded by a square. For example, *Intention for responsible handover, Professional writer for documentation, Understandable contents, Update history, Quick correspondence for the review, Check by other similar documents*, and *Review the handover documents* share the objective of creating quality documents.

Figure 5 also describes the relationship between the groups. Time is necessary to create quality documents, to thoroughly communicate knowledge to the successor, and to have the successor fully understand. For these reasons, time includes necessary conditions for the document, communicating, and understanding groups. The communication group and the understanding group affect each other. On the other hand, the dealing with defective documents group will be used if a quality document is not prepared. Since support for surroundings is necessary for the successor to face defective documents, the deal with defective document group needs to have a good organization group.

This pattern map was inspired by a couple of workshops at Waseda University [13] and a Focus Group at PLoP 2016 [14]. Additionally, the workshops revealed 22 new patterns outlined in Sect. 6. The rest of this section describes 3 patterns of the 25 patterns in detail. Appendix B outlines class diagrams, which depict how the patterns solve a problem.

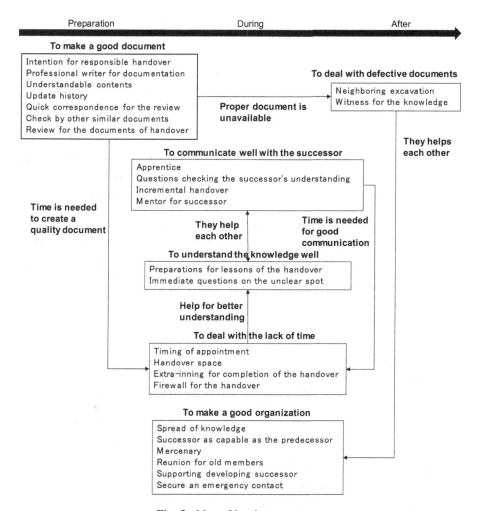

Fig. 5. Map of handover patterns

Spread of Knowledge

In the preparation phase, the predecessor prepares to handover responsibilities by sharing basic knowledge about the system to third parties. This helps the predecessor ensure important details are covered.

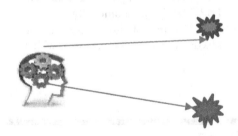

Hiro has been in charge of the financial system since its inception, but he will soon transfer overseas. There is insufficient time for a handover. His successor will be Kei, who has never worked on the financial system. Since Hiro is the only expert of the system, no one can review his documentation for the handover and help the successor.

***

How Can Hiro Best Support the Handover Process in Order to Transfer Sufficient Knowledge to Kei so She Can Take over the Financial System?

Compared with Hiro, Kei has less experience and knowledge. Kei may require training prior to and some help after the transfer.

Yoshiaki and Joe understand parts of the financial system and are also responsible to make sure the system is maintained properly. However, they do not have a sufficient understanding to fully maintain the system or pass knowledge onto Kei.

Hiro has no reservations communicating his knowledge about the financial system to Joe and Yoshiaki because there is a horizontal atmosphere in the organization and he has a solid relationship with both. However, the handover must happen within a limited amount of time because Hiro, Joe, and Yoshiaki are very busy.

Therefore:

The Predecessor, Hiro, Starts to Organize His Knowledge About the Financial System and Begins to Share Core Knowledge About the System to Responsible Third Parties Such as Joe and Yoshiaki Before the Handover with Kei.

As he prepares for the handover, Hiro begins by spreading knowledge about the financial system to Joe and Yoshiaki, who have a rudimentary understanding of the system. Hiro defines the roles of Joe and Yoshiaki as actual operations and future visions, respectively. Both become more knowledgeable about the business side and the technical side of the financial system.

Neither Joe nor Yoshiaki will become an expert on the financial system. Together they become fairly knowledgeable about the system and are capable of reviewing Hiro's documents. Before the transfer, Hiro communicates the roles of Joe and Yoshiaki to Kei. After the transfer, Kei can ask Joe and Yoshiaki for help about the technical side and the business side, respectively.

Spread of knowledge can be implemented informally like a daily chat. However, this type of *Spread of knowledge* often lacks detailed information. Therefore, it is important that the predecessor shares knowledge with more than one person. During these sharing sessions, many questions are asked. Additionally, notes and documents are prepared. The necessary level of detail in the documents depends on the knowledge to be transferred and the complexity of the situation. Third parties have their own tasks, and it is impossible for them to become experts of the system. Note that *Spread of knowledge* is not the spread of responsibility. The only responsible person for the system is Hiro, and his responsibility will be transferred to the successor, Kei.

The predecessor should choose third parties who at least have a basic understanding of the system and responsibilities. In this scenario, Joe and Yoshiaki are in the same section with Hiro, but they have their own responsibilities for the financial system. During this *Spread of knowledge*, the third parties gain a better understanding of the system and can apply this knowledge in their everyday work. The predecessor needs to ensure that the third parties can share the knowledge with the successor.

***

Spread of knowledge can also help identify reviewers of the handover documentation. *The Group Validation* [12] and *Creator-reviewer* [15] assist with the *Spread of knowledge* because they recognize the need for a third party. Thus, *Spread of knowledge* is a necessary condition for *Review of the handover documents, Handover space, Firewall for the handover, Support developing the successor,* and *Witness for the knowledge. Spread of knowledge* is effective for dealing with many of the problems noted in the handover anti-patterns [3]. Yoshiaki, the third party, might use a *Mercenary* or *Successor as capable as the predecessor* to avoid shortcoming of the successor.

Spread of knowledge aims to mitigate the organizational issue of a limited number of knowledgeable people, which is a main cause for the *Background is omitted* [3] and *Necessary knowledge is omitted* [3]. Thus, *Spread of knowledge* can be an effective countermeasure to help avoid these anti-patterns.

Handover Space

Handover space occurs when the predecessor uses a separate space to limit interruptions during the handover process. The third party's gained knowledge about the system allows the predecessor to concentrate on the handover with fewer interruptions.

As soon as Hiro accepts the overseas transfer, he prepares by initiating *Spread of knowledge* to Yoshiaki and Joe. Hiro then begins the handover with Kei. However, the handover is often interrupted by phone calls and people coming to Hiro's desk to ask simple questions. These interruptions prevent Hiro from concentrating on the handover.

***

How Can Hiro and Kei Minimize Distractions so they Can Focus on the Handover Process?

Kei is not as knowledgeable and experienced as Hiro about the financial system. Hiro needs to make sure that he communicates sufficient core knowledge about the financial system to Kei without overwhelming her.

Because Hiro knows the system well, he can answer questions quickly. The normal path is to call Hiro's desk for any issue related to the financial system. Consequently, Hiro spends a lot of time responding to requests, preventing him from preparing for the handover. Because there is no strict rule that bans Hiro from leaving his office, he can use a vacant meeting room in the internal system department office.

Often available meeting rooms or other spaces are limited within an organization. Thus, finding available unoccupied space can be challenging.

Therefore:

To Concentrate on Communicating the Predecessor's Knowledge to the Successor Without Interruptions, Hiro and Kei Use an Available Meeting Room During the Handover Process. If a Meeting Room Is Unavailable, Hiro and Kei Find Open Space Such as a Local Coffee Shop to Discuss Handover Issues Without Regular Interruptions.

Hiro temporarily moves into a vacant meeting room to concentrate on the handover with Kei. Before the move, Hiro asks Joe and Yoshiaki to act for him while he is away from his desk. Joe and Yoshiaki substitute for him between their normal jobs. They answer basic questions and deal with normal operation issues. Anything they cannot answer, they forward to Hiro at a later time unless it is an emergency. Because Hiro and Kei can concentrate on the handover without interruptions, the handover can be substantial and more successful.

***

This pattern requires *Spread of knowledge* because the third party cannot act for the predecessor without the necessary knowledge. Thus, the predecessor must carry out *Spread of knowledge* before *Moving to a different room*. Even if they move to the room, other people may interrupt to ask a question.

To minimize this, Joe and Yoshiaki become *a Firewall for the handover*. Because third parties have other responsibilities, this pattern has limitations. To avoid these problems, handovers must be completed in a timely fashion. Otherwise, the third parties might become overwhelmed and unable to perform their normal tasks. *Daycare* [12] enhances the performance by concentrating on system development, while the professional is taking care of a new member. *Handover space* is similar to *Daycare* because it enhances the handover quality by allowing the predecessor and the successor to concentrate on the handover, while third parties temporarily act for the predecessor.

Handover space aims to enhance communications between the predecessor and the successor by limiting interruptions. Insufficient communication is one of the main causes for the *Background is omitted* [3] and *Necessary knowledge is omitted* [3]. Thus, *Handover space* can be an effective countermeasure to help avoid these anti-patterns.

Firewall for the Handover

The third party uses *Firewall for the handover* to protect the predecessor and the successor during the handover. The predecessor has many job responsibilities, which must be performed during the handover, interfering with the handover process. The third party stands in for the predecessor to support the handover.

As soon as Hiro accepts the overseas transfer, he begins his handover. Since knowledge about the financial system is very important, Joe and Yoshiaki want Hiro to allot a sufficient time for the handover. However, Hiro is very busy and has many interruptions, preventing him from devoting sufficient time for the handover.

***

Hiro's Regular Tasks Involving the Financial System Often Keep Him Very Busy and Do Not Allow Much Time for the Handover. How Can Hiro Find the Time Necessary to Ensure a Good Handover to Kei?

Compared with Hiro, Kei is less experienced and knowledgeable. If Hiro cannot find the time to communicate sufficient core knowledge about the financial system, she cannot support the financial system. There is very little time left before Hiro's transfer. Joe and Yoshiaki need to help create an environment where Hiro can effectively communicate his knowledge about the financial system to Kei.

Because there is a sense of unity in the internal system section, Joe and Yoshiaki feel that it is natural to help with Hiro's handover. It is important that the financial system keeps operating and people have their questions answered.

Therefore:

Joe and Yoshiaki help Hiro by Acting as a Firewall for Hiro During the Handover. They do this by Assisting with Some of the Normal Operations, Including Answering Regular Inquiries.

Joe and Yoshiaki start by asking Hiro how they can help him. Hiro thanks them and forwards calls and inquiries about the financial system to them. Joe and Yoshiaki learned some important information about the financial system when Hiro executed *Spread of knowledge*.

Therefore, they are able to assist Hiro by answering his phone and responding to questions, especially the simple ones. This allows Hiro to spend most of his time communicating knowledge to Kei. After Hiro's transfer, Kei is accomplished in the role of Hiro's successor.

***

Spread of knowledge is a necessary condition for *Firewall for the handover*. However, third parties must be careful not to be overly assertive as they are not experts. When third parties cannot adequately address a situation, they must judge its urgency. If a situation is urgent, the handover must be interrupted to ask the predecessor for help.

Since the third party has his or her own work, becoming a *Firewall for the handover* can be problematic because this requires a balance between helping with the handover and performing his or her normal duties. The firewall person works to be as flexible as possible by assuming the roles of *Firewalls* [12] and *Gatekeeper* [12].

A cohesive team is crucial for success. The third party should assume that the predecessor's job is temporarily part of his or her job. *Breaking Down Barriers* [16] contributes to the performance of the *Firewall for the handover*. This pattern is an effective countermeasure against the *Background is omitted* [3] and *Necessary knowledge is omitted* [3].

Firewall for the handover aims to mitigate the issue of insufficient time, which is one of the main causes for *Unsupported to review* [3] and *Necessary knowledge is omitted* [3]. Thus, *Firewall for the handover* can be an effective countermeasure to help avoid these anti-patterns.

5   Case Study

To examine the effectiveness of these patterns, we sent a questionnaire to five people in three different large Japanese companies and a government agency. The questionnaire targeted businesspersons working for the systems department for more than three years. This questionnaire was the beginning of a case study to help validate our patterns and elucidate other possible scenarios and patterns. Table 2 shows the results of the questionnaire.

Table 2. Results of the questionnaire

	Effectively used	Ineffectively used	Not used
Spread of knowledge	3	0	2
Handover space	4	0	1
Firewall for the handover	3	0	2

Our limited survey indicates that the patterns proposed in this paper are effective. To better illustrate this, we introduce one of our experiments as a case study of these patterns. We interviewed one of the responders, Responder *Mr. Tarou*. He shared his experience using *Spread of knowledge* and *Handover space* during the handover process.

5.1 Scene

Mr. Tarou works for one of the biggest computing companies in Japan, which develops and sells database management systems. Because *Mr. Tarou* will be retiring in the near future, it is important that he handover his responsibilities. *Mr. Tarou* is in charge of the development for part of this system, which consists of multiple modules that are developed using the process described in Fig. 6.

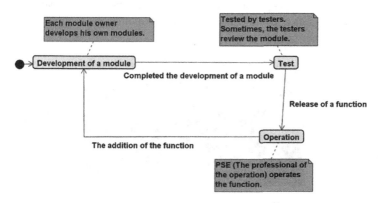

Fig. 6. Development process

Each module has an owner (developer) who is responsible for its development. *Mr. Tarou* is a module owner and has developed various modules. The module owner is the only person who can edit the modules. During the handover, *Mr. Tarou* used the *Spread of the knowledge* and *Handover space*. He felt that these patterns are very effective during the handover process.

5.2 Experience with Spread of Knowledge

Many people, like testers and developers, are involved in the development of a system. *Mr. Tarou* thinks it is natural to share knowledge with coworkers. In particular, two parties are very interested in *Mr. Tarou*'s work and have a vested interest in a successful handover.

The first party is responsible for maintaining the system and adding new features. When *Mr. Tarou* needs to add new features, he must understand the knowledge about the previous release. However, sometimes *Mr. Tarou* cannot communicate immediately with the people who are responsible for defining previous features. Therefore, the developers are required to write plan specifications and code comments so that anyone can understand the knowledge at a later date. This is a kind of *Spread of knowledge*.

The second party is other module owners (developers) who are working on various modules related with *Mr. Tarou*'s modules. For example, other modules may use features from *Mr. Tarou*'s modules or need to integrate with *Mr. Tarou*'s modules. Therefore, it is important that *Mr. Tarou* shares knowledge about his modules with other module owners. By applying *Spread of knowledge*, many colleagues can review

Mr. Tarou's work, reducing issues and helping his successor better understand the modules that he or she will be responsible for after the handover. The company's *Spread of knowledge* policy has assisted in successful handovers.

5.3   Experience with Handover Space

During a handover, *Mr. Tarou* moved to a different room when sharing knowledge with his successors or third parties. The main reason *Mr. Tarou* moved to a different room was to avoid bothering other people since the handover may be noisy. However, an added benefit was that *Mr. Tarou* could concentrate on communicating without interruptions.

Picture 1. Workshop at PLoP 2016

6   Workshops About Our Pattern Language

We held two workshops for our pattern language for handovers at Waseda University and held a focus group at PLoP2016. The goal of these workshops was to consider the relationship of the patterns and to mine new patterns. We recruited people interested in handovers, and about 25 people participated in our workshops in Tokyo and Illinois (Picture 1).

In the workshops, we divided the participants into groups. We distributed pattern cards that briefly described our 25 patterns. Then each group created a pattern map by organizing the pattern cards into related sequences. In addition, we asked the participants to write any new patterns they found on blank cards. Finally, they shared their results, including pattern maps (Picture 2) and any issues.

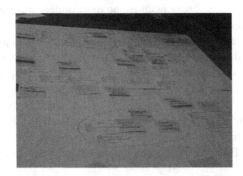

Picture 2. Example of the pattern map gained in the workshop

This led us to find various pattern sequences. A sequence is a path through the pattern language. It is the process that we follow to build something [17]. Therefore, the task of creating a pattern map to find a new pattern has a significant meaning.

Table 3. New handover patterns

	Pattern name	Summary of the pattern	Num of groups
1	Simplify the system	Keep the system simple, allowing knowledge to be easily handed over	1
2	Automate Away	Automate the work to avoid a handover	1
3	Hire a Maintainer	Keep the predecessor inside the organization	1
4	Relief pitcher	Find temporary substitutes from the company	1
5	**Ability check**	**Check the ability of the successor before the personnel change**	3
6	Vacation chaos monkey	Randomly give someone vacation to see what happens	1
7	Find another successor	Find another successor in case the initial successor is inadequate	1
8	Work as a team for a while	Before the predecessor leaves, work as a team to aid in a seamless handover	1
9	**Pair working**	**For critical tasks, avoid handovers by using a pair programing**	3
10	**Cross training**	**Work with a rotation between two people and share their work**	2
11	Make key person dependencies visible	Clarify the ownership of knowledge	1
12	Develop a review process	For example, create a review manual	1
13	**Matching the knowledge**	**Successor takes notes to confirm the understanding is right**	3
14	**Prioritize**	**Prioritize knowledge when there is insufficient time for a comprehensive handover**	2
15	Handover evaluation	Evaluate and visualize risks for handover failure	1
16	Get motivated	Recognize the successor's contributions to increase amount input	1
17	Official project by sponsor	Recognize a handover as an official project to secure the time and human resources	1
18	Order of transfers	The most knowledgeable and experienced person leaves last when most of a team transfer	1
19	Meeting together	Have the successor and predecessor meet prior to a handover	1
20	Professional questioner	Include a person who asks insightful questions to avoid loss of tacit knowledge	1
21	**Create new knowledge**	**Recreate lost knowledge**	2
22	**Accept reduced capacity**	**If the knowledge is lost, accept the reduced capacity**	2

From the workshops, we outlined 5 pattern maps with 22 possible new patterns. Picture 2 shows an example of a pattern map, while Table 3 shows the new patterns. The "Num of groups" shows the number of groups that proposed the same pattern. According to the table, seven patterns are proposed by multiple groups; these seven patterns are shown in bold fonts in the table. These patterns might have some universality. However, some patterns proposed by a single group were evaluated as ingenious and interesting; for example, some participants had a positive impression of *"Evaluation of the handover"*. We received excellent feedback from the workshops, and the participants might have gained some insight on how to achieve better handovers.

7   Conclusion and Future Work

Herein we outlined a Pattern Language for Handovers. We explain three anti-patterns (*Unsupported to review, Background is omitted,* and *Necessary knowledge is omitted*) to describe the problems in the handover process. We then described three patterns from our pattern language in detail (*Spread of knowledge, Handover space,* and *Firewall for the handover*) as they help mitigate issues found in the anti-patterns. We also expressed the pattern sequences in a pattern map. To better understand these patterns in relation to handover issues, we used a concrete scenario and presented our questionnaire to four organizations. The results revealed that the three patterns introduced in Table 2 are common practices in these companies. As a case study, one person shared his experience, confirming that these patterns are very effective during the handover process. We are now assessing the effects of each pattern.

There are four future works for a pattern language for handovers. First, our pattern language defines the third party as an indirect person for the handover. In reality, there are various kinds of indirect persons for handovers. We need to define the roles of these other people. Second, our pattern language does not address important questions as part of the handover process, "What is the conversation and what should be formally documented?" Third, other unidentified patterns may exist. In the workshops, we identified 22 possible new patterns. Fourth, we need to continue to investigate implicit/explicit handover patterns and practices in companies, especially software outsourcing companies since they often have their own well-defined internal processes to deal with knowledge transfers and personnel changes.

To find additional patterns, we have opened a wiki site on the handover pattern language. This site can be edited by anyone. The URL of the wiki site is: https://www65.atwiki.jp/handover/.

The purpose of this wiki site is to activate discussions on handovers and to create new patterns. We invite you to visit our wiki site.

Acknowledgement. We thank all the respondents of the questionnaire and the participants of our workshops. We would also like to thank our AsianPLoP 2016 shepherd Foutse Khomh and PLoP 2016 shepherd Lise Hvatum for their valuable feedback during the shepherding process. Additionally, we thank reviewers for their valuable comments during the review process. Finally we'd like to thank the writers' workshops at AsianPLoP 2016 and PLoP 2016 for all of the valuable feedbacks.

Appendix

Here we introduce three anti-pattern figures (Unsupported to review, Background is omitted, and Necessary knowledge is omitted) and three pattern figures (Spread of knowledge, Handover space, and Firewall for the handover). The three anti-pattern figures describe the mechanism of handover problems. These figures express how they are resolved. By using UML, readers can easily understand where problems exist, how a pattern works, and what problems are resolved.

Appendix A: Anti-pattern Figures

We describe the result of an ideal handover and an anti-pattern handover by a class diagram. The diagram reveals the gaps and identifies the location of the problem easily be visualized. Herein we explain three anti-pattern figures (Fig. 7).

Unsupported to review

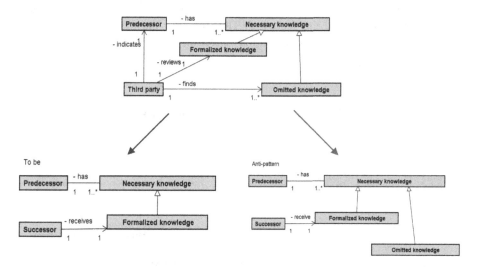

Fig. 7. Unsupported to review

First, a third party reviews the formalized knowledge. They indicate whether the predecessor omits some necessary knowledge. Because the successor cannot inherit omitted knowledge, the predecessor should reflect on the third party's feedback to verify all necessary knowledge is included (Fig. 8).

Background is omitted

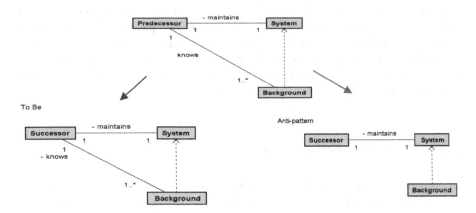

Fig. 8. Background is unclear

The background impacts the system. The predecessor who has been engaged in the system for many years knows such knowledge, which may not be included in the documents handed over to the successor. The successor must maintain the system without the background knowledge that may affect the system (Fig. 9).

Necessary knowledge is omitted

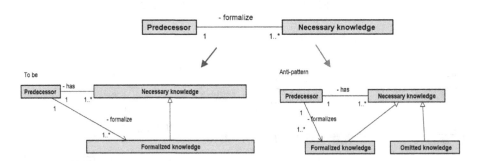

Fig. 9. Necessary knowledge is omitted

In many cases, the predecessor formally conveys necessary knowledge in documents. All the necessary knowledge should be communicated to the successor. However, some omissions may occur unintentionally due to forgetting to write down crucial information. In such a case, the omitted knowledge is lost.

Appendix B: Pattern Figures

In this section, we describe the before and after situations of the patterns' use by class diagrams. To easily understand the impact of the patterns, the class diagrams depict the before and after situation. Herein we outline three pattern figures (Fig. 10).

Spread of knowledge.

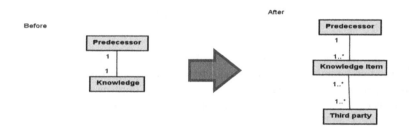

Fig. 10. Spread of knowledge

Before using the patterns, "Knowledge" and "Predecessor" are one-to-one relationship. That is, only the predecessor has "Knowledge". However, this pattern subdivided "Knowledge" into "Knowledge item", which is shared by several third parties. "Knowledge" is subdivided because it is inappropriate for third parties to have all the knowledge as the responsibility may become ambiguous. By using this pattern, the predecessor's knowledge is backed up after the personnel changes (Fig. 11).

Handover space

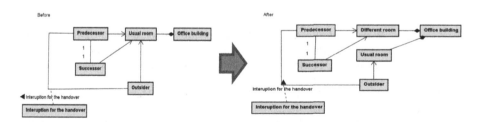

Fig. 11. Handover space

Before using the pattern, the predecessor and the successor are handing over in the "usual room". The handover may be interrupted when outsiders come to ask the predecessor questions. Therefore, the predecessor and the successor move to a "different room" and hand over there, making it more difficult for outsiders to interrupt the handover.

Firewall for the handover

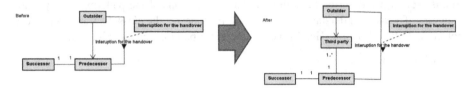

Fig. 12. Firewall for handover

Before using the pattern, outsiders can easily contact the predecessor. However, by relaying the communication between outsiders and the predecessor via a third party, outsiders cannot directly contact the predecessor. The third party acts as a relay to avoid unnecessary interruptions. In other words, the third party becomes the *Firewall of the handover* (Fig. 12).

References

1. Volleman, T.: Transitioning from development to maintenance. In: Proceedings of International Conference on Software Maintenance (ICSM 1990), San Diego, USA, pp. 189–199 (1990)
2. Khan, A.S., Kajki-Mattsson, M.: Core handover problems. In: Proceedings of the 11th International Conference on Product Focused Software 2010 (PROFES 2010), Limerick, Ireland, pp. 135–139 (2010)
3. Ito, K., Washizaki, H., Fukazawa, Y.: Handover anti-patterns. In: Proceedings of the 5th Asian Conference on Pattern Language of Programs (Asian PLoP 2016), Taipei, Taiwan (2016)
4. Gill, T.G., Cohen, E.: Research themes in complex informing. Informing Sci. Int. J. Emerg. Transdiscipline **11**(1), 147–164 (2008)
5. Yoder, J.W., Wirfs-Brock, R.: AsianPLoP Pattern Writing Bootcamp (2016). http://pl.csie.ntut.edu.tw/asianplop2016/files/AsianPLoP2016BootcampPatternWriting.pdf
6. Manns, M.L., Rising, L.: Fearless Change: Patterns for Introducing New Ideas. Addison-Wesley Professional, Boston (2004)
7. Manns, M.L., Rising, L.: More Fearless Change: Strategies for Making Your Ideas Happen. Addison-Wesley Professional, Boston (2015)
8. Khan, A.S., Kajki-Mattsson, M.: Taxonomy of handover activities. In: Proceedings of the 11th International Conference on Product Focused Software 2010 (PROFES 2010), Limerick, Ireland, pp. 131–134 (2010)
9. McCormick, H.W.: AntiPatterns, a brief tutorial (1998). http://www.antipatterns.com/briefing/index.htm
10. Brown, W.J., Raphael C.M., "Skip" McCormick III, H.W., Mowbray, T.J.: Anti-patterns. Wiley, Hoboken (1998)
11. Alexander, C., Ishikawa, S., Silverstein, M.: A Pattern Language: Towns, Buildings Construction. Oxford University Press Inc., New York (1977)

12. Coplien, J.O., Harrison, N.B.: Organizational Patterns of Agile Software Development. Pearson Prentice Hall, Upper Saddle River (2005)
13. Ito, K., Washizaki, H., Yoder, J.W.: Workshop at Waseda University (2016). http://www.washi.cs.waseda.ac.jp/?page_id=3056
14. Ito, K., Washizaki, H., Yoder, J.W.: Focus Group at Pattern Language of Programing (2016). http://www.hillside.net/plop/2016/index.php?nav=program
15. Rising, L.: The Pattern Almanac. Addison-Wesley Longman Publishing, Boston (2000)
16. Yoder, J.W., Wirfs-Brock, R., Washizaki, H.: QA to AQ part three shifting from quality assurance to agile. In: Proceedings of the 10th Latin American Conference on Pattern Language of Programs (SugarLoaf PLoP 2014), Brazil, Ilhabela (2014)
17. Harrison, N.B., Coplien, J.O.: Pattern sequences. In: Proceedings of the 6th European Conference on Pattern Languages of Programs (Euro PLoP 2001), Kloster Irsee, Bavaria, Germany (2001)
18. Nonaka, I.: Management of Knowledge Creation. Nihon Keizai Shinbun-sha, Tokyo (1990)
19. Polanyi, M.: Personal Knowledge - Towards a Post-critical Philosophy. University of Chicago Press, Chicago (1974)
20. Fries, C., Biskoup, A., Augustin, N.: Handover guidance and handover note outline (2016). https://usaidlearninglab.org/library/handover-guidance-and-handover-note-outline
21. Dunn, R.: Internal work package handovers and effective knowledge transfer (2012). http://projectmanager.com.au/effective-knowledge-transfer-on-a-construction-project/
22. Laine, M.: Best practices for project handover in middle-size organizations. Thesis, Master's Degree Programme in Information Systems, HAGGA-HELIA ammattikorkeakoulu (2012)
23. Kalkan, V.D.: Knowledge continuity management process in organizations. J. Bus. Econ. Res. 4(3), 41–46 (2006)
24. Ito, K., Washizaki, H., Yoder, J.W., Fukazawa, Y.: A pattern language for handovers. In: Proceedings of the 23rd Conference on Pattern Languages of Programs (PLoP 2016), Monticello, USA (2016)

Author Index

Printed in the United States
By Bookmasters